Everybody's Guide
to
Great Wines
Under $5

JAMES NELSON

Everybody's Guide
to
Great Wines
Under $5

Second Edition

McGRAW-HILL BOOK COMPANY

New York   St. Louis   San Francisco   Bogotá
Guatemala   Hamburg   Lisbon   Madrid   Mexico
Montreal   Panama   Paris   San Juan   São Paulo
Tokyo   Toronto

The first edition of this book was titled
The Poorperson's Guide to Great Cheap Wines

1 2 3 4 5 6 7 8 9 F G R F G R 8 7 6 5 4 3

ISBN 0-07-046222-4

LIBRARY OF CONGRESS CATALOGING IN PUBLICATION DATA

Nelson, James, 1921–
Everybody's guide to great wines under $5.
Updated ed. of: The poorperson's guide to great cheap
wines. c1977
Bibliography: p.
1. Wine and wine making.   I. Title.
TP548.N44 1983   641.2′2   83-9373
ISBN 0-07-046222-4

For my wonderful, beautiful mother,
who, at 91, lives in Denver, and
enjoys the smell and taste and color of wine
when I visit,
although deep in her dear heart
she'd rather have
a Rum Collins . . .

Contents

Preface to the Second Edition

Changes on top of changes! That's what has happened to the wine business since the First Edition of this book appeared in 1977. Fortunately, these changes mean that you, the seeker after wine experiences that are both extraordinary and affordable, have a whole new world of wonderful choices!

What has changed since the First Edition came out? For one thing, the book itself. First time around we titled the book *The Poorperson's Guide to Great Cheap Wines*, and our price ceiling was $3 a bottle. This time the title is *Everybody's Guide to Great Wines Under $5*.

Why the changes? We raised the price ceiling to compensate for inflation and to bring in a number of new, outstanding, and highly affordable wines that were just out of reach with our old ceiling. We modified the title because, in the current economy, a wine that sells for $5, while not expensive, is not "cheap" either.

What else has changed? Here's a list:

• You're drinking more wine. If you were an average American when the First Edition appeared, you were drinking 1.8 gallons of wine each year. Today, you're closing in on 2.5 gallons. That's a 39 percent increase!

• You're buying more imported wines. In 1977, 17 percent of the wine you drank came from abroad. Today, nearly a quarter of it comes from outside the United States. Although the largest segment of this growth is a gusher of Italian Lambruscos, many other new wines are pouring into this country in ever-increasing quantities from every corner of the globe. In this book we'll cover wines from 18 countries, including, of course, the good old U.S. of A.

• You're drinking more white wine, less red. Some people call this the "white-wine revolution." Others call it the "cold-wine revolution." They point to the increasing number of pink wines and Lambruscos being consumed and argue that the common denominator in the wine revolution is not color but chill factor.

• You're drinking more varietals, wines made principally or totally from the single grape variety that gives the wine its name. Varietal whites are wines with names like Chardonnay, Chenin Blanc, Sauvignon Blanc (also called Fumé Blanc), Johannisberg Riesling, and Gewurztraminer, to name a few. Red-wine varietals include Cabernet Sauvignon, Pinot Noir, Zinfandel, Gamay, Barbera, and others.

The opposite of a varietal wine is a generic wine. This doesn't mean the wine isn't made from varietal grapes, because every wine has to come from *some* grape variety. It just means the grape variety may be so humble that mentioning it doesn't cause much of a stir. Or the wine may be a blend of one or more different varieties, no one of which is present in sufficient quantity (75 percent) to permit the winemaker legally to call the wine by a varietal name.

Imported generic wines are frequently called *Vin Rouge, Vin Blanc, Vin de Table, Vino da Tavola, Tafelwein, Vino Tinto*, Red Wine, or White Wine, or are designated by a brand name, such as Demestica or Simpatico. Generic American whites are generally called Chablis, Sauterne, Rhine, White Wine, White Table Wine, or Vintage White. Labels for generic American reds may read Burgundy, Claret, Chianti, Red Wine, Red Table Wine, Big Red, or Vintage Red.

The fact a wine is generic and not varietal doesn't mean it can't be terrific. An increasing number of California generics are being made from blends of high-quality varietal grapes. Sometimes the vintner goes so far as to tell you on the label just what varieties went into the wine, and in what quantities. As you will see from the Wine Index, some of these wines offer extraordinary value.

• You're drinking more vintage-dated wines. These are wines that say 1977 or 1983 on the label to tell you the year the grapes were harvested and pressed. The reason you're drinking more of them is that the California wine industry has decided that vintage-dated varietal wines are the surest route to the pocketbook of the increasingly sophisticated wine drinker. I think they're right.

Vintage-dating may raise a question in your mind in regard to this book. A year from now, when new bottles with brand-new vintage dates begin to appear on store shelves, will this book's Index of 505 red, white, and pink wines be suddenly obsolete?

The answer is no. Sure, no two harvests are exactly alike, and some differences will occur in wines from year to year, but *the most significant factor in the wine equation is not the year but the winemaker.* He—or in an increasing number of cases, she—is the person who puts the strongest imprint on the wine. The winemaker is the person who selects the grapes, decides when to pick them, monitors the fermentation, speeds it up, slows it down, decides whether or not the wine will age in oak, and if so, how long, and makes the hundreds of other decisions that affect the style and content and personality of the wine.

Winemakers are not flighty—they tend toward consistency. Thus, if you liked, say, Beaulieu Vineyard's fine 1978 Burgundy, chances are excellent, despite harvest variations, you'll like their '79, their '80, their '81, and so on, because the same hand that guided production of the '78 will have controlled production of these subsequent vintages. This factor, even more than the amount of sunshine or rain that fell on the Napa Valley, will determine the quality of the wine you are going to find on your store shelf.

• Another thing you've started to do is drink white wines made from red-wine grapes. How did these wines get started? Well, what is a poor winemaker to do when his vineyard is full of Cabernet and Zinfandel grapes, and the world is crying for white wines? Surprisingly, some of these wines are very good.

• Because you're concerned about your weight, you've begun drinking "light" wines—wines lower in both alcohol and calories than ordinary wines. The "lights" are principally whites and rosés, and whereas ordinary wine has some 76 calories per 100 milliliters (about 3.3 ounces), the lights range from 57 down to 48 calories for the same amount.

• You're buying wine in new kinds of packages—wine-in-a-box, for example. On the outside of the box there's a plastic spigot, and inside, of course, a plastic pouch containing the wine. Pouch sizes range from 4 to 20 liters, and for some vintners this is a fast-growing new area of their business.

The principal question to be asked about bag-in-a-box wine, of course, or wine in any other kind of packaging for that matter, is whether you *like* the wine to begin with. If you do, then buying it in a box can be a great idea, especially if you're giving a party or picnic, want ease of handling and serving, and expect to use most of it up. Relatively fast turnover is important, because, despite technological advances, a bag sitting too long on a counter or in your refrigerator may permit air to find its way in through the bag membrane or the plastic spigot, spoiling the wine before the box is empty.

Wine in cans is another kind of new packaging, not much in evidence yet. Yes, with pop-tops and everything—take home a six-pack today!

• Another change: You're now completely metric, of course. Gone is the "fifth." The standard of the industry today is the 750-milliliter bottle, followed closely by the 1.5-liter "magnum" and larger metric sizes.

• While we're talking about magnums, incidentally, let me point out that you have a whole new category of wine to investigate. This is the affordable and often excellent 1.5-liter bottles of red and white generics from vintners who normally concentrate their attention on vintage-dated varietals that cost $10 to $20 or more per bottle. Many of these new wines don't deserve to be called "jug wines," because they're several steps up from jugs. They are, in fact, a whole new species.

• You have more and better places to buy wine. Several states have recently changed their laws to permit the sale of wine in food stores, something that has been standard operating procedure in many other states for years. And only one state—Connecticut—still has a fair-trade law on the books to keep wine and liquor dealers from competing in terms of price. The rest of these restrictive price-maintenance laws have been struck down, and "discount" has become the name of the game.

Thus, as long as you don't live in Connecticut or in a "control" state—where the state operates the stores and sets the prices—you'll find increasing numbers of scrappy independents and smaller chains competing for your business. In the East you'll find that many tough-minded independents have banded into groups to buy and advertise jointly. This keeps costs down, volume up, and prices competitive. In the West, California and Arizona have seen the emergence of a new super-chain called The Liquor Barn, expected to number 100-plus stores by the end of 1983 and keep right on growing. These enormous stores, owned and operated by Safeway, offer an almost bewildering array of domestic and imported wines.

What's more, in many cities a whole new breed of wine retailer has evolved: the wine shop. The wine shop may also handle distilled spirits, but whether they do or not, the emphasis is definitely on wine. Many of these shops feature wine bars, where, for a modest sum, you may sample a number of different wines without having to buy a full bottle.

With all these new outlets available to you—wine shops, discount groups, chains—the key to getting the best wine at the lowest price still lies in shopping around. *No single store can have the lowest price on everything*.

• The last and best change to take place since the earlier book is the happy fact that there is much less bad wine being made today than used to be the case. To turn that thought around, let me say that many wineries, both here and abroad, that used to pump out oceans of nondescript, charmless wines are now turning out wines of remarkable quality. Chalk it up to better-educated winemakers, to better vineyard management, to improved winery procedures, for much of which thank such institutions as the University of California at Davis and the University of Dijon in France. It is also due, however, to a somewhat tardy realization by many vintners that in the long run—and generally in the short run as well—the surest way to grow rich and famous in the wine business is to make the very best wine you can.

Now for the crystal ball. It's my firm opinion that, with more and better wines constantly coming into the market, both from domestic producers and from overseas, with nearly every wine-producing country in the world turning up an annual surplus, and with the dollar relatively strong, we may, for a few years at least, be living in a wine drinker's paradise.

So, prepare to enter this paradise—with this book under your arm, of course. And even if you read the book the first time around and know how to find, evaluate, and serve wines, let me make one modest suggestion: Please reread Chapter Six, "Disclaimers, excuses, and more disclaimers." It has a few new thoughts not carried in the First Edition that may prove helpful in understanding and using the recommendations in the Wine Index.

Now, go to it! Good hunting!

Introduction to
the Original Edition

Another book
about wine?

I wrote this book because I like wine.

I like to drink it, I like to sniff it, I like to look at the light through it and marvel at how beautiful (or clear, or murky, or golden, or ruby red, or whatever) it is.

I like red wines, I like white wines, I like rosé wines. I like apéritif wines before dinner, and table wines with dinner, and dessert wines with dessert. I like sangría in the summer and hot mulled wine in the winter, and I like sangría in the winter and hot mulled wine in the summer, or whenever there's any hot mulled wine around.

However, according to reliable reports (or perhaps unreliable; I can never remember which), there are in print at present over 1,400 books on wine. The world can hardly be said to be holding its breath for yet another book. Why on earth, therefore, would anybody write or publish, or worse yet, *buy* another book about wine?

Well, the book would have to be different from all the others. This book is such a book. It solves an unsolved problem, namely, that the wine the wine lovers love to write about always turns out to be a Château Latour '61 or a Robert Mondavi Cabernet Sauvignon Reserve 1975. Marvelous as these wines are, I can barely afford to read about them, let alone drink them. Maybe, if you're reading this book, you're in the same boat. And the other books on inexpensive wines? *Their* problem is that they all seem to think "inexpensive" means a wine that "only" costs $8.00 to $25.00 a bottle.

I grant that most of these books have a chapter on jug wines, and they nod benignly in the direction of a few California vintners from whom you might expect to get "decent quality in the lower price range." But then they get back to their main topic, which is those $8.00 to $25.00 wines that they consider drinkable by people for whom drinking a $4.99 bottle of wine is dangerously close to slumming.

In doing so, these writers ignore more than 90 percent of all the wine that is consumed in the United States today. They are ignoring vast numbers of new labels that are spreading out from California as a result of the greatly increased planting of wine grapes—mostly of very high quality—that has taken place in recent years. And they are ignoring the enormous influx of new, low-cost wines from Europe, South America, Africa, Australia, and many other wine areas where good harvests and heavy production have put more good, low-cost wines on the market today than have been available to the U.S. consumer in years.

This, therefore, is a book that deals with these wines. Old wines, new wines, undiscovered wines, wines whose prices have plummeted, wines whose prices were low to begin with.

How do you find these bargain wines that you can put on your table for $5.00 a bottle or less? How do you know when you've found one? How do you sift out the awful and the ordinary, and come up with high-quality, low-cost wines you'd feel comfortable serving at your Saturday-night dinner party?

This book is designed to help you answer each of these questions. It will tell you where to look for wine bargains, and how to sniff out the stores that offer unusual wine values. It will tell you whom to talk to in your area, and what to ask them, and how to get a wine or liquor dealer to run down good, low-cost wines they may not have in their current stock.

It will tell you how to evaluate wines, how to put your eyes, nose, and mouth to work to help you separate the low-cost, sensational wines from the low-cost bummers. And it will tell you how to serve wines so that you get the utmost quality that each wine has to offer.

Finally, it will give you an Index of low-cost wines, all listed by name and recent market price, together with a numerical evaluation of their quality and a brief paragraph commenting on their outstanding virtues or defects. This is a book that deals with wines named Premiat, Demestica, Trakia, Langenbach, Concha y Toro, Barossa Valley, Simpatico, Folonari, and many more.

I have read and enjoyed many books on wine, but I have never seen these names or many of the others you will find in the Index of low-cost wines at the back of this book. Until now, no one has taken the time to taste them, evaluate them critically, and write about them.

The principal idea of the book, however, is not to give you a long list of decent, reasonably priced wines from which you can choose at random. The real idea of the book is to show you how to construct your own personal catalog of sound, affordable wines, available where you live, together with suggestions for making sure that your great $3.50 Chenin Blanc comes off to its best advantage at your Saturday-night supper party.

Using the tools provided in the book, you can not only serve pleasing wines at your dinner parties, but you can discover highly enjoyable, highly afford-able wines to wash down the Wednesday tuna cas-serole or the Thursday leftovers. And you can do it without risking either your palate or your pocket-book. All it takes is some time, a willingness to exper-iment, a not-very-arduous amount of record-keep-ing, and an average amount of ingenuity, judgment, and self-confidence.

What's more, you'll have fun doing it. You'll be-come much more aware of wine wherever you come in contact with it, in your own home, a friend's home, or in a restaurant. In addition, you'll derive a pleasant extra dividend, because in wine experiments, unlike chemistry experiments, you get to drink the results!

I had a lot of fun writing this book, not only because I love wine, but because I also dearly love a bargain. I recently found a pair of handmade English shoes on sale in New York for half their original price. They fitted perfectly, so I bought them, and the whole experience made me feel wonderful.

That same week I also found an extraordinarily pleasant white wine you can serve at your next dinner party—and so can I—at a cost of slightly less than $2.00 a bottle. That made me feel wonderful, too. And that's what this book is all about.

PART ONE

All about Great Wines Under $5

HOW TO FIND THEM,
HOW TO RATE THEM,
HOW TO SERVE THEM.

1

What makes a bargain?

A friend of mine recently confided over lunch how lucky he felt to have found a case of 1979 Château Margaux for only $36.00 a bottle. It was a real bargain, and naturally he'd snapped it up, because he knew he'd have to pay twice as much in a year or two.

I had no doubt it was a bargain. It's the same kind of bargain I once heard of from an acquaintance at a cocktail party, who told me that the only truly economical car was the Rolls-Royce. He cited maintenance statistics, depreciation schedules, resale value, and so forth, and actually built a pretty strong case for the fact that a Rolls was a bargain at almost any price.

Despite its bargain status, I still don't have a Rolls, nor have I laid in a supply of those $36.00 bargain bottles of Château Margaux. And it's not because I don't like bargains. It's just that one person's bargain is another person's major capital investment. You and I want sound wines on our table, enjoyable wines, affordable wines, wines we're not ashamed to serve to dinner guests. But, we don't want to mortgage our furniture or our children to get them.

In the quest for wines that I could afford, and subsequently, in doing the extraordinarily enjoyable research for this book, I believe I have tracked down and sampled more different kinds of inexpensive wine that any person in this country. Red wines, white wines, foreign wines, domestic wines, familiar wines, wines I'd never heard of. But all affordable wines.

Are these wines any good? Take my word for it, a few are absolutely ghastly. Then there's a group of moderate size that won't dissolve your gold fillings or corrode the lining of your stomach, but is still very, very ordinary.

Finally, within a very modest price limit, there is a group of wines that are extremely good, some that would be pronounced excellent by experienced, professional wine tasters. Some of these wines, in fact, are the equal of wines selling for $8.00, $10.00, or $15.00 a bottle!

What are we looking for?

There are lots of words to describe the kind of wines we are looking for: inexpensive, affordable, low-cost. But we want more than that. A low-cost wine is no bargain if it delivers a low degree of satisfaction. If it doesn't look, smell, and taste terrific, who cares how little it costs?

So, we are looking for something else: value. Value is a smooth, rich wine, perfect for serving at your next dinner party, that costs you $2.00 a bottle.

Value is a brilliant, fruity, golden wine that costs $3.50 a bottle and has your guests asking, "Hey, what is this? It's *good!*"

In short, value means the great wine discoveries of the world, the underrated wines, the hard-to-find wines, the underpriced wines, the well-constructed, sound, highly drinkable wines that complement a good dinner and would, if they came out of a bottle with a more aristocratic label, make a devoted wine drinker nod thoughtfully and say, "Very nice. Very, *very* nice."

Fortunately, friend, there are a lot of those wines out there, and you and I are going to find them. But first, let's take a look at what is happening in the world of wine, and how we got to where we are today.

 What have *you been drinking?*

We'll start with the fact that, if you're an average American, you've been tossing down 182.5 gallons of *something* every year since you reached adulthood.* Not just wine, but all the many different kinds of liquids you pour down your gullet.

Back in the year 1953, if you were around then, your tastes were relatively simple. You drank 28.5 gallons of milk each year, 36 gallons of coffee, 7.2 gallons of tea, 3.5 gallons of juice, and 76 gallons of plain old water.

* According to John C. Maxwell, Jr., the leading industry source for data on consumption trends, as published in the magazine *Beverage Industry*.

You also had a fondness for soft drinks, but you managed to keep your habit under control and consumed only 12 gallons of Coke, Pepsi, Seven-Up, or whatever each year.

You didn't drink many alcoholic beverages, but when you did, your preference ran heavily to beer, of which you drank 12.5 gallons, and distilled spirits, of which you drank 1.2 gallons.

You also drank 0.6 gallons of wine, you old devil, you! Your taste in wine ran heavily to the sweeter, higher-alcohol varieties, like Sherry and Muscatel, and unless your family was rich and worldly, or you came from an ethnic background where wine was a customary accompaniment to a meal, you hardly drank any of those funny, not-very-sweet table wines at all.

There is, in fact, a strong feeling that much of the wine consumption of this earlier period was based on the fact that, because there wasn't much demand for wine, it was very cheap. And because it was cheap, a bottle of Muscatel, for example, offered more "proof per penny" than a bottle of whiskey or gin, a fact that had not escaped the notice of the majority of poor alcoholics living along the various skid rows of the nation.

How your tastes changed in twenty-eight years
During the next twenty-eight years, your tastes changed drastically. You still couldn't choke down more than 182.5 gallons of liquid each year, but you began to drink more of this, less of that. By the year 1981, in fact, your consumption of milk had gone down from the 1953 figure of 28.5 gallons to 20.6 gal-

lons. Your coffee drinking had also dipped markedly, from 36 gallons to 26, while your use of tea had declined from 7.2 gallons to 6.5. Your fondness for juices had climbed appreciably, from 3.5 to 6.9.

Your consumption of soft drinks had zoomed even more sharply. You now consumed 39.5 gallons a year, compared with 12 in 1953. This may have been one reason why you now drank only 46.1 gallons of water, against 76 gallons twenty years before.

But there were other reasons. On the alcohol beverage front, you were guzzling 24.6 gallons of beer, against 12.5 gallons in 1953, and your intake of distilled spirits had jumped from 1.2 to 2 gallons.

And then there was wine. In twenty-eight years you had become so interested in the fruits of the vine that you had quadrupled your intake. From the 0.6 gallons you put away in 1953, you were now drinking 2.4 gallons. The vintners were pleased—you'd come a long way, baby!

In fact, it seemed as though the whole country was suddenly drinking wine. Stockbrokers, kids in college, afternoon bridge groups. Instead of being the drink of the very rich and the very poor, plus a few ethnic minorities, wine had become everybody's drink. And it had become the perfect gift for housewarmings, or for a hurried Christmas present, with the recipient often gauging the strength of the friendship by the name and year on the label.

 Spain, Italy, France: Where they really drink wine!
But even as we watched ourselves knocking back the seemingly incredible quantity of 2.4 gallons of wine

per person per year, one look across the ocean told us that, when it came to wine, we were practically teetotalers. Because the average Argentinean drinks 20 gallons a year, the average Italian 24 gallons, and the average Frenchman, lucky dog, 25 gallons. Thus, our country's wine industry—hustling, growing, busting out at the seams—is still outproduced by Italy, France, Spain, the Soviet Union, and Argentina. To winebibbing Americans, this is a humbling thought, and many a patriot has made a solemn vow to do his bit to try to help America catch up.

My own discovery of wine parallels the national trend. During the first decade of my life, wine barely existed at all as far as I was concerned, because I was young, and so was prohibition.

During the second decade of my life—the thirties—wine still didn't appear on my personal horizon, except in church. I was an occasional altar boy for the local Episcopal parish, and from time to time I got a faint taste of something unusual on the wafer that was dipped into the chalice just before being deposited on my outstretched tongue. Frankly, it didn't taste very good.

Wine became compulsory during the early part of my third decade, because this was the United States in World War II, and wine was something a sailor had to buy three bottles of in order to earn the right to buy one bottle of a rotgut called Four Feathers. What to do with the unwanted three bottles was always a problem. Someone usually suggested tracking down a sailor with an Italian surname. The only time I ever tried it, it turned out he had the same problem I had. It never occurred to any of us to try drinking it.

Half a dozen years later, however, my wine perceptions underwent a radical change. In the process of marrying my lovely wife, I also married a charming set of parents-in-law, who served no hard liquor in their house. Instead, before dinner, they served chilled Spanish Sherries dry enough to wither your tonsils, while the dinners themselves were often accompanied by bottles of such unfamiliar wonders as Piesporter Goldtröpfchen, Bernkasteler Doktor, Châteauneuf-du-Pape, and Château d'Yquem.

 The author makes a modest discovery about wine
At last, the light bulb went on above my ignorant head. Wine was not just a compulsory purchase to get a bottle of bourbon. Wine was good in itself! It was for drinking! Even before dinner! Even while eating!

Two years after this milestone discovery, my wife and I moved to the Sonoma Valley in California. Suddenly there was wine in profusion. Within a twenty-mile radius there were at least twenty wineries, and believe me, the price was right!

True, there was no Château d'Yquem, but there was an astonishingly good wine that resembled it in many pleasant ways, and cost about one-tenth the price.

True, there was no dry Sherry to compare with my father-in-law's Tío Pepe, but over in the nearby Napa Valley there was a vintner making a Sherry that tasted good even to my father-in-law's discriminating palate. It made him offer the following enthusiastic, if somewhat left-handed compliment: "Why, Jim, this almost tastes like a *real* Sherry!"

Naturally, it cost about a third the price of the fine Spanish Sherries. Even today, its still an outstanding bargain, representative of the kind of unrecognized values that I plan to talk about in the next few chapters.

The life of a wine drinker is filled with problems

The growing popularity of wine in the United States has not been without its problems. One is how to pronounce all those difficult names, like Cabernet Sauvignon and Pouilly-Fuissé, and another is how not to lose face in a restaurant while trying to decide between a 1977 and a 1980 vintage.

Not to mention the problem of deciding whether it is more chic to have red with meat and white with fish, or to be the kind of person who knows all the rules but conspicuously ignores them.

The wine ceremony; or, customer vs. waiter

Then there is the problem of the wine ceremony, as conducted in an expensive restaurant. This is a stylized drama, not unlike the Japanese tea ceremony, in which a restaurant waiter shows the requested bottle to the customer, uncorks it, offers the cork for the diner's inspection, wipes the mouth of the bottle with extravagant care, and finally, pours a tiny sample into the customer's glass.

The ball is now in the customer's court, and it is up to him to determine whether it is, or is not, fit for his table. It is of no consequence to the ceremony that the customer never rejects a bottle, not even when it tastes like fusel oil. The diner's problem, of course, is that he's totally unsure whether the stuff they've poured into his glass is what he's ordered. His second problem is his belief that the waiter knows everything there is to know about wine, and will sneer, no matter what course of action the diner takes.

True, the waiter may sneer, but chances are his wine knowledge matches that of the legendary diner who, after sniffing and swishing and sipping the sample at some length, turned to the waiter with a bright look of discovery, and said, "Wine! Right?"

It is possible to send a bottle of wine back without suffering ignominy or bodily harm, and everyone should do it at least once during one's lifetime. I did it for the first time a number of years ago, and the incident gave me courage, confidence, and a good story to tell at dinner parties.

 Winesmanship: Nelson & Friedman vs. the Fior d'Italia

It came about through my having lunch—and a bottle of wine—about once a month with my good friend Mike Friedman. We were discussing the apparent boredom with which our waiter had carried out the wine-tasting ritual, when an idea occurred to me.

"Mike," I said, "have you ever sent a bottle of wine back to the cellar?"

"No," he said. "Have you?"

"No," I said. "But I think it's about time."

Then we hatched our plan. The next time we had lunch in our accustomed restaurant, we would reject the bottle, no matter how it tasted.

I could hardly wait for our next luncheon, especially since it was my turn to pay for lunch, which meant that, as host, I would be in charge of the wine tasting.

When the day arrived, I selected a modest California Zinfandel and sat back, waiting for our waiter to run through his act. He uncorked, splashed a few thimblefuls into my glass, and waited.

I sniffed the wine casually, swished it in the glass, took a sip, and tried to look thoughtful. I lifted my eyebrows slightly, ran through a few mouth movements, and took another sip. I paused.

"Mike," I said, "I think you'd better taste this. It seems a bit off to me."

Mike looked properly surprised. "Oh?" he said.

The waiter suddenly came to life. The monotonous pattern of his day had been interrupted. He looked at me, he looked at Mike.

"Give the doctor a taste of the wine, please," I said.

The waiter poured a sample in Mike's glass, and Mike held it up to the light. He swished it around in the glass, sniffed it, and looked at me.

"Hmmm," he said.

He took a sip and looked out over the dining room. He took another sip, rolled it around in his mouth, and put his glass down.

"I see what you mean," he said. "Off. Definitely off. Too acidic. Just not right."

"Better bring another bottle," I told the waiter.

The waiter was dumbfounded. The incident was apparently a first for him, too.

"Another bottle?" he said.

I looked him in the eye. Friendly, cool, James Bond through and through.

"Can't drink this one," I said.

It took some little time for the next bottle to arrive. When it did, it was accompanied not only by our waiter, but by the maître d'.

"I'm sorry about that bottle of wine," he said. "You were right. I tasted it. It was too acid. It happens." He shook his head. "Here, try this bottle."

We repeated the tasting ceremony. Mike and I looked at each other judiciously and nodded.

"This bottle is just fine," I said. The maître d' looked relieved. The waiter still looked stunned.

The maître d' nodded thoughtfully.

"It happens," he said, as he started to move away. "It happens."

I'm sure the kitchen drank and enjoyed our rejected bottle of wine, and I'm sure that, from our continued patronage, the restaurant has recouped its loss. The waiter, though, may never be the same.

 Decisions, decisions! California vs. the United Nations

There are, of course, lots of problems besides the restaurant wine ceremony and the pronunciation of difficult names that face anyone with a growing interest in wine. There is the question of whether to stick to traditional French wines and "be safe," or whether to go exclusively for American wines, or whether to admit both to your cellar (even if your cellar is three bottles stashed in the broom closet). There is the question of whether a wine from Yugoslavia is any good, and even if it is, whether you look like a dummy serving it to company. And so on. In fact, a diligent winesman, playing winesmanship, can find an infinite number of things to worry about.

The problem we're worrying about in this book, however, is *good wines at a price*. If we had unlimited incomes, we'd have no problem finding good wines.

A Bill of Rights for Prudent Wine Lovers
But since we don't, we're going to adopt the Wine Lover's Magna Carta, which will set down some basic principles from which we will not deviate.

The first article of the Wine Lover's Magna Carta is that wine is going to be a pleasure, not a mystique. We are not going to make a religion out of it, nor are we going to use it as a means of snowing our friends (except now and then).

The second article of our Magna Carta is that we're going to drink the wine, not the label. This doesn't mean we won't serve wine in labeled bottles, because sometimes we will, and sometimes we won't. What it does mean is that we're going to judge our wines solely on how they look and taste and smell, and whether they fit within our budgetary limit.

Third, we are going to become detectives and shoppers, not just buyers.

Fourth, and finally, our Wine Lover's Magna Carta states that we are not under any circumstances going to drink, serve, or otherwise fool around with any wine we can't put on our table for $5.00 per 750-ml bottle, or less.

Ours is a pleasant, humanitarian mission. We start it, secure in the knowledge that we can afford it, since most of the world's wine is drunk by people poorer than ourselves, and all but the tiniest fraction of it is inexpensive. Surely, we are entitled to think of ourselves as explorers, setting out bravely across a vast, uncharted sea of wine, domestic and imported, in search of the Golden Bottle.

2

How to find great wines under $5,
AND WHAT TO DO WHEN YOU FIND THEM

You might think that the wine that comes from next door should be cheaper than the wine from thousands of miles away, but that's not always the case. I recently discovered a Bulgarian red wine that was extraordinarily pleasant, selling for $2.99 a bottle. I discovered it by reading a wine newsletter that ordinarily concerns itself only with very fine, very expensive wines of the kinds that almost never find their way into my home. The writer of the newsletter gave an unusually warm recommendation for the $2.99 wine, because it represented such an outstanding value.

You might think that the bargain Bulgarian wine was a freak, but this is not so. This kind of bargain will be repeated again and again during the next twelve months. It's up to you and me to track these bargains down, evaluate them to make sure they're really the bargains we hope they are, and, if they are, buy them.

How much do the experts know?

Let me tell you about a wine tasting that took place not too long ago under the auspices of a well-known consumer magazine. First, the magazine assembled a panel of wine experts. Some were professionals who made their living through their wine expertise, and some were private individuals whose cellars and wine knowledge were widely recognized. In a blind tasting—that is, the experts tasted various white wines without any knowledge of which wine was which—the wine that placed fifth, trailing after four lower-priced U.S. wines, was a well-known French wine selling, at the time, for $8.50 a bottle. The wine the experts placed in the number-one spot was an American wine costing only $2.49 for a full 750-ml bottle.

Chances are, the experts were red-faced when they discovered what they had done. The lesson for us is that even the trained palates of experts help prove the fact that you don't have to spend a bundle to get a good wine.

So, the first question to be answered is this: Now that you've agreed to pay as much as $5.00 a bottle for a sound, presentable wine, where do you start?

Your liquor dealer can be a big help

Well, your number-one starting place is your friendly neighborhood liquor dealer. Depending on which state you live in, this person may be your supermarket operator, your druggist, a government employee, or simply your friendly neighborhood liquor dealer.

Whichever he or she is, he is a person you want to make friends with, because if he's any good, he can be a big help. Many liquor dealers, particularly those who operate stores with large wine sections, take the trouble to taste their merchandise. Thus, many of them have acquired a knowledge of wine that enables them to give their customers a good bit of fairly expert help. Often, this applies equally whether the customer is wondering which $12.95 Pouilly-Fumé to serve with the fish course, or which of three Burgundies in the 4-liters-for-$4.99 range is the best value.

Taking notes is important
Okay, so you've come to your neighborhood liquor store. Now it's time to go to work. I mentioned earlier that the pursuit of high-quality wines with low price tags involves a modest amount of record-keeping, and here's where it starts. Obviously, you have to go about it in your own way, but in case you don't have a way, let me tell you how I do it. I keep a small, thin notebook with me at all times—well, almost all times—and although I occasionally use it for other purposes, I use it principally to record names, prices, and other information about wines that I see on the shelf or taste in a restaurant. Some typical entries might look like this:

> Nov. 29. Don's Liquors: Sonoma Vineyards Red Table Wine. Don recommends as crisp, lively, fruity. $3.99 for 1.5 liters.

Nov. 29. Also at Don's: Bollini Chardonnay. Italian white, nice bottle and label. Don hasn't tried yet. $3.99 for 750 ml.

Dec. 4. Covington Bar & Grill. House red is August Sebastiani Country Zinfandel. Dry, velvety, nice bouquet. Should try.

For better or worse, that's the way I keep my "source" record. You'll devise your own way.

Keeping this kind of record also helps you compare prices from one store to another. That's important to a bargain hunter, because not every retailer sells the same wine at the same price. Example: One day recently I found the same California 1.5-liter table wine selling for $3.49 in one store and for $6.49 in another!

So there you stand, notebook and pencil in hand, just inside your liquor dealer's front door. You are now ready to start your systematic (and very pleasant) research into the world of bargain wines.

Naturally, the first thing you do is to start listing all the wines you see that are in 750-ml bottles and sell at a shelf price of $5.00 or less. You can list them by winemaker—all the Inglenooks in one list, for example—or you can list them by type, putting all the Burgundies together, all the Zinfandels together, and so on.

Of course, just because you've said you would pay as much as $5.00 doesn't mean that you're going to start forking out $5.00 right at the start. Actually, you're going to try to beat that figure as much as possible. Nevertheless, you might as well get acquainted with the "top of the line" as far as your particular budget is concerned, and then work your way down to the real bargains.

In my nearby Safeway supermarket, which has a fairly routine wine department, I recently found 143 different wines that fitted our $5.00-a-bottle budget. That didn't include any "pop" wines or sangrías, nor did it include a very large number of wines in containers larger than 750 milliliters—no. 1.5's, no jugs, no bag-in-a-box, etcetera.

The incredible variety of wines available
Incidentally, while we're talking about variety, let me point out that in your U.S. wine shop you'll find more different kinds of wines, from more different foreign countries, and from more different regions of the United States, than you will find in wine shops anywhere in the world.

If you lived in Madrid, for example, you would naturally find lots of Spanish wines on the shelves, plus some Port from nearby Portugal, plus a smattering of French wines at very high prices, plus, if you were lucky, a German or Italian wine or two. And that would be it.

If you lived in Paris, you would find a bewildering variety of marvelous French wines, plus a bewildering variety of French wines not quite so marvelous, plus some Spanish wines, and some from Germany and Italy. In a very fashionable shop, you might even find, moldering on the shelves, a few lonely bottles of wine from the United States.

The story would be the same in other countries. In an Argentine wine shop I recently found an unlimited quantity of very good Argentine wines, but only a few from Bolivia, a couple from Chile, and that was it. Period. Nothing from Europe, Africa, the United States, or anywhere else.

 Where they come from

But let's take the United States. In my Safeway, the one I mentioned just a few paragraphs ago, a store that is not by any person's definition a haven for wine connoisseurs, I recently found wine from Spain, Portugal, Italy, France, Australia, Germany, Japan, Israel, and of course, a large number from the good old U.S.A.

On my way home from Safeway, I stopped in a very fancy, large-volume shop not too far from where I live and found wines from all the countries I've mentioned so far, plus a substantial representation from Bulgaria, Yugoslavia, the People's Republic of China, Hungary, Greece, Canada, Mexico, Czechoslovakia, Chile, Argentina, South Africa, Denmark, and Morocco!

Many of them, of course, go over our budget. But enough will fall within our limits to make our efforts worthwhile. So, after you're sure your notebook contains a catalog of the store's offering of $5.00-and-under wines, the next thing to do is have a chat with the man or woman who runs the store. Be frank about what you're doing, and you stand a very good chance of enlisting his or her help. This kind of help can often save you both time and money, as well as giving you some ideas about buying wine that may never have occurred to you.

How your dealer can help

You may find, for example, that your liquor dealer has some wines in his back room that haven't yet made it out to the selling floor. If he thinks they fit the specifications of what you're looking for, he'll go into the back room and drag them out. If you've got a particularly tolerant and cooperative dealer, he may even let you look at his price book, containing the printed listing of all the wines available through distributors in his area.

You can't taste a wine that's only a name and a price on the printed page, but if you find one that looks interesting, you can ask your dealer to order some for you, so you can give it a try. In some cases, he can order a single bottle for you, but the main thing is to get him interested in your project. He may turn out to be as curious about the unknown, low-priced wine in the price listings as you are. And if you need a partner in this particular type of research, you couldn't find a better partner than a liquor dealer!

I cannot emphasize too strongly the importance of trying to get a look at the price listings. In California alone, there are some 8,000 different kinds of wine for sale, and since many of them come in different sizes, you get a rough total of 10,000 to 15,000 different kinds and sizes of wines available for you to choose from!

No single retailer can carry even a fraction of this bewildering variety. But every retailer in the state can order a case of any wine carried by the wholesalers with whom he deals. So if your friendly neighborhood wine merchant lets you take a peek at his price postings, and if you find a wine from Ithaca or

Iceland that you'd like to try, and if you can talk this friendly neighborhood wine merchant into ordering a bottle or two or three, you can try all kinds of wines from all kinds of places at a very modest out-of-pocket cost.

Some store operators know quite a bit about wine and are only too glad to pass their expertise on to a willing listener. Others may never have progressed beyond bourbon-on-the-rocks-with-a-twist. If this is the case with the particular wine merchant who serves your neighborhood, you may as well recognize and accept the fact that you're going to have to find another more wine-oriented dealer.

But don't let that discourage you. Because, even if your first dealer turns out to know quite a bit about wine, you will still want to make a wine safari through a number of other liquor stores. And you'll want to talk to as many knowledgeable wine-oriented store operators as possible, because it's a good idea to get as many informed opinions as you can.

 Different stores, different wines
Wisdom is not the only reason for canvassing other stores, however. Wine variety is another. No two stores carry precisely the same wines. This is frequently true even of different stores in the same chain. The variation in wines stocked is often the result of the differing tastes of different neighborhoods, differing tastes of different store managers, and sometimes, as in everything else in life, simple inefficiency and confusion.

So, pencil and notebook in hand, scour the shelves of as many liquor emporiums as your time and patience can stand. Take a Saturday afternoon, or several Saturday afternoons, and visit different areas of your city. Often where you least expect it, you will find a wine you've never heard of before. It may be the store's own "house brand"—wine available only in that store, or chain of stores, and nowhere else. Sometimes, these wines can be very good. Or, it may be a wine from Europe or South America or South Africa, or from a town you've never heard of in California or New York State. But whatever it is, if you haven't seen it before, you'll feel a little like Admiral Peary finding the North Pole.

Does your town have a Latin Quarter?

If there is a section of your city populated by an ethnic minority accustomed to wine drinking, take a look in the liquor stores in that area. Sometimes you'll find a wine or two in these shops that are sold nowhere else in town. Buy a bottle and enter it in your taste-test sweepstakes.

Thus far, I've only talked about those wines that, as they stand on the shelf in their 750-ml bottles, cost $5.00 or less.

The magic of rebottling

But let's do some mathematics, because the real leverage in putting commendable wines on your table for $2.50 a bottle, or $1.50, or even less, lies in the strategy of buying wine in larger containers and rebottling. Instead of buying a 750-ml bottle for, say, $3.29, you buy a 4-liter jug for $8.99, and, unless you're giving a party where you're going to use it all up at once, you put the contents of the jug into five 750-ml bottles and cork them.

I have in my cellar right now (my cellar is my garage, in case you thought it was something fancier) eleven bottles of an extremely pleasant, medium dry, slightly fruity white wine that cost me exactly $1.25 a bottle. The bottles are green and attractive. The labels are suitably home-made. Our guests love it. They can't identify it, and they usually don't ask. My wife and I love it, and frequently find it a more-than-adequate accompaniment to a party dinner, a weekday hamburger, or a pizza from the nearby Lo Coco's Pizza emporium.

Here's how I found it. In poking around through a liquor store I had never been in before—notebook in pocket—I came across an Italian wine whose name was new to me. The price: $4.99 for three liters. You couldn't say the price wasn't right! Of course, I would have preferred to buy 750 milliliters of this wine to take home and try, but it didn't come that way. So, I took home a 1.5-liter bottle and blind-tested it against another good-tasting, somewhat more expensive wine of which I was quite fond. I found I liked the new, unfamiliar label, which was the cheaper of the two, more than I liked the more familiar wine.

For me this was a little bit like Edison inventing the electric light. I was delighted with my find, and, that same evening, so were our next-door neighbors, who came over and helped us finish the test samples over meatballs and spaghetti.

The following day, I went back to the store and bought three 3-liter jugs of this same Italian wine. The 1.5 liter sold for $3.79, the 3-liter sold for $4.99. I took the three jugs home, rebottled them into twelve empty 750-ml bottles I had been saving for just such an occasion. I then laid them carefully on their sides in one of the numerous cardboard wine cartons I use for storage in the garage.

Out of the three 3-liter jugs I got, naturally, twelve 750-ml bottles of wine. Eleven of them are still resting in the bottles I have mentioned. The twelfth, as you might have suspected, disappeared the night of the rebottling, along with a succulent dinner of red snapper, broccoli, and fried potatoes.

Now, when a 3-liter jug of wine costs $4.99, a 750-ml bottle of that same wine costs only $1.25. Provided, of course, that you, and not the winery, have put it into the 750-ml bottles.

Try it and see. The results will demonstrate that you can really afford to put much better wine on your dinner table than you thought possible, and still stay below—well below—the upper reaches of your budget.

The New Math for wine buffs

Look at it this way. You've already agreed that, for certain especially good wines, you'd be willing to shell out as much as $5.00 a 750-ml bottle. Well, how many 750's in a 3-liter bottle? Four. If you multiply $5.00 by four, you get $20.00. That means that you can pay as much as $20.00 for a 3-liter bottle of wine and, by rebottling, still stay within your $5.00 budget.

Don't expect to find many wines selling at $20.00 for three liters, however. The more expensive a wine gets, the less likely it is to come in jug sizes. Nevertheless, a large number of very good wines do come in 3-liter sizes, and in other sizes larger than the standard 750 ml, and if current trends continue, there will be many more high-quality wines put out in larger containers. With wine consumption increasing, and inflation chipping away at our pocketbooks, more and more people are finding that they don't really want to buy their wine in smallish, costly, 750-ml containers.

So, what do you do if the wine you want to buy at $20.00-or-less per 3-liter jug isn't available in that size? All is not lost. You can still save yourself money by rebottling from 1.5-liter bottles.

Let's talk about the 1.5-liter "magnum." This size bottle yields two 750-ml bottles, and two times $5.00 is $10.00. This means you can spend as much as $10.00 for a magnum of a wine that pleases your palate, rebottle it into 750-ml bottles, and still be within your $5.00-a-bottle budget.

A note of caution. If you're rebottling from 4-liter bottles, or from a larger bag-in-a-box container, you may end up with a bottle that's only partly filled. If so, use it at your next meal. If you cork it and store it partially full, you'll be leaving too much air in with the wine, and the wine will almost certainly go bad.

 The case discount may help
Another cost-cutting device is the 10 percent case discount, if you don't mind laying in some inventory. Let me give you an example, just to explain the mathematics.

I'm very fond of a particular California Cabernet Sauvignon, but since it has recently been selling at $5.99 for 750 milliliters, it's over my Poorperson's budget. Even if I buy a case of twelve bottles, and therefore get the customary 10 percent case discount, that only brings the bottle price down to $5.39.

This particular wine also comes in 1.5-liter bottles, however, at a price of $10.49 per bottle. If I buy a case of six magnums, the case discount brings the price down to $9.44 per bottle. That's clearly under our maximum price of $10.00 for a magnum, and puts me back within the confines of our Magna Carta. So what do I do? I buy the case—I generally have to place a special order with my liquor dealer—and when I get it, I leave three magnums as is, and bottle the other three into six empty 750-ml bottles. Then I'm ready for any occasion!

Let's sum up all this messy financial information in a table. As long as you buy in the quantities indicated at the top of the table, you can select wines having shelf prices up to the maximums listed in each column and still be putting wine on your table for $5.00 a bottle, or less. Let's take a look:

Allowable shelf price per bottle to stay within a wine lover's guidelines

Bottle size	If you buy a single bottle	If you buy a case of 12 bottles	If you buy a case of 6 bottles	If you buy a case of 4 bottles
750 ml	$5.00	$5.56		
1.5 l	$10.00		$11.11	
3 l	$20.00			$22.22

Supplies for rebottling

So, let's do some rebottling. First, you need empty 750-ml wine bottles, which I'm sure comes as no surprise. You can buy full wine bottles and drink the contents or you can buy new bottles.

You also need corks, which you get in the same way. If you like wine and drink wine, chances are you may have a few empty bottles around the house, and maybe even some corks. In any event, today is the day you stop throwing away corks and empty wine bottles!

If you don't have enough bottles yourself, you can ask neighbors and friends to start saving their empties—and their corks—for you.

If you have a friend in the restaurant business, you might see if there is some way you can get a supply of empties from him. But be careful, because in some states it's against the law for an eating or drinking establishment to do anything other than break empty bottles in which alcoholic beverages of any kind have entered the restaurant.

Finally, of course, when all else fails, you can buy new or used bottles, and new corks. New bottles currently cost about $4.50 a dozen, corks go for about $11.00 to $12.00 per hundred. Once bought, they can be used over and over again—more true of the bottles than the corks, of course, but even a cork can be used two or three times before it's finished.

You'll find a list of suppliers of bottles, corks, labels, and corking machines at the back of the book. Write them for price lists and catalogs. They're well accustomed to handling mail orders.

Okay, so now you have a big collection of empty wine bottles, and some corks, new or otherwise, and some 3-liter bottles of a fine Chenin Blanc or Burgundy or Zinfandel that you want to put into the bottles.

Why rebottle? Spoilage is one reason

Maybe, as you start the process, you're wondering why you're rebottling at all. Why not just open up the 3-liter bottle, use what you want, recap it, and put it away for another day?

The answer, of course, is that the large amount of air in the partially emptied 3-liter bottle will cause the wine to deteriorate. Then, next time you invite your friends over for dinner, the wine won't taste half as good as it did when it was first opened. By rebottling, you can open a small amount at a time, while the rest sits safe, fresh, and we hope, cool, in your cellar, garage, closet, or basement.

Rebottling: Psychology is another reason

Another reason for rebottling, which really belongs in the chapter on serving wines, is that the effect of opening a 750-ml bottle and putting it on the table at dinner is quite different from the effect you get by plunking a 3-liter jug on the table.

Even if a jug is freshly opened, and your party is going to empty it before the evening is over, there's something psychologically more pleasing about pouring from a nice, green, unlabeled or home-labeled 750-ml bottle than from a big jug. It's a little like the difference between having a single, beautiful ruddy apple served to you on a china plate, with appropriate silverware and a napkin, or taking the same apple out of a bulky paper sack.

Same apple, different experience. Same wine, but it doesn't *seem* the same!

The first thing you want to do before rebottling is to wash the bottles inside and out. If you're fussy or if you're planning to store the wine for a year or more, you may want to sterilize them. If you don't know how to wash and rinse a bottle, I'm not going to help you, but you may need help on how to sterilize one. All you do is wash the bottles and put them in the oven—make sure the oven is cold—and then heat the oven to about 450 degrees. Let the bottles "bake" for an hour or so; then turn the oven off and let them cool down. When it's all over, you will have some nice, clean bottles that are free of any yeasts, bacteria, or other adulterants that might cause some change in the wine you're going to store.

Now, the corks. As we mentioned earlier, they can be new, or they can come from previous bottles of wine you may have opened. If they're used, but in pretty good shape, considering what you did to them with the corkscrew, then they'll do for rebottling. If you mangled them excessively in getting them out of the bottle, you might as well toss them out.

At this point let me put in a plug for the "Ah-So" opener. It's an unusual device that has two flat legs that you insert on either side of the cork, between the cork and the bottle. Once the legs are inserted, you twist the opener and pull, and out comes the cork, completely unpunctured, unharmed, and ready to go again. It's better than most corkscrews, and easy to use. If you *don't* care about saving the cork, however, an even better opener is the Screwpull. The way it works is almost magical.

Using a clean funnel, fill your five bottles. If the jug you're pouring from doesn't quite seem to stretch, fill four bottles to within half an inch of the cork, and let the fifth bottle fill as much as it can. If it falls short of the half-inch-from-the-cork mark, don't worry. At least you've confined your air-deterioration problem, if any, to a single bottle, rather than spreading it evenly over all five bottles. Drink the slightly short bottle soon, with the Wednesday hash perhaps, and save the other four for nobler occasions.

Corking bottles

We now come to the problem of corking the five bottles. There are two ways to accomplish this: (1) brute force; (2) a corking machine.

Which of these two methods you use is up to you. I used the brute-force method for quite a while, accompanying it with grunts, groans, and various expletives. Subsequently, I bought a hand-held corking machine for about $11.00 and have been happy ever since. You can get a simple two-stage corking machine (the first stage is compressing the cork, the second driving it into the neck of the bottle), for prices ranging from $7.98 to $70.00 from various of the equipment sources listed in the back of the book. In my book, they're worth it.

Either way, brute force or machine, you should

soften the corks in warm water before you try putting them into the bottles. Some counselors advise you to boil them before putting them in. Others say that boiling destroys significant amounts of cellulose in the cork. However, since we are not laying down a Château Latour to mature some twenty years down the road, but rather are simply trying to assemble a small, drinkable cellar without going to debtor's prison, we need not be quite as fussy about our techniques as the château bottlers. Be clean, be careful, but don't turn it into a religion.

Now that you know how to rebottle from jugs into 750-ml bottles, let's get back to the business of how to find wines worthy of rebottling. Let's see how many ways there are for finding sound, enjoyable wines, and getting them at the right price.

 House wines can aid your search
Well, one thing to consider is the fact that almost every restaurant nowadays has a "house wine." In fact, given the state of the economy, many *bon vivants* who always used to call for the wine list and spend twenty minutes deciding whether to have a Cabernet or a Pinot Noir now simply ask for a carafe of the house red. They frequently get a pretty good wine in the bargain.

For the bargain hunter, a restaurant's house wine is simply another chance to evaluate a wine that you can probably afford to put on your own table. Even restaurants with very high standards are now serving house wines poured from larger-than-750-ml containers, wines that cost less than our top allowable prices. So, next time you have a restaurant meal, have a glass of the house red or the house white along with it. If you enjoy the wine, ask the waiter about the brand and type. If the waiter leaves you wondering whether or not he got the answer to the question right, go to the bar and ask the bartender on your way out. In almost every case, provided it appears that you're asking the question because you enjoyed the wine, you'll find the bartender happy to haul out the bottle from which he poured your glass and let you have a look at the label.

Then, out with the notebook. Write it down: the type of wine, the maker, any special information on the label, the name of the restaurant, and the date. Also write down anything else that you thought significant about your enjoyment of that particular glass of wine.

For example, did they fill your glass at the table from a carafe? If it was a white wine, did they supply you with a chilled glass? Was there anything special about the glass itself—its design, color, ornamentation? And so forth.

Through ordering house wines and asking questions later, I have found a number of wines of which I think very highly. I now regularly decant these wines from 3-liter jugs into 750-ml bottles, cork them, and lay them down in my garage-cellar. At the same time, from dining in an expensive restaurant and watching an experienced, knowledgeable waiter serve half a liter of house wine, I have confirmed over and over again my long-time belief that the enjoyment of a good glass of wine is only about 50 percent dependent on the wine itself.

Wine tastings

How else to find good wines? Go to wine tastings. If
you happen upon a wine you like especially, find out
if it's available in the larger sizes. Even if it isn't,
write it down in your notebook. When your ship
comes in, you may be willing to pay a good bit more
than $5.00 a bottle for your table wine.

 Winery towns

If you live near wine country, go visit the wineries.
Visit the big ones, and visit the small ones. Taste everything in sight. Ask questions about sizes and
prices, and be sure to ask about any wines that are
available only at the winery. The Louis M. Martini
winery in St. Helena, California, for example, makes
an excellent dry Sherry that used to be available at the
winery in bulk sizes, but through liquor outlets only
in 750's. Alas, Martini gave up that practice some
time back, and 750's are now the only size available.
The winery is still the only place you can buy Martini's delicious Moscato Amabile, a lovely white dessert wine, but alas again, it doesn't fit our wine
lover's budget. Why do I give you this example of a
size that's discontinued and a wine we can't afford?
For the principle of the thing—so you'll remember,
when you take a wine tour, to ask about special
wines and special sizes available at the winery, and
nowhere else.

 Pricing in a fair-trade state

People who live in states that have axed their "fair-
trade" laws will feel a swell of compassion toward

those unfortunates who live in Connecticut, which still has one. Fair-trade laws, in case you're not familiar with them, are statutes that give manufacturers, and in some cases wholesalers, the right to set a price below which it is against the law to sell their products.

The fair-trade laws came into being during the Depression of the 1930s, ostensibly to protect the small retailer from the price onslaught of the big chains. While this was a commendable objective, it has been argued that, at present, the fair-trade laws simply provide a convenient mechanism for price fixing, and for frustrating the noble principle that the price of a product is a function of supply and demand.

If you live anywhere outside Connecticut, except in a "control" state, nobody has to tell you that you can save money by shopping around. When retailers are free to set the prices of their goods, you frequently find wide variations in prices for identical products. Naturally, what's true for electric razors and Sony television sets is also true for wine. In the 49 states without fair-trade laws, therefore, it pays to read the ads, watch for bargains, and check shelf prices of the wines you want to buy, before you buy them.

You'll also occasionally find in non-control, non-fair-trade states that you can "deal" with the store operator. Thus, if your individual order is big enough, or if business is bad enough, or if you can get a bunch of friends to pool orders so that your business is of unusual significance to a dealer, you can often buy your wines at savings even greater than those of the advertised specials.

Even in fair-trade and control states, however, there are bargains. Retailing being what it is, when a product doesn't move, you have to have a clearance sale. In a fair-trade or control situation, this often doesn't look like a clearance sale, in that the price cut may not be advertised, and the store may not have a bargain basement. So, you've got to look, and you've got to ask.

As an example of what can happen, let me tell you the story of a fine French wine with a long name that got a big promotional push not long ago. The wine, a high-quality white, was advertised as the perfect complement for fish dishes, and a good bit of money was spent trying to promote its popularity.

Unfortunately (fortunately, say the bargain hunters!), the campaign laid an egg. The wholesaler, who had posted a minimum resale price in the $5.25-per-750-ml range, finally got tired of carrying the inventory. A big retail dealer with several stores offered to take the inventory off his hands at a very low figure. The wholesaler agreed.

The wholesaler then posted a new minimum resale price with the state Alcohol Beverage Control Commission, and suddenly it was legal to sell this $5.25 wine for $1.99 a bottle, which the big retailer proceeded to do. For such a fine wine, the price was ridiculously low, but that's the force of circumstance. And that's what keeps us bargain hunters on our toes.

 Outside the law
There used to be another kind of bargain in a fair-trade state, but unfortunately it's slightly illegal. I do

not want to encourage the citizens of Connecticut to disobey the law, but at the same time it would only be telling part of the story if I didn't let you know that there is a substantial volume of price-controlled liquor and wine that moves regularly through retail channels at prices well below the official fair-trade prices. These dealers—sometimes known as "bombers"—probably do four times the volume in half the floor space occupied by their legitimate brothers operating two blocks up the street, simply by selling their merchandise at 10 to 30 percent below the prices the wine and liquor companies post with the state.

I won't tell you how to locate these stores, because what they do is against the law. And anyhow, your Uncle Al or your cousin Fran or the couple who lives next door know a lot more than I about which stores are doing it.

By now your notebook should be brimming over with useful information. You have long lists of wines that fit within the $5.00-a-bottle limit we've put on your expenditures, both those that cost $5.00 or less when sold in 750-ml bottles, and those that qualify when you buy the larger sizes and rebottle. You have names of house wines from your favorite restaurants, and the recommendations of wine dealers and bartenders and knowledgeable friends.

So now the problem changes. It becomes: Which of these many wines should you buy?

You *are the final judge*

Actually, the answer is up to you. Because in the final analysis, you are the person who is going to drink the wine. You are the person who is going to serve it to your guests. And, let's not forget, you are the person who is going to pay for it. Therefore, you're the person who, aided by whatever judgmental mechanisms we can come up with to help you, has to make the final purchase decision.

Actually, it isn't all that hard. And as I mentioned before, it's fun. In the next chapter I'll tell you how to go about it.

3

Evaluating what you find:
"IT COSTS ONLY $1.99, BUT IS IT ANY GOOD?"

Once, during the time that my wife and I lived in the wine country of California, we gave a party built around our guests' senses of taste, smell, and touch.

Each guest was given a pencil and paper and was then conducted individually through a series of tests designed to give him an idea of how discriminating or undiscriminating his senses were. We didn't fool around with sight or hearing, because we use these senses so actively and so often that they're usually pretty well honed. Our other senses, however, don't get this same vigorous daily workout.

For the touch test, each guest was given ten small fabric bags, each containing a different familiar article, such as a paper clip, a clothespin, a rubber eraser, and so forth, and securely closed with a tied drawstring. The object was for the guest to identify the item in the bag, simply by feeling it with his hands. Our guests did pretty well on the touch test.

The smell test consisted of uncorking and sniffing the contents of ten different bottles, and then writing down the identity of the item sniffed. Again the smells were all familiar, everyday smells—rubbing alcohol, wintergreen, vanilla extract, ammonia, bourbon whiskey, and the like.

Our guests didn't do as well on the smell tests as they did on the touch test, but they still did fairly well.

The items in the third test—taste—included milk, Coca-Cola, bicarbonate of soda, plain water, tea, coffee, and four other items. We blindfolded our guests so they wouldn't get any visual clues and served them the ten different drinks, one at a time, letting them taste each one as many times as they wanted. Also, to eliminate clues that had nothing to do with taste (coffee is hot, Coke is cold and carbonated, etc.), we served each beverage at room temperature, and in the case of soft drinks, let the fizz disappear.

How did our guests do on this test? They went bananas. They tasted milk and swore it was bicarbonate of soda. They tasted Coca-Cola and called it tea. They made positive identifications and doubtful identifications, but for the most part they made outrageously wrong identifications.

They couldn't believe it. Neither could we. It seemed that nobody could do as badly as almost everyone had, and yet the evidence was unmistakable. People who had sworn they could tell Coke from Pepsi blindfolded could barely tell it from ginger ale. We moved on to dinner and discussed the shameful results over many bottles of good, cheap, Sonoma County wine.

For our present investigation, the fact that emerges from this simple-minded party game is that, almost without exception, taste is everyone's least reliable sense. Furthermore, second place in the unreliability sweepstakes goes to our sense of smell. When you stop and think that taste and smell are what everyone uses in deciding whether a wine is a great wine or an absolute dog, you'll begin to realize that very few people know very much for certain about wines, or how to evaluate them.

In this chapter, therefore, you're going to learn something about how to sharpen up your taste buds, and how to discipline your sense of smell. And you're going to learn how to compare one wine with another in a way that, if not exactly scientific, is at least logical, and likely to produce results that you can live with happily ever after, and maybe be extremely proud of.

The first step in the process is an easy one. You simply stand in front of a mirror, look yourself in the eye, lift your chin, straighten your shoulders, and say, "Never again will I underestimate the ability of my precious taste buds. And that goes for my nose, too."

If you need encouragement in thinking that your nose and taste buds are as good as anyone else's, consider the great French Wine Scandal of 1974.

Mon Dieu! Trouble in the French wine trade!
The scandal erupted in the Bordeaux area of France, a district from which come some of the world's finest,

most famous, and not surprisingly, most expensive wines. The French government levied charges against some of the most prestigious winemakers and shippers, charges that included the most heinous crimes known to dedicated wine drinkers, far outstripping murder, rape, and plunder.

It was alleged, for example, that the Bordeaux vintners had promoted some of their wines from buck private to brigadier general simply by falsifying a few legal papers. A few quick strokes of the pen, and cheap red wines from the south of France became members of the Bordeaux nobility, bearing cherished names and price tags to match. Other wines, so poor that they were fit only to be made into vinegar, were "recovered" through treatment with chemicals, and were then sold for fancy prices.

Still others, it was alleged, were upgraded simply by switching the labels. And some costly Bordeaux reds that were in very short supply suddenly became plentiful through the judicious and totally surreptitious addition of less costly white wine.

Many of these wines were then, predictably, shipped to the United States.

The real scandal, according to one American wine connoisseur who commented on the affair, was that nobody, including the experts, seemed to have noticed the difference. The villains went merrily on, adulterating, switching labels, and in general making silk purses out of sows' ears. The wine bibbers, or at least those sophisticated enough to want the wines in question and well-heeled enough to afford them, tipped back their glasses and drank to one another's health, completely unaware that their joy was counterfeit.

"Wine experts?" said one American connoisseur. "About all that most wine experts can tell about a wine is whether it's good or bad, whether it has turned vinegary or smells skunky."

Another renowned U.S. wine pundit agreed heartily that most experts can't really tell the difference between a tampered wine and the real thing. "Even if the wine was authentic Bordeaux, there are many variables involved. The taste of a wine can change from bottle to bottle in the same case. The light in the room, the glass from which it is drunk, the cork, all have an effect."

The best thing to do, he concluded, was to relax and enjoy the wine, whatever the label might say.

If the experts are confused, where does that leave you and me? Well, it leaves us dependent on our own palates, our own noses, our own taste buds. Actually, that's not a bad dependence, because the kind of wine we want to drink and serve to our friends is the kind of wine that tastes good to *us,* and not necessarily what appeals to those people generally referred to as "the experts."

This is not to put the experts down. We need experts, and they are not dummies. Without people who care about the quality of wine, there would be no wine, because the first expert needed in the wine equation is the winemaker himself.

We need the wine connoisseurs and critics, too. They, because of their long experience and exceptional sensitivity to smells and tastes, can offer the rest of us some general guidelines that will help us evaluate wines and separate the good from the bad. They can even help us separate the very, very fine from the just plain good.

You, and only you, know what you like

What they can't tell us, however, is what we like and what we don't like. After all, there's no expert in the world who can give an authoritative pronouncement on whether chocolate tastes better than vanilla. You wouldn't believe him if he did, because it's an individual judgment. In other words, the final judgment on matters of taste preference is completely and totally up to you.

So, let's start evaluating some wines.

Let's say you've gone out on a wine-collecting mission, and you now have three or four bottles of different white wines that fall within our price guidelines. Now you want to check them out to see whether to buy some more of them—say, for example, buy 3-liter containers and then rebottle—or strike them off your list and avoid them forevermore.

The best way to judge these wines—or any wines, for that matter—is to judge them in a side-by-side comparison. In other words, the most effective way to judge a wine is to compare it with other similar wines, and not to judge it all by its lonesome.

The remembrance of things past

If your eyes, nose, and mouth have a rough equivalent of that rare quality of the ear known as perfect pitch, then side-by-side comparison probably isn't all that important to you. Perfect pitch is really nothing more than perfect memory of a previously heard sound that has been adopted as a standard against which to measure other sounds.

Thus, if your eyes can remember the visual qual-

ities, good and bad, of the wines you tasted yester-
day and last week and last year, and if your nose and
mouth can do the same thing for the wonderful smells
and tastes of wines you've consumed in your check-
ered past, then your wine evaluation standards are
more or less built-in.

The rest of us, unfortunately, don't have it that
easy. We find it hard to remember smells precisely.
Our taste buds shrug and look the other way when
asked to recall a complex taste experience from the
past. Sure, we have pleasant memories of a good dinner, an exotic perfume, an enjoyable bottle of wine,
but our recollections are usually general, not specific
enough to serve as reliable standards against which
to measure the various merits and demerits of a new,
untested bottle of wine.

Side-by-side testing

The moral is: Whenever possible, test two, three,
four, five, or more similar wines on a side-by-side
basis. As you do more and more evaluations, you will
probably find that you have a few favorite wines that
become standards. Thus, if you are going to evaluate
three new white wines, toss in your "standard"
white as a reference point. That way, when you're
through judging, you'll know whether each of the
other three is, in your opinion, better or worse than
the wine you have designated as your standard in
that category. You may even find that such a comparison will persuade you to make a different wine your
standard.

Before you can judge the merits of four or five

wines, however, you need to know how to judge just a single bottle. You need to know what to look for in terms of sight, smell, taste, and mouth-feel. You need to know how to consider the various aspects of a wine one at a time, and then again as an integrated whole. And you need to know some words to help you describe your perceptions, so you can write something useful in your wine log.

So, let's open just one of your bottles of white wine. Since it's white, it should be cold. How cold? About as cold as wine gets after two or three hours in the refrigerator. (Not in the freezer, of course.) The first step, of course, is to uncork your bottle. The word "uncork" may not be totally accurate, because the bottle you're going to evaluate may have come with a metal screw-type closure. For many years, I used to think that this kind of metal closure was somehow technically inferior to a cork, but this is not the case. True, you'll generally find metal closures on bottles of lower-priced wines, and corks in the necks of the more expensive ones, but that's not necessarily related to their abilities to preserve wine over a long period.

 Air is the enemy
Both closures keep wine's old enemy, air, from getting into the bottle and spoiling the wine. The metal closure keeps air out, period. The cork closure, some winemakers feel, allows the wine to breathe a bit, permitting, over the many years that a wine may lie aging on its side in a cool cellar, imperceptible amounts of air to pass through the wine-soaked cork

(in which direction I'm not sure) for the ultimate greater glory of the wine when it is drunk.

Whether this is the absolute truth or a winemaker's fairy tale, I don't know. What I do know is that there is a great deal more ceremony, drama, and pleasant tribal ritual in withdrawing a single purpled cork from the neck of a bottle than there is in unscrewing fifteen patented metal closures.

Sniffing corks

Got your bottle open? Okay, if you opened it by withdrawing a cork, you might as well sniff the wet end of the cork to see if it gives you any clues. Actually, it will only give you clues of the grossest type. For example, if the end that's supposed to be wet is dry and crumbly instead, this could mean that the bottle has been stored standing up rather than lying down. The result is that the cork has dried out, and when the cork dries out, the air gets in, and there goes the neighborhood.

On the other hand, if the cork is nice and moist, it probably means that the wine has been properly stored on its side. A moist cork is no guarantee that the wine hasn't turned to vinegar, but if it has, you'll probably get a vinegary whiff from the cork.

If you don't get any whiff at all, don't worry. Neither do a lot of other people who sniff corks. So sniff it, pause, look suitably thoughtful, and then put the cork down beside the bottle. The great wine ritual has begun, and you've already scored two points for corksmanship.

Choosing glasses
Now, pour some wine into a glass. You can taste wine
in a cut-crystal tumbler or a plastic orange-juice glass.
However, since the way you serve wine can affect the
way you perceive its quality, you might as well give
it the best possible chance to succeed, by serving it in
a fair-sized, simple, clear, slightly tapered wineglass
with a stem. For years I have used a simple, inexpensive, and I think handsome restaurant glass, which I
buy by the dozen. Libbey Glass makes them. They're
called Citation, and the item number is 8456. Now,
fill your glass about a quarter full. You are about to go
through the kind of scoring procedure that the professors of viticulture and enology—grape growing
and winemaking—use at the University of California
at Davis.

The University of California scoring system
These professors are renowned for their wine expertise and use a scoring system that looks complex at
the outset. Actually, after you've worked with it for a
while, it's not that hard at all. It's only one system of
several you can use (we'll talk about another one
later), but it's a good one, because it breaks the wine
experience down into its individual component
parts. Long term, you may find you'd rather use a
simpler system for your judging, but you'll also find
that a short-term use of the University of California
system will acquaint you with each of the various
basic wine characteristics the professors and critics
and connoisseurs think are important.

The system rates wines on ten separate characteristics, and assigns points for each. Here are the categories and the maximum number of points allowed:

Characteristics:	Maximum points:
Appearance	2
Color	2
Aroma and bouquet	4
Acescence	2
Total acid	2
Sugar	1
Body	1
Flavor	2
Astringency	2
General quality	2

We'll take up each characteristic one at a time. But in the meantime, you should know that the system uses a scorecard, and if you want to use this system, you will, too. It doesn't matter whether you record your scores in a loose-leaf notebook or a file of 3 × 5 cards. The main thing is to establish a written, dated record of how you rate various wines on the scale from zero to 20.

A perfect wine, if there is such a thing, would score a full 20 points in the U.C. system. A wine that scores zero would undoubtedly clean the rust out of your car radiator.

For a sample of what your scorecard should look like, more or less, take a look at page 62.

Okay, your glass is now about a quarter full of an unevaluated white wine, and you're ready to begin. So, let's judge the wine on the first characteristic: appearance.

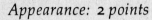 *Appearance:* 2 *points*

Hold the glass up to the light and take a look. You'll need good light and a white background in order to get a really good look at the wine. If your kitchen, dining room, or parlor doesn't happen to have a white background, you can always hang up a sheet, a tablecloth, or a big swatch of white shelf paper.

Does the wine look clear? Is it cloudy? Or is it somewhere in between? If there is no sign of any suspended material floating around in it (pieces of cork don't count), and if it has a nice, sparkling, clear look to it, you can say that the wine is *brilliant* and give it 2 points. Two points is the most a wine can earn for its appearance.

If the wine has a slight haziness, but not enough to cause you to notice it the first instant you look, you call it *clear* and give it 1 point. If you notice the haziness right away, however, you call the wine *dull,* and if it's worse than just hazy, and has quite a bit of suspended material, you call the wine *cloudy.* In either case, dull or cloudy, you score your wine with a big fat goose egg in the appearance category.

Does that sound difficult? If it does, I've misled you, because all it means is this: Is the wine nice and clear (2 points)? Or is it cloudy (zero)? If you can't make up your mind whether it's clear or cloudy, give it 1 point, and move on to the next scoring category, which is color.

 Color: 2 *points*

If you're judging an $18.00 bottle of Bernkasteler Doktor, the color may give you some problems. The reason is, some people have been drinking and judging this famous German white wine for years and years, and they know what it "ought to look like." Fortunately, this is unlikely to be a problem for us. All we really need to decide, therefore, is whether the color is pleasing to our eye, and whether, in some only slightly definable way, it's matched to the taste of the wine.

The color range of white wines runs from light straw yellow, which is the lightest shade of the lightest wines, such as Chablis, through medium yellow, light gold (we're getting darker now), and on into light, medium, and dark amber.

Judging the color of whites

If the white wine you are judging, therefore, has a pleasing color, principally yellow, gold, or straw (amber is for Sherries, Ports, Muscatels, and the like), give it the full 2 points. If it's bleached looking, almost colorless, give it 1 point or none. Nobody likes a watery-looking (or -tasting) wine. You can also give it 1 point or none if it looks brownish, or has any other unpleasant color overtones. If a white wine looks a tiny bit green, don't worry. In fact, you can even feel slightly good about it, because it may just be residual chlorophyll, which in many cases is a desirable characteristic.

Portugal is famous for its *vinhos verdes,* or green wines, which are called green because they are made from grapes that have not fully matured. Sometimes they have a greenish cast, although not always, and to round out their theme of greenness, they are drunk

very young. California has its green wines, too, and
they generally score a solid 2 points on the rating
scale.

Judging the color of reds

Red wines range from low pink, which means
washed out, through medium pink, low red, and medium red, to high red. Medium pink is what most
rosé wines are supposed to be, and medium red is the
standard for the great bulk of red wines. So, if you've
bought a bottle of wine that's labeled Burgundy or
Claret or Zinfandel, it ought to be a nice, rich, red
color and you should score it 2 points. If it has a few
hints of purple, you're into what is known as the
high red area, and there's still no need to knock off
any points. On the other hand, if your Burgundy is
pink instead of red, better give it 1 point, or none,
depending on how light the color is. Naturally, it's
the other way around for rosé wines. If they're too
red, you'll want to knock off a point or two. Same
thing goes in case they're "watery pink." Don't worry
about whether or not you're doing it right. You'll develop a feeling for color after you've looked at a number of wines—*really* looked, that is, which is something you may not have done much—and swirled
them in a glass and held them up to a good light.

Aroma and bouquet: 4 points

We now move on to aroma and bouquet, a category
otherwise known as "Does it smell good?" Since
smell is such an important part of the wine evaluation
process, your wine has an opportunity to score 4

points for this characteristic. This is more points than we award for any other single characteristic.

Swirl the wine in your glass. This gives it a chance to "breathe," and to release its fragrance. It also gives you a chance to ponder the difference between aroma and bouquet, which are really not the same thing.

If the news surprises you, don't be concerned, because the difference is not really that important. Still, as a budding wine bore, you ought to know.

Judging aroma . . .

Aroma is that odor which comes from the fact that what you are smelling is, in actual fact, the juice of crushed grapes. The experts describe this grapey smell as the wine's aroma. If the wine smells nice and grapey, but not like any specific variety of grape, you describe the aroma of the wine as being *vinous*.

If you are knowledgeable enough to be able to smell a wine and detect that it is indeed made from a particular variety of grape, then, even if you can't identify the variety, you call the aroma *distinct*. If you can actually identify the grape as a Zinfandel or a Cabernet or a Pinot Noir, you go to the head of the class and announce that the aroma is *varietal*. Naturally, in assessing aroma, the intensity of the aroma gets evaluated, too. It can be light, medium, or high, and as you might already have guessed, high is best.

. . . and bouquet

Now we come to bouquet. Bouquet is a product of the aging of wines. It is what happens after the wine is put into the barrel, or subsequently, the bottle, and it has to do with the reaction between its alcohols and acids.

It often results in a somewhat sweet, fruity, unusually pleasant smell. To some noses a wine may have a bouquet that makes them think of violets, or clover, or roses, or any of a number of other agreeable smells. When such a bouquet is strong, you'll find you can get a lot of pleasure from just sitting and sniffing, long before you take your first taste. Just remember, however, if you want to be precise in describing this smell, not to call it aroma, because it isn't. It's bouquet.

How should you score your wine on aroma and bouquet? Well, some professional judges say that, as a starter, they give a wine 2 points if it smells pleasantly vinous, 3 if it has some varietal overtones, and 4 if it has a nice, recognizable varietal aroma. At the same time, since aroma and bouquet share the same four points, the judges admit that they are mixing their perceptions of bouquet in with their perceptions of aroma and at the same time are scoring the intensity of both these factors. How they make this extraordinary computation is their own mysterious secret. How *you* make it is yours.

 In simpler terms . . .
My own way is to ask myself, "Does this wine smell *really good?* Is the good smell *really strong?*" If the answer to both these questions is an unqualified yes, the wine scores a 4, no matter whether the pleasantness of the smell comes from its being vinous, distinct, varietal, or from bottle aging.

If the smell, on the other hand, is very, very weak, and not all that good anyway, I give the wine a zero. And if it's in between, I give it in between.

Let me interject something that applies to judging all these categories. After you've judged half a dozen bottles, trying to think about all these individual qualities of aroma and bouquet, as well as clarity, color, and all the rest, you'll find that the whole thing gets easier. Practice, even if it doesn't make perfect, will at least make you comfortable, confident, and if you keep at it, quite competent.

Acescence: 2 points
You're not through sniffing the wine, however, because you still have 2 points to award—or withhold—with your nose. These points are for the presence or absence of vinegar. In fancier language, you are testing for acescence, or volatile acid. So, take a sniff of the wine in your glass, and if you don't smell any vinegar, give the wine 2 points. If you smell vinegar very, very faintly, just the barest, tiniest whiff, give the wine 1 point. And if the vinegar smell is strong, give it zero. So much for acescence.

Now we're going to do what you wanted to do all along, namely, taste the wine.

The question of how to taste a wine has been discussed exhaustively in any number of learned books. In this book, however, neither you nor I is going to become exhausted by the subject.

If, as a result of your experimentation with wine, you want to delve into which area of the tongue contains the taste buds that detect and measure the presence of sugar, and other interesting technicalities, you will find the subject a rewarding one. But it won't make an enormous difference in your ability to judge wine.

 Developing your own tasting procedure
Each person has to determine just what constitutes his or her most productive tasting procedure once the wine gets into the mouth. Some people chew it, some people inhale through the mouth, thus aerating the wine (and occasionally getting a dollop down the windpipe), some press the tongue against the roof of the mouth and raise their eyebrows expectantly. Some purse their lips and suck in their cheeks as though they had just bitten into a green persimmon. Some gargle.

I recommend them all. That is, I recommend that you experiment with your wine and your tongue and the roof and sides of your mouth, and a little bit of air and a little bit of solemnity, and see what happens. Because, only by experimentation, trial and error, the pragmatic approach, can you determine whether there is, or is not, a preferred system of tasting for you.

Myself, I run the wine around in my mouth with my tongue, hold it, breathe through my nose, and think. I try very hard to remember other wines I have tasted, and I try to think just what words best describe whatever it is that is going on inside my mouth and nose. It's not a ritual. It's simply an attempt to let my senses do the job they're supposed to do, namely to identify and catalog those sensations that please them most.

To spit or not to spit

When a professional wine taster has evaluated his mouthful of wine, what does he do? Correct! He spits it out.

We won't do that.

Recently I read a book on wine that outlined the procedure for giving a sit-down wine-tasting party. The author recommended "spitting buckets . . . one for every two guests."

Forget your bucket, gentle reader. You are the bucket. That's half the fun of tasting wine.

True, your ability to discriminate subtle differences between wines diminishes as you drink more of them, but it also diminishes, though not so rapidly, as you taste more and more wines and spit them out. There is a fatigue factor in both tasting and smelling, and it's pretty hard to avoid. So, unless you are tasting a dozen or more wines in a side-by-side tasting, or judging wines for the Los Angeles County Fair, you can forget about spitting them out.

That doesn't mean that you can gulp your wine, however. Take a middle road. Take enough wine into your mouth to get a good, honest taste, evaluate it, think about it, put your evaluation into words, and then swallow.

Acidity: 2 points

In our battery of taste tests, the first thing we try to evaluate is called "total acid." This is a test of whether the wine feels refreshing to your mouth, or flat, or soapy, or sharp.

Your wine, as you might suspect, shouldn't be

too sharp or too flat. Too much acid content makes it sharp, too little makes it flat. To be pleasant, the wine should hit somewhere in the middle ranges, making your mouth feel refreshed. A wine may have a fairly high acidity and still be considered good, provided it is well balanced. It will taste agreeably fresh, and the words that will spring to your mind as you hold it in your mouth are these: "pleasantly tart."

At first, total acid is a tough category to which to assign your zero, 1 point, or 2 points, chiefly because you have probably never tried to assess a wine that way before. But after you've tried a few bottles with that particular characteristic in mind, concentrating for a moment or two solely on that single aspect, you should begin to be able to mark your scorecard with aplomb, and get on to the next category.

Sugar: 1 point

The next category is sugar. It's worth 1 point.

Actually, sugar and acid have to balance one another. If a wine is too sweet, you won't want to serve it with a meal, except perhaps with the dessert. And if it's totally devoid of sugar content, the acidity may come through in a rather unpleasant fashion.

So, how sweet is just sweet enough to win the 1 point we have to offer for the sugar category? What I do is ask myself whether the sweetness is so pronounced that it's the first thing I notice about the wine. If so, I will probably score a zero for sugar. Similarly, if the sugar content is so low that I'm left only with a sensation of acidity, I again give it a zero. Everything in between scores 1 point.

Body: 1 *point*

Body, the next category, is easier to score. Like sugar, it's only worth 1 point. You should award that point to your wine if it is pleasantly full and viscous, or put another way, if it is not thin and watery. Body is something you feel in your mouth, not something you taste. It's the texture of the wine, and if your wine doesn't have any texture, give it a zero.

There's another way you can judge body, and that's by swirling the wine in the glass to make it climb the sides. When you stop swirling, watch the wine slide down the side of the glass. If it leaves a thick transparent film that is slow to rejoin the rest of the wine, and if there are a large number of fat, slow-moving "legs" moving down the sides of the glass, you have another indication that the wine has good body. If the wine is watery, the film will break up into streaks rather quickly. Incidentally, you should expect red wines to have considerably more body than whites.

Flavor: 2 *points*

We come now to flavor, a 2-point category. This should be a very complex and difficult category, but it isn't. Because, in the final analysis, it simply consists of answering the question "Does it taste good?"

"Good" is pleasant, clean, fruity, rich, balanced, full, spicy, tasty, yummy, any way you want to put it. Your mouth knows what tastes good to you, so trust it. And if the wine tastes really yummy, give it 2 points. Fairly yummy, give it 1 point. Not yummy at all, zilch.

Astringency: 2 points
We are now closing in on the final two scoring categories. The next to last is a 2-point category called "astringency," and if your wine makes your mouth feel rough or puckery, it won't win any points. If you wish to impress your friends, you can say that the tannin content is too high.

A small amount of astringency is not too bad a thing. In fact, a moderate amount of astringency is desirable in red wines. Wines tend to have more astringency when they're young, less as the wine ages. Wines with low astringency are described as being smooth or soft; wines with a higher astringency level are described as slightly rough, and highly astringent wines are called very rough. Obviously, very rough scores zero.

 General quality: 2 points
The final category is a 2-pointer which enables you to adjust for having been too generous in any one of the preceding categories, or to improve the score of a wine that you really think is a knockout. This scoring category is called "general quality," and that's precisely what it means.

Did you really like the wine? Would you like to have another glass right now? Would you like to salt a few bottles away in your garage, closet, cellar? Would you like to serve it to your friends? If the answer to any or all of these questions is yes, give the wine the 2 points for general quality. You'll also know when to give it 1 point, and when to award it the golden zero.

What your total scores mean

Your scoring is now over. You've awarded your wine up to 20 points in ten separate categories. Now all you have to do is add up the score and compare it with the University of California's standards, which go like this:

17–20 points: Wine of outstanding characteristics

13–16 points: Sound commercial wine—no outstanding merit or defect

10–12 points: Commercially acceptable wine with noticeable defect

0–9 points: Commercially unacceptable wine

How did your wine score?

Incidentally, it's a good idea to put the date and a full description of the wine on the scorecard, verbal comments as well as the numerical scores. You should also include the price and the name of the store where you bought it. And if you have a wine you aren't quite sure about after judging it, forget it for a while.

Then, later, get another bottle and put it through the 20-point ordeal again without referring to your original scorecard until you've finished. When you compare the results of the two tastings, you should have a better answer as to whether this particular wine is of sufficient quality to earn a place in your cellar.

It is possible, of course, that you may feel slightly resentful about the elaborateness of the University of California 20-point evaluation system. In fact, you may be telling yourself, "Wow, I don't want to go through that rigamarole every time I open a bottle of wine!" If this is the case (and it is with me), you may

		SEVEN OAKS ZINFANDEL $2.79 / 1.5 liter SAM'S 6.22.83		LAKEVILLE ZINFANDEL $2.99 / 750ml DANTE LIQUORS 6.22.83		SANTAREEN ZINFANDEL $4.99 / 1.5 liter SAM'S 6.22.83	
Brand Type of Wine Price Supplier Date Tasted							
Appearance	0-2	VERY CLEAR	2	FAINT, FAINT HAZE	1	VERY CLEAR	2
Color	0-2	A BIT ON THE LIGHT SIDE	1	RICH, RUBY RED	2	MEDIUM RED	2
Aroma, Bouquet	0-4	PLEASANT, FRUITY A BIT RELUCTANT	2	ACCEPTABLE, BUT A BIT STUFFY, DANK	1	FAINT BUT NICE CLEAN, MATURE FRUIT	2
Acescence	0-2	OKAY	2	OKAY	2	OKAY	2
Total Acid	0-2	SLIGHT SHARPNESS	1	A TRACE FLAT	1	REFRESHING, PLEASANT	2
Sugar	0-1	DRY	1	SWEETISH	0	DRY	1
Body	0-1	GOOD "LEGS"	1	GOOD	1	GOOD MOUTH-FEEL	1
Flavor	0-2	PLEASANT, BUT FAIRLY ORDINARY	1	MUSTY TASTE	0	OKAY - NOTHING SPECIAL	1
Astringency	0-2	A LITTLE ROUGH	1	SOME ROUGHNESS	1	CRISP, PLEASANT	2
General Quality	0-2	SOUND, AVERAGE	1	BELOW AVERAGE	0	SLIGHTLY ABOVE AVERAGE, OKAY	1
TOTAL	0-20	PERFECTLY OKAY BUT NOT FOR PARTIES	13	DON'T BUY AGAIN	9	BETTER THAN AVERAGE. AN ENJOYABLE WINE AND A GOOD BUY.	16

wish to move on to a somewhat simpler system that may, in the long run, do the job just as well.

The value of the U.C. system, of course, is that it makes you think about a great many individual wine characteristics, one at a time. This is something that most people have never done, and I am highly in favor of everyone who is interested in wine learning and practicing the U.C. system until he or she feels comfortable with the idea of sorting out the complexities.

The Nelson 2-3-4-5 *system*
The shortcoming of the U.C. system is that it is rather cumbersome. So, in case you don't have the time or the inclination to go through each of the steps, you may wish to go with what I call the Nelson 2-3-4-5 system. It's simple and easy to remember, and if you've tried the U.C. system enough times so that you're familiar with each of the components that go to make up a good wine, you'll find that they all fit into the 2-3-4-5 system.

As a little simple addition will show you, the 2-3-4-5 system is a 14-point system. It scores like this:

Eyes	2 points
Nose	3 points
Mouth	4 points
Brain	5 points

Obviously, the eyes category covers clarity, color, and visual assessment of the wine's body. The nose is responsible for aroma and bouquet. The mouth handles body, flavor, and acidity.

That leaves the brain with five big points to give out for overall quality. My own practice is to award these points by taking a second look, a second smell, a second taste, and deciding just how well these first three categories combine to make me smack my lips and say, "By George, *that* is a good wine!"

For a sample of a marked 2-3-4-5 scorecard, see page 65.

 Your eyes, your nose, your mouth, your brain
There are, of course, many other ways to score wines, and many kinds of scorecards. In the end, however, all the systems come down to the same thing, namely, taking evidence with your eyes, your nose, your mouth, and integrating these impressions with your brain.

At the beginning of this chapter, assuming you can remember back that far, I said that the best way to evaluate a wine is in the company of other similar wines. Naturally, if you and your luncheon companion are evaluating a restaurant bottle, you won't have a second wine standing by to serve as a standard.

If, on the other hand, you are in your own kitchen, staring at four red wines that call themselves Burgundies, and you want to figure out which, if any, you should buy more of, then you'd better resign yourself to the joyful task of opening all four bottles and testing each wine against the others.

Enlist some confederates
The best way to do it is to enlist some confederates. This means your wife, husband, paramour, alternate-

	VIRAGO	BROOKFIELD	RIVER HILL	EL VERANO
Brand				
Type of Wine	BURGUNDY	BURGUNDY	BURGUNDY	BURGUNDY
Price	$1.99/750ml	$3.49/1.5 liter	$2.29/1.5 liter	$3.99/750ml
Supplier	LOU'S LIQUORS	LOU'S	BIG M LIQUORS	TORRANCE SUPER
Date Tasted	5·3·83	5·3·83	5·3·83	5·3·83
👁 2	CLEAR DEEP RUBY — 2	CLEAR MEDIUM RED LOTS OF "LEGS" — 2	WATERY, LOOKS LIKE A PALE ROSÉ. CLEAR, HOWEVER — 1	DEEP, RICH RED, ALMOST PURPLE — 2
👃 3	FAINT BUT PLEASANT. SLIGHT FLORAL OVERTONES — 1	FRUITY, PLEASANT, SIMPLE, A BIT RELUCTANT. — 1+	GODAWFUL! ACRID, CHEMICAL — 0	PLEASANT, FRUITY, WITH SPICY OVERTONES; OUTDOORSY! — 2+
👄 4	DRY, ACIDIC, ALMOST ROUGH; TART, FRESH — 1+	A LITTLE SWEET, A LITTLE FLAT, BUT NOT BAD — 2	COTTON CANDY, THIN, FLAT, VULCANIZED — 0	LIVELY, SLIGHTLY TART, SMOOTH, PLEASANT AFTERTASTE — 3
🍷 5	SIMPLE, CLEAN TASTE. OKAY BUT NOT SPECIAL. — 3	SOUND AND PLEASANT. MIGHT BLEND WITH SOMETHING ACIDIC — 3	UNDRINKABLE, EVEN BY ME! — 0	A REAL FIND! A NICE WINE FOR COMPANY. — 4
14	7+	9	1	11+

life-style chum, neighbor, fellow bargain hunter, or whatever. From two to half a dozen people make a nice group. Larger than that becomes a production, except when you're giving a wine-tasting party, in which case you expect a production.

 Letting red wines breathe . . .

Naturally, you want to have all four of your red wines at the same temperature. And you want to open them all at the same time. Opinions vary, but some professionals suggest you open them about thirty to forty-five minutes before you plan to taste them. Supposedly, this gives them time to breathe and develop the maximum amount of aroma, bouquet, and flavor. And it's true, a wine that tastes sharp on opening may smooth out after it's come in contact with air for a while.

 Anonymity is important to success

Another thing you want to do is to make sure that your fellow judges (and you yourself, if you can arrange it) never actually see the bottles, or, more important, the labels. The problem is that when any one of us sees a bottle of wine bearing a label that reads Margaux or Château Latour, we unconsciously predispose ourselves to think that the wine is going to be pretty good. And, like a self-fulfilling prophecy, the wine often has to be pretty bad before we stop thinking it's pretty good.

Naturally, there are limits to our credulity, but we want to eliminate as many variables as possible in our quasi-scientific test. So, one we will want to eliminate is any possible identification of the wine through seeing the shape of its bottle or its label.

Obviously, someone has to run the test, so someone has to know which wine is which. Unfortunately, if you want the test to run right, this person frequently turns out to be you.

Okay, let's say you've assembled a few fellow scientists, and you've opened your four bottles of red wine.

You should, if you've got enough glassware, give each taster four glasses, so he or she can have all four wines available simultaneously in order to make the side-by-side comparisons we've already talked about. It's nice if the glasses are all alike, and nicer yet, if all are more or less like the standard 8- or 10-ounce wineglass you encounter in most restaurants. If you haven't got sixteen or twenty identical glasses, however, don't worry about it. You can taste wines in tumblers or old jelly glasses, if necessary, because the chief ingredients of a tasting are the wines and the tasters, and the glasses are merely vehicles for bringing the two together.

Number bottles and glasses

Warn your guests that they should be very careful to keep their four glasses in their original order, so that the results of the tasting don't get more than normally confused. Or, to be safer yet, attach a numbered piece of masking tape to the stem of each glass. This will completely eliminate the possibility of your guests mixing up the wines. It will help you keep them straight, too, for that matter, because once you've got everyone else fitted out with four kinds of wine, you fit yourself out, and the evaluation begins.

Since you're in charge, you can conduct your evaluation procedures any way you want, either by asking your guests to rate the wines according to the University of California system, or the Nelson 2-3-4-5 system, or simply by tasting the wines and talking about them. I'm partial to the Nelson system myself, because it's easy to explain, and because it makes even the most inexperienced guest think about at least three separate aspects of each wine without my having to deliver a long and boring lecture.

Have your scorecards ready

For either system, U.C. or 2-3-4-5, each taster needs a pencil and paper to go along with his four glasses of wine. It's not a bad idea to make up scorecards in advance, so you're sure each taster is following the same procedure.

Let's assume that you've decided to use the 2-3-4-5 system, and that you've already filled the numbered glasses. If you haven't, now's the time to do it.

Naturally, it's handy to keep the bottles nearby, in case you have to refill the glasses. If you do, you should disguise them somehow—mask them with paper, wrap them in a napkin, do whatever is necessary to make sure none of your fellow adventurers knows which is which. Some tasters soak the labels off—in room temperature water, so as not to heat or chill the wine unduly—and then mark each bottle with a piece of tape and a number corresponding to the numbers on the glasses.

This is a lot of folderol, but the anonymity is important. You now start by making your visual evaluations of all four wines, and marking your scorecard. Then you let your nose evaluate each wine in terms of aroma and bouquet, and mark your scorecard for the nose category.

Finally, of course, you taste each wine in order, going back and forth as many times as you want. After you've marked your scorecard, you're ready to chew on a piece of bread or a plain cracker, to cleanse your palate and get your taste buds back into shape for your second eye-nose-mouth evaluation, and the awarding of the final five points.

Words to drink by . . .

It's an excellent idea to write down a few words about each aspect of each wine, provided you can think of the words that describe the wav the wine 'ooks or smells or tastes.

You'll find the words hard to come by at first, and you may feel a bit affected saying that the wine has "a rather astringent mouth-feel," but it's like anything else: once you do it awhile, it gets easy.

Besides, the words are usually more useful than the numbers in helping you remember just what it was you liked about the smell of a particular wine— was it that you liked its strong, fruity aroma, or did it have an unusual spicy smell, or again, did it remind you of fresh-cut clover? If you wrote it down, you'll know.

The real pleasures of tasting

After everyone has scored the four wines, two of the greatest pleasures of wine emerge. The first is talking about them, comparing your evaluations with those of your fellow tasters. The second, of course, is drinking what's left in your glass, and refilling it and drinking some more. If someone found the first wine had a dry, fruity taste, and you thought it was a little on the sweet side, there's plenty of opportunity for both of you to taste the wine again and talk about it, and see if you feel your original evaluation still holds.

At some point, of course, you'll want to bring out the bottles and identify which was which. This will probably start another round of conversation and still more tasting, and before you know it, you will have invested a lot of very pleasant time in a very genial activity.

 Other methods, other thoughts . . .

There are lots of other ways to compare wines, as well as ways to compare the abilities of different wine tasters. One such procedure is called the "triangular test" and consists of presenting a taster with three glasses, two of which contain the same wine, while the third glass contains a different wine. The taster is then asked to tell which of the three glasses contains the odd sample. This is a system that is often used in choosing people for a taste panel. It's slightly complicated, since to get a good taster it's necessary to present him with five to ten different triangular tests to make sure that he is consistent in picking the right wine. This takes a lot of time, a lot of glasses, a lot of different wines, and a lot of money. I suggest you get into this kind of testing only if you decide that the life of a professional wine taster is the only life for you.

There are a number of differing schools of thought about wine tasting. Some authorities, for example, feel that your senses are at their most discriminating when you're reasonably hungry. Some feel that tasters do their best work in the morning, when most of the rest of us are busily engaged in doing something that can't be half as much fun. Yet, there is another body of opinion that says your senses are sharpest between six and twelve in the evening, and says further that women consistently surpass men in their ability to discriminate between different tastes and smells.

The opinion that counts: Yours

Fortunately, you're at liberty to form your own body of opinion. As we agreed at the outset, what really counts is how the wine tastes to you. So, no matter what your fellow tasters may say as they sit there, sipping your wine and marking your scorecards, you are the ultimate authority. Don't forget it.

4

How you serve it:

THE OTHER HALF OF THE WINE EQUATION

Once upon a time I read the results of an experiment in which men and women were asked to evaluate four separate cups of coffee in order to decide which of the four cups was best.

The cups into which the coffee had been poured were identical, and each was sitting in front of an opened can that was half full of ground coffee. Each can was color coded, one can brown, one blue, one red, one yellow. Nobody actually said that each cup of coffee had been made from the contents of the can in front of which it stood, but the cup placements implied it strongly.

Each person, after tasting the four cups of coffee, was asked to rank the coffees 1, 2, 3, 4, in order of preference, and to list those attributes that made the taster like or dislike each cup.

When the results were tabulated, it was found that a large majority of the tasters gave first place to the coffee sitting in front of the red can. They described it as rich, full bodied, and satisfying. The coffee in front of the brown can was adjudged a trifle strong, the coffee in front of the yellow can a bit weak. The coffee in front of the blue can, said the tasters, was bitter.

As you have probably already guessed, the four cups of coffee were identical, poured from the same pot.

The researchers concluded, as they had suspected all along, that the color of the container from which the coffee was thought to have been made was a much more powerful factor in influencing the brain's decision than the actual taste.

Put another way, the tasters transferred their visual sensations into what they believed were their taste sensations. For some reason—don't ask me why—it seemed to make a lot of sense that coffee from a red can should be richer than coffee from cans of other colors. This fact has not been lost on marketers of coffee, which is why, when you walk down the coffee aisle in any supermarket, you will see a lot of cans sporting a fair amount of red.

Coffee marketers aren't the only people who worry about their packages. It is a commonplace of consumer marketing that the look of a package will influence not only a consumer's readiness to put it in the shopping cart, but the consumer's ultimate evaluation of the product itself.

Naturally, if something tastes awful, you can't make it taste wonderful simply by putting it into a wonderful package. Within certain limits, however, since the average set of taste buds walks on extremely shaky ground, you can influence the brain's response simply by altering the size, shape, color, or general graphic design of your package.

What's the message for us impoverished wine drinkers? The message is that the enjoyment of a wine is not determined solely by the wine itself. The message is that the visual clues we give our guests when we serve them wine will most assuredly influence their perceptions. The container from which we pour the wine, the glassware into which we pour it, the manner in which we serve it, all these things will, within limits, influence our guests' evaluation and enjoyment of the wines we serve them.

Amazingly enough, you will find that these same visual cues will influence your own perceptions, even those of wines with which you are already familiar. Thus, although you're dining alone, eating last night's leftovers, the wine with which you accompany your meal will taste better if you pour it from a Swedish glass carafe into an 18-ounce balloon goblet, rather than if you slop it out of a gallon jug into a jelly glass.

Please understand that I'm not asking you to adopt a set of affectations. After all, there is absolutely nothing wrong with pouring wine from a jug into a jelly glass and enjoying it. Serving and drinking wine is not a matter of right and wrong. Thus, the suggestions I am about to make are not aimed at enabling you to "fool your friends" or "put on the dog." They are simply ideas to help you maximize your own enjoyment of the many different kinds of wine that you can afford to buy and serve, and your friends' enjoyment of them, too.

The power of confidence

The first thing to remember about serving one of your wines is this: Never apologize for a wine you are about to serve. Serve it confidently, with a smile, and without too much foofaraw. If you serve it hesitantly or say something like "Gosh, I hope this wine's okay . . . ," your guest will probably get an uneasy feeling which he may transfer to his evaluation and enjoyment of the wine itself.

It's the old self-fulfilling prophecy. If you think you're going to fail, you probably will. But if you think you're going to win, well, you may not win, but you stand a much greater *chance* of winning, simply because you have a positive attitude and you're not thinking failure.

Do you remember the old story about the gold rush? A mischief-maker comes into a bar in Alaska and fabricates a rumor that they've struck a rich vein of gold on the North Fork of the Whatsis River. The effect is electric. The bar buzzes with excitement and rapidly clears as the patrons rush to get their picks and gold pans. The rumormonger watches, chortling with wicked glee, until the bar is empty. Then suddenly, he bolts for the door to get his own equipment and head for the Whatsis.

"You never know," he says, "a rumor like that could have some truth to it!"

The same psychology that applies to rumors of gold strikes also applies to wines. If someone tells us,

"I want you to taste a really superb wine," or if we are offered wine from a bottle labeled Chambertin-Clos de Bèze, or if the sommelier in a fancy restaurant pours our wine from a sparkling crystal pitcher into an elegant Baccarat wineglass, we generally figure we're in for a treat.

Our expectations are part of the treat, part of the machinery that helps make the wine taste good. We transfer our visual perceptions—and the expectations these perceptions generate—into the realm of our taste sensations, without even knowing it.

Question: Would the Chambertin-Clos de Bèze have tasted as good poured out of a Mason jar into a toothpaste glass, and served timidly with the remark, "Gee, this is all we've got, I hope it's okay . . ."?

The answer is no. But it still wouldn't have tasted bad!

 Packaging the wine experience

I have picked up many ideas about serving wine from restaurants. For example, in one of my favorite restaurants, when you order the house wine, assuming you order more than a single glass, your waiter will bring it to you in a simple, green 750-ml bottle. The bottle will already be open; in fact, without your knowing it, it has just been filled from a 3-liter jug behind the bar. Nevertheless, it has a plain, decent, authentic look to it, honorable yet without pretense, and even though you have not gone through the ceremony of the cork and the tasting, there is considerable satisfaction in seeing your wine poured from this simple, unlabeled green bottle into the waiting, stemmed glass.

There is another advantage to the procedure at this restaurant. You're charged only for what you pour out of the bottle.

Order the house wine at Le Bistro in New York, and your waiter will bring it in a handsome glass pitcher with straight sides and no ornamentation. The glass into which he will pour your wine will also be plain and traditional, and the whole experience will be extremely pleasant.

There are many, many kinds of pitchers suitable for serving wine, and one of the important things to remember is that there are no rules on the subject. This was brought home to me several years ago when I was charged with setting up an informal luncheon in San Francisco for fifteen visiting Frenchmen and an equal number of Americans. I selected a small Neapolitan restaurant called Tommaso's, and since I had to operate within a budget, I suggested that we have the house wine rather than something more expensive.

Lino Costa, who was in charge, immediately produced several flowered pottery pitchers, and announced that he would use them to serve the wine. Because I had never before seen wine served from flowered pottery pitchers, I suffered about five seconds of doubt. Then, as the sixth second ticked by, I realized that they were not only suitable, they were an absolutely perfect complement to the country informality of the meal, the restaurant, and the occasion.

The luncheon was a huge success, and the moral of the story is obvious: When you serve wine, you make your own rules.

At home, my wife and I serve wine from many different containers. Sometimes it's a plain green wine bottle. Sometimes the plain green wine bottle wears a handwritten label noting what kind of wine it is, when it was rebottled from a larger container into the smaller bottle, and occasionally the wine's rating on the 2-3-4-5 scale.

Sometimes we use our Italian *litros*, the common garden variety of wine carafe in which house wines are often served in restaurants. They're made of heavy glass and feature a circular glass blob on the front with a piece of lead sealed into it. They also have a line scribed near the top of the neck, showing exactly how full the jar should be in order to contain exactly one liter.

We have two of them, a green one we use for white wines, and a clear one for reds.

We also use a flowered pottery pitcher, not quite like the ones at Tommaso's, a couple of smallish cut-crystal pitchers that look very handsome when filled with red wine, one Danish decanter, very modern, and one beaker that looks as though it would be more at home in a chemistry lab than on a dinner table. It would be, in fact, because that's where it came from, and I guess that's why I like it.

We also have one large, green, unlabeled glass bottle, magnum size, and one large clear one that I bought filled with bargain Frascati, and which looks great on the table, filled with either red or white. And we have several wicker-enclosed bottles in sizes varying from 750 milliliters to 3 liters. I occasionally fill them and put them on the table when the menu in-

cludes spaghetti, lasagna, or some equally suitable
dish. I also take them on picnics.

None of these serving containers cost me very
much, but that isn't the principal reason I like them. I
like them because they have a modest amount of style
and charm without any particular affectation, and because they somehow make our rebottled reds and
whites taste a little better than they ought to.

Take a look around your own house or apartment. Chances are you already have some pitchers or
other containers that you never thought about using
to serve wine, but which will do the job very nicely.

Great, cheap glasses for great, cheap wine
You can also add a little extra fillip to the occasion by
the way you use your containers. For example, you
might want to put two unlabeled bottles on your table, one red, one white, so your guests can have their
choice. Or, if you're having more than one course,
you might want to give each guest two glasses, and
serve the white wine with the first course and the red
with the second. Or, if you really want to freak everyone out, you can give each guest three glasses, one for
the white, one for the red, and one for the sweet,
slightly charged dessert wine you serve with the cherries jubilee.

This latter effort will require quite a bit of glassware, so this is probably the right time to pass along a
purchasing tip. This is simply that when you are
looking for glassware, you might try your local restaurant supply house. Restaurants go in and out of

business with fair regularity, which means that all kinds of wineglasses move in and out of the supplier stores with the change of the tide. To find these stores, look under "Restaurant Supplies" in the yellow pages.

When you visit this kind of store, look for simple, classic glasses that hold at least 10 ounces when filled to the brim. I told you in Chapter Three about the Libbey glasses I use. You might also take a look at the larger, 18-ounce balloon glasses. They cost a little more, but their extra size gives them an extra touch of class, in addition to which they're great for swirling and sniffing wine. Whichever glasses you pick, however, they'll be a little thicker than the fine crystal goblets the Queen drinks from, but for you that's an advantage, not a disadvantage. You can run your stemware through the dishwasher with minimum fear of breaking them, and the Queen can't.

One way or another, however, no matter how careful you are, you'll break some glasses. My advice is to buy an oversupply—they're fairly cheap—and not to worry.

As for pitchers, if you don't like those offered by the restaurant supply house, fortunately there are lots of attractive pitchers available in many different kinds of stores at relatively modest prices. So, use your own judgment, indulge your taste, preference, or prejudice, and you should be able to put your wines on the table in a way that gives them every possible chance of succeeding in their pleasant, humanitarian mission.

My own tastes run in favor of simple containers and simple glasses, and against serving wine from any kind of metal pitcher. I freely admit that this last is my own irrational prejudice, amply proved by the fact that I used to enjoy a particular kind of Beaujolais that came in a pull-top can. I would probably still enjoy it if it had been successful enough to survive in the U.S. market, although now that I've learned to buy in bulk and rebottle, I probably couldn't afford it any more.

Wine on picnics
While we're talking about serving wine, we should not overlook the fact that not all wine is consumed at luncheon or the dinner table. Wine is also consumed on picnics at the beach, during romantic trysts in the woods, aboard motorboats and sailboats, and just about any place that people sit down to enjoy an informal meal. One of nature's most beautiful sights, in fact, is a pair of naked green bottles lying on their sides in the shallow edge of a mountain stream, letting the icy waters cool the fragrant white wines inside.

Some purists, in fact, maintain that wine on a picnic should be drunk from the same stemmed glassware used at the dinner table. I have to admit that it makes for a pretty classy picnic, and not only the wine, but the fried chicken or peanut-butter sandwiches take on a gourmet dimension you didn't know they had. Getting the glasses back and forth without breaking them is a bit of a chore, and if you let them clank around in the trunk of your car it may be more than you can put up with. Still, if you've never sat idly beside a mountain stream, sipping cold

Chablis out of a classic wineglass, maybe you ought to try it at least once.

 Take a bota *to lunch*
Of course, there are lots of ways to take wine on a picnic. Take, for example, the *bota*.

I came into contact with my first working *bota* just outside an amusement park in San Sebastián, in the Basque area of Spain. A *bota*, to keep you in suspense no longer, is one of those leather flasks, nowadays usually lined with plastic, slung on a shoulder cord and intended for carrying wine wherever you want to take it.

Emptying wine from a *bota* is only slightly harder than filling one. You remove the cap, hoist the *bota* to a position slightly higher than your head, point the nozzle in the direction of your mouth, and squeeze.

With practice, you become skilled. You hit your shirt only one time in four, and finally not at all. And, most amazing of all, the whole idea of drinking wine from a *bota* will gradually stop being a parlor trick and become a very sensible way to take wine to places where wine has never gone before.

The *bota*, you see, has licked the problem of air attacking the remaining wine in a partially emptied container. The *bota* collapses as the wine supply diminishes, with the result that there is no more air in the *bota* when you've drunk half the wine that there was when the *bota* was full. It's the same idea as today's bag-in-a-box packaging.

Like a wine bottle, a *bota* can be immersed in a

stream to cool it. Even better than a wine bottle, however, the *bota* continues to cool the wine after it has been withdrawn from the stream, thanks to the gradual evaporation of the water that has soaked into its leather cover.

Another nice thing about a *bota* is that you can forget your stemmed glassware, you can forget styrofoam cups or tin cups or plastic-coated paper cups. The *bota* is the serving container, and each person becomes his own drinking utensil. Is it hygienic? You bet! Any number can drink from (or be bathed by) the same *bota* and still preserve the strictest standards of hygiene, since mouths and lips never touch the *bota* itself.

Botas come in many sizes, from tourist-souvenir-tiny to authentic-Spanish-large. I recommend the latter highly to anyone who likes hiking, cycling, picnicking, and the concomitant pleasures of dining al fresco with wine.

Have dinner with a porrón
The *porrón* is the indoor equivalent of the *bota*. My wife and I saw our first *porrón* in action in an elegant restaurant in Barcelona called Los Tres Gatos. A *porrón* is a large glass container shaped like a badly squashed ball. A conical glass spout protrudes from one side of the *porrón*, and a slightly flared tube rises out of the top, serving not only as a means of filling the *porrón*, but also as a handle for picking it up.

I had to marvel at the unerring accuracy and complete insouciance with which each person at a table near ours directed the stream of red wine through a long, looping arc into a slightly opened mouth. My own mouth would have been gaping as though the dentist were repairing a nether inlay.

I have seen *porróns* on sale in the United States, but only very small toylike ones, and as a result I don't have one.

If you're really adventurous, you can score a lot of points in the gee-whiz-look-at-him category by storing your wine in a wineskin. In the average American city, however, a wineskin may be a hard item to come by.

 About wineskins

I have seen only one set of authentic wineskins in my life, and that was in a restaurant in Madrid called Mesón de San Javiar, which stores its house wines in several large bullskins. A bullskin is a large skin with the bull removed and the skin sewn back together so that it is watertight, or as it turns out, winetight, and then filled with wine.

At the San Javiar, the skins rest on a big table, and when you order the house wine, the waiter takes a pitcher over to one of them, opens a spigot that has been inserted into a foreleg, and fills the pitcher. He then returns to the table and pours, and you sit for a long time staring at your filled glass, wondering whether or not to drink the wine. In the end, of course, you do, and it tastes just fine.

Like the *bota* and the bag-in-a-box, the wineskin solves the problem of keeping air from attacking the wine remaining in a partially emptied container. The wineskin simply collapses as the wine pours out, leaving the wine safe from air damage.

Neither you nor I will probably ever serve our wine from a wineskin. For us, the wineskin will simply serve to symbolize the fact that with a little investigation, thought, and experimentation, you can devise your own serving techniques to heighten your enjoyment of the wine experience.

What the wine-serving equation boils down to is this: If there was once a right way and a wrong way to serve wine, there isn't any more. Now there are only interesting ways and unimaginative ways, and you don't have to stand on your head or pour wine from a hiking boot to make the way you serve wine interesting.

The simple ways of serving wine have plenty of charm, and the principal thing to do is to make sure you give the serving process all the care and thought it deserves. If you do, those good, sound, $5.00-or-less wines that you have selected so carefully will add a measure of enjoyment to your meal far out of proportion to their cost.

5

Bargain-wine miscellany,
OR EVERYTHING THAT DIDN'T FIT INTO
ANOTHER CHAPTER

I am now going to serve you a mismatched potpourri of wine information that somehow just didn't seem to fit anywhere else.

You don't have to read it if you don't want to. If you reached this page without skipping, you have already acquired the basic tools for finding, judging, and serving great cheap wines. So, if you're in a hurry, you can omit this chapter and jump ahead to page 106 and start reading my listings of bargain wines, great and otherwise, together with my evaluations and comments.

On the other hand, if you have a few more minutes, you might as well hang around while I divest myself of a few more thoughts about wine that may or may not fit into your own ways of acquiring and appreciating wine.

Blending your own wines

The first thought I would like to offer to those splendid individuals who have kept on reading is the idea of blending your own wines. Let's say you have bought three liters of wine that tastes pretty good, that has a clear, ruby color, good body, and a pleasing aroma, but lacks a feeling of freshness. It's just a bit flat, a bit innocuous, a bit lacking in the tartness that would make it seem well balanced enough to score the extra points necessary to put it in your Winner's Circle.

Well, take a look at your past wine-scoring records and see if somewhere you haven't come across a wine that seemed sound, smelled and tasted good, but lost points because it was too sharp, too rough, too tingling when you swished it around your mouth and swallowed it. If you're like me and hate to pour a bottle down the sink unless it's totally undrinkable, you probably have a few fifths of such a wine hanging around the house. Maybe you bought three liters of such a wine, used some for tasting, and rebottled the rest, simply because even cheap wine costs money, and you figured the time might come when you'd be glad you had it around.

Tart helps flat, flat helps tart

Well, now is the time. Open a bottle of the flat wine and a bottle of the tart wine, and do a little experimental blending. Take three glasses, number them, and into the first glass pour one jigger of the flat wine and three jiggers of the tart one. Into the second glass pour two jiggers of each. Into the third glass, pour three jiggers of the flat wine and one jigger of the tart one.

Now you're ready to evaluate three totally new wines. You've never tasted any of them before, and neither has anyone else. You set about your task in exactly the same manner as though they were three new wines you had just brought back from your friendly neighborhood wine merchant. You score each of them on the basis of an evaluation with your eyes, an evaluation with your nose, then with your mouth, and you conclude your investigation by integrating all this sensory data in the convolutions of your brain.

Many results are possible. One of them, unfortunately, is that none of the blends will taste worth a damn. However, it is highly unlikely that the blending of these two wines will turn out to taste less good than either one of the two wines tastes separately. And it may happen that you'll stumble onto a combination that's better than either of the wines drunk all by itself.

That's what you hope happens anyway, and it's really not a far-fetched idea. After all, that's what the winemakers do. A Cabernet Sauvignon made in California, for example, only needs to contain 75 percent Cabernet grapes in order to be labeled "Cabernet Sauvignon" (unless the label states specifically, as some labels do, that the wine is made 100 percent from grapes of the Cabernet variety). As a result, most winemakers who offer a Cabernet Sauvignon do a little blending, mixing the pure Cabernet with wines from different (and sometimes cheaper) grapes, and tasting the results until they find the blends they want.

It takes care to grow good grapes, skill and experience to press and ferment them, and a talented palate to blend them into an interesting, well-balanced wine. Fortunately, you as a wine fancier don't have to grow the grapes or make the wine, and just as fortunately, you now have the talent and the judging criteria for deciding which wines look, smell, and taste good to you. So try some blending. Blend some reds together. Blend some whites. Blend a red and a white and make your own rosé. If you think a particular wine needs a little more flavor, try adding a fractional amount of Sherry or Port or whatever strikes your fancy. It's a lot of fun, and the wines you will then be able to put on your table will not be available on any other dinner table in the world!

I said you don't have to grow the grapes or make the wine, but many people do just that—particularly the latter. I recently ran into a friend on an airplane and found that he and three friends had bought 16 acres of Zinfandel grapes in Sonoma County, California. They bought it half as an investment, half as a lark, and it was rich in both. They were not only selling grapes to local vintners, but were holding back enough so that each of the four families was able to make 200 gallons each year! That's a lot of Zinfandel!

It's quite possible you may not be situated geographically or economically to repeat my friend's adventure. If you were, we might never have met in the pages of *Everybody's Guide to Great Wines Under $5*. Poverty, nevertheless, need not keep either of us from making our own wines if that's what we feel like doing, because it is not an expensive process.

Making your own wine

Do not fear, gentle reader, that I am now going to take you step by step through the process of making your own wine. All I am going to do is suggest that, if the idea of making your own wine intrigues you, you will probably find that it's a lot easier and a lot less expensive than you ever dreamed. You don't have to live in California or the vineyard area of New York State in order to get the ingredients, the equipment, and the know-how you need to embark on your project.

Don't forget the Feds

But first, a word from your friendly neighborhood attorney: Although you no longer need a permit from the Treasury Department to make wine at home, you do have to obey the Treasury's limits on how much wine you can make. I don't know who comes around to check up on you, but whoever it is had better not find you making more than 200 gallons per year, if you are the head of a household, or 100 gallons if you're a single person living alone. It seems like a generous enough quantity, especially since you can only make it for personal use, not for sale.

Getting started

Unless you live in the Napa Valley, the easiest way to start making wine at home is from—in descending order of desirability—frozen grapes, frozen juice, or juice concentrates. As you can imagine, the closer you get to fresh, ripe grapes straight from the vineyard, the better your wine is likely to taste. And the higher the quality of the frozen grapes or grape juice you buy, the greater the likelihood your wine will taste like Château Latour.

Obviously, making wine from frozen juice doesn't have the same degree of romance as trampling the vintage with your own bare feet. Nevertheless, if you work at it, and if you're careful, you'll find you can produce some very fine, very interesting, and sometimes very unusual wines.

Besides, if you live in an apartment in New York City, you may find that one of those small-print clauses in your lease specifically prohibits, along with denial of your right to drive nails into the walls or keep a goat in your kitchen, the trampling of grapes.

Two ways to go about making wine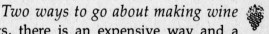
As in all things, there is an expensive way and a cheap way to go about making wine at home. The expensive way is to go to your wine equipment supplier and outfit yourself with a deluxe setup, everything new and shiny from the ground up. The other way is to look around your house or apartment and see how many crocks or other large stainless steel or unchipped enamelware containers you may have, in order not to have to buy any big barrels or carboys. Also, in time, you will find plenty of use for those big 3-liter jugs from which you have rebottled those many cases of wine.

You'll also need some corks, some rubber stoppers which you will fit with short lengths of glass tubing, some plastic tubing, some cheesecloth, and lots and lots of bottles for the finished product.

Naturally, you have to know what to do with all this stuff. Well, there are lots of good books on making wine, and some of them are listed in the back of this book. They range from the famous University of California Professor Maynard Amerine's *Technology of Winemaking* to Richard Vine's *Commercial Winemaking*. Basically, they're all concerned with the same process, but of course each winemaker-writer has a few tricks that are his or her own special technique for achieving perfection. As you get deeper into making your own wine, you'll undoubtedly develop tricks of your own.

 Polynesian Barsac?

Making your own wine opens up all kinds of new horizons as far as your nose and mouth are concerned, because some of the people who supply extracts seem to try to outdo each other in coming up with new and exotic formulas. Recently, for example, I received a notice from a West Coast mail-order supplier, offering extracts that will enable home winemakers to make "June Mead, a strawberry and honey combination, sure to please on a summer evening or for a casual party . . . California Gamay, a new twist on an old favorite . . . Polynesian Barsac, a white wine that even your most knowledgeable wine snob friends won't be able to identify . . . and Date Madeira, one of our latest discoveries, great for sipping in front of the fire."

With homemade Polynesian Barsac on your table, poured from your cut-glass pitcher into your balloon goblets, how can you lose?

A last resort: Real grapes

Even though frozen juice may be the easiest way to make wine at home, you shouldn't rule out the plain, old-fashioned way of making wine from real, honest-to-God grapes. Obviously, where you live has something to do with the availability of grapes in quantity. But even if you live far, far away from the vineyards of California or New York, you can still take a crack at buying grapes in quantity at your local wholesale produce market, providing you get up early enough to get there when your town's grocery-store operators are buying their daily supplies of fruit and vegetables, including grapes. It doesn't always work out, but it has been my general experience that most wholesalers don't mind selling in quantity to ordinary mortals, provided the mortals behave in a confident manner, as though they were accustomed to buying in the wholesale market every day, and pay cash.

Wine drinks

Now that you know all about how to make wine, let's move on to another subject: recipes for wine drinks. There are at least a thousand of them, but in an Olympian effort to simplify, let me state my gross generalization that they are all variations of two great basic concoctions, sangría and hot mulled wine.

Sangría, as you undoubtedly already know, is a Spanish mixture, usually consisting of red wine, citrus juice, and sugar in varying quantities, and always drunk cold. Mulled wine, on the other hand, is generally a mixture of wine, sugar, and spice-cupboard miscellany, and is always drunk hot.

 ## Sangría: The classic recipe

Let me start you off with what I consider to be the classic recipe for sangría. Let me also state at the outset that there are at least 99 recipes for sangría, all of which are claimed as classic recipes by the people to whom they are near and dear. I found this out in Spain one long, hot summer by ordering a lot of sangría, and by doing a lot of watching, question-asking, and many liters worth of tasting. It was an arduous task, but when you love your work, you're willing to make certain sacrifices.

The classic recipe, therefore, is simply the recipe I liked best, and here is how you make it. Take two oranges, one lemon, one 750-ml bottle of good red wine, a bottle of brandy (no, you won't use the whole bottle!), and the family sugar bowl (you won't use all the sugar, either).

Juice the oranges and the lemon. Before you do, however, cut a nice round slice out of the middle of the lemon and one out of the oranges. You'll float these on top of the pitcher of sangría when it's all finished. Pour the lemon and orange juice into a glass or pottery pitcher, add about three heaping table-spoons of sugar and some brandy ("some" is up to you; I generally put in 3 to 6 ounces), and stir the mixture up with a long-handled wooden spoon. Fi-nally, pour the wine in, and stir some more.

Now taste your concoction. Chances are it may need a little more sugar, but that will depend on whether you like it a little on the sweet side, as I do. When tasting, it's not a bad idea to pour a little bit of your sangría over some ice and taste it after it has cooled, because that's the way you're going to drink it, and it may taste slightly different when cold.

When you have your sangría at the desired de-gree of sweetness, float the orange and lemon slice on top of the mixture, and you're ready to serve. Take several tall glasses, put three or four or five ice cubes into each one, give the sangría a final stir with the wooden spoon, and fill the glasses.

I presume you will know what to do next.

Sangría is an informal drink, but even informal-ity can be elegant. So, if you managed to make a great buy on those 18-ounce balloon goblets from the res-taurant supply store, trot them out right away. The sangría will look wonderful in them, and they'll make a mighty good thing taste even better.

In time, the wooden spoon with which you stir your sangría will acquire a reddish-purplish color from having sat in the pitcher, waiting to give the mixture a stir before you serve the next round. Some-how, when you open the kitchen drawer on a cold, wintry day and see this stained implement lying

there, reminding you of all the good sangrías you
made the summer before, it will give you a psycho-
logical lift. Mine does, anyway.

Now for the variations on the classic recipe. They
are as numerous as religious sects, and each has its
disciples. The first area of potential variation has to
do with the fruit. Some people feel that a sangría is
not a sangría unless it has a lime in it. You can substi-
tute it for a lemon, or you can use a lime in addition
to the lemon, or, if your taste buds march to a different drummer, you can make your sangría with nothing but limes, and forget the oranges and lemons.

Or you can slip in a grapefruit. Or some tanger-
ines or tangelos or mandarin oranges. Or strawberries or raspberries or blueberries or ollalieberries. You
can try making it with pineapple juice and call it Hawaiian Sangría. Or you can use peach nectar or
crushed cherries or cranberry juice. You'll be putting
a lot of distance between your sangría and the sangrías of Spain, but who cares? They're your taste
buds—use them! I have been served sangrías with
fruit cocktail floating in them, and a spoon to fish it
out and eat it with. It was awfully good, and I made a
mental note to try it at home sometime.

The next area of variation, and one the Spanish
monkey around with quite a bit, has to do with the
brandy. For example, you can omit it entirely and still
have a wonderful sangría. Or you can make it with
gin instead. (That's the way they made it for me once
in Toledo—the one near Madrid, not the other one.)
Or you can add a combination of brandy and gin, or
rum, light or dark, or a touch of fruit-flavored liqueur
or a trace of crème de menthe or orange curaçoa, or

whatever you happen to have in your liquor cabinet that seems as though it might fit.

Concentration vs. dilution

Since the objective of a sangría is to refresh you, not to make you drunk, you don't want to add so much liquor that you turn the concoction into a bomb. The addition of a hard liquor is for flavor and character, and it's up to you to decide just how much flavor and character your particular sangría needs. Some people, in fact, like to go in the other direction and make the solution more dilute by adding ginger ale, a lemon-lime or other fruit-flavored soft drink, or plain old club soda. Experimentation is the order of the day.

White-wine sangria

Speaking of noble experiments, last summer the Nelson Laboratory of Sangría Research came up with a white-wine sangría, a notable invention that I now offer to a waiting world. You make it in exactly the same way as red-wine sangría, except that you use any one of your inexpensive white wines instead of one of your inexpensive reds. I served mine in our balloon glasses on one of the hottest afternoons of the summer, and there are now rumors floating around that I may be a candidate for a Nobel Prize.

As far as I know the Nobel Prize for Sangría made with Rosé Wine has yet to be considered. So there's still time for *you* to make *your* mark in this world.

Now, about hot mulled wine. Hot mulled wine

goes with skiing, sledding, rainy days in November or March, and that terrible feeling you have in your throat just before you get a cold. In other words, it is a refresher when your hands and toes are cold, and an effective medication to boot.

 Hot mulled wine: the classic recipe
So here's the classic recipe for hot mulled wine. Like all other classic recipes, every hot mulled winemaker has his or her own formula, which to his or her own taste is the only real classic recipe.

Mine starts with cloves, nutmeg, and cinnamon, all of which have to be ground up pretty well before you can begin. I use about a teaspoon of cloves, a single cinnamon stick two or three inches long, and a small amount of whole nutmeg—about one-eighth of one, if you're good at subdividing nutmegs.

Grind them up any way you want, but grind them well. You can grate the cinnamon stick on a kitchen grater as a starter, and then put the smallish pieces into a nutmeg grinder along with the cloves and the nutmeg. If you haven't got a nutmeg grinder, try a pepper grinder, and if you haven't got a pepper grinder, try a mortar and pestle. If you haven't got a mortar and pestle or a pepper grinder or a nutmeg grinder, you're in deep trouble.

Okay, you have now ground up the cloves, nutmeg, and cinnamon, one way or another. Put these spices into the top of a double boiler along with half a cup of sugar, three tablespoons of lemon juice, a bottle of inexpensive red wine, and a cup and a half of Port wine. Heat up the mixture, stirring occasionally, until the sugar is completely dissolved and the whole thing is nice and hot. It takes about twenty minutes, more or less.

Serving hot mulled wine

Once the mixture is heated, you're on your own, except for the fact that I never like to let you go off on your own without a word or two about serving. Hot mulled wine is frequently served in pottery mugs, because they help keep it hot, or in little glass cups, because that's what your local liquor store will rent you if you don't feel you have appropriate vessels for your guests to drink their hot mulled wine out of.

Like everything else, however, you can drink hot mulled wine out of a lot of different containers. Mugs are nice; little glass cups with handles are nice; but wine glasses can be nice, too, especially the smaller sizes. The big sizes let the hot wine cool off too fast. The smaller size, however—say, the 10-ounce—holds a suitable amount of hot mulled wine, and the stem lets you hold the concoction without getting second-degree burns.

It's nice to float a lemon round on top of each serving. True, it tends to get in the way when you drink it, but it adds a touch of style that your guests will just have to learn to put up with.

Variations on a theme

Hot mulled wine, how do I alter thee? Let me count the ways. If this were a recipe book, I would fill it with formulae for Fish House Punch, Wine Syllabubs, and other exotic hot wine drinks. Since it is not a recipe book, I will simply direct you to cookbooks, other wine books, books for the home bartender, and the like, where you will find a bewildering array of recipes for hot mulled wine, not to mention wine punches, and where you are sure to find at least one mixture whose name, or ingredients, or general horsepower appeals to you.

In order not to put you completely at the mercy of other books, however, I will simply state that, in general, adulteration of the classic hot mulled wine recipe begins in the area of the spices used. There is ample precedent for fooling around with mixtures that contain allspice, mint, peppermint, bay leaves, sweet basil, dill, cardamon, paprika, and you-name-it.

The next step in fooling-around-with-hot-mulled-wine gets into the kinds and amounts of fruit you use. My classic recipe calls for lemon juice, but you can't go wrong with the addition of orange juice, lime juice, grape juice, cherry juice, cranberry juice, pineapple juice, and so on.

The final adaptation, naturally, has to do with the basic ingredient of hot mulled wine, namely the wine itself. My classic recipe calls for some red wine and some Port. Instead of the red wine, however, you might try some white wine, especially if you stay toward the citrus side of things in the rest of your mixture. Hot white-wine punch is as rare as white-wine sangría, and you'll never know how good it is until you try it.

 The frontiers of science
Instead of adding Port to the classic recipe, you can try adding Sherry instead, or Muscatel or Tokay, or even a bit of rum or brandy. Or you can try mixtures.

The true scholar and scientist, which is what you must be to have read this far, is never satisfied with stock answers. The true scientist presses on to the very limits of knowledge, questioning, experimenting, adding champagne or ginger ale or whatever strikes his fancy, and then submitting to his or her taste buds the responsibility for answering the awesome question: Does it really taste good, or did I blow it completely?

Instant champagne: The light that failed

So much for hot and cold running wine. Let me tell you about my brilliant concept for making champagne in a seltzer bottle.

I bought my seltzer bottle in a secondhand store in San Anselmo, California, and my CO_2 cartridges from the liquor store. I then washed my new toy, filled it with white wine, inserted a CO_2 cartridge, and put it in the fridge to cool off. Two hours later, I started filling glasses.

The result? Well, some ideas are brilliant in conception and real dogs in execution. This one was a dog. All that came out was foam. When it settled, it was flat and ordinary. The moral, therefore, dear reader, is simply that while one must be resourceful and adventuresome in one's attitude toward wine, one cannot expect to score a touchdown on every play.

The end nears

We are now approaching the end of the book. Alas, says the wordy author, who has an irresistible urge to keep on talking about wine indefinitely. Hurrah, says the faithful reader, who wants to *get on with it!*

The author's brow wrinkles. He asks himself: What have I left out? Some words of wisdom, perhaps:

 Great wines under $5: Nothing stands still
I counsel you not to expect anything in your personal wine equation to stay the same forever. This applies to the sources of good, affordable wines, because the sources will change. As I mentioned in the Preface, new wine outlets are springing up in many areas of the country, large stores that specialize in wines— cheap wines, expensive wines, wines that were once expensive and are now being "closed out" at bargain prices because they didn't sell, wines by the bottle and wines by the case. Look for these stores, they're spreading.

The same goes for rating the wines you find: Don't expect the evaluations you make this year to hold up forever. For one thing, the wines themselves will change. Even the vintners who try to maintain a constant product year after year find that they can't always do it. And the small winery whose wine you consider outstanding this year may be gobbled up next year by a giant company more attracted by the equity in the label than the red stuff in the bottle. This, too, can change the product.

What's more, your own taste preferences may change. This is a common and very normal circumstance, and you shouldn't let it bother you. All it means is that your appreciation of smells and tastes, like your appreciation of music or art or literature or sports or fashions, is bound to change over time. So don't worry if one day you find that one of your favorite red wines doesn't hold the same charm for you that it once did. Maybe your tastes are maturing. Don't chalk it against the wine. Chalk it in favor of your educated taste buds, and set out to find yourself some new wines to enjoy.

The agony and the ecstasy
In the end, you'll find that nothing in the wine equation ever really stands still. Not the finding, not the evaluating, not even the serving. That's part of what makes the pursuit of good, affordable wines so enjoyable. Every bottle, every glass can be a richly anticipated experience, either a new and pleasant meeting with an old friend, or an introduction to a mysterious stranger who must be sized up, and who may, in time, become another valued member of your inner circle.

But now the time has come for you to get started. Are your eyes sharp, your nose clear, your taste buds quivering in nervous anticipation? They are?

Good! Go to it! And good luck!

PART TWO

The Wine Index

AND ALL THAT

6

Disclaimers, excuses, and more disclaimers

What follows is a list of 505 wines I have bought, tasted, evaluated, loved, hated, been fascinated by, or found boring. I picked them from a much larger list of wines I have evaluated, as being broadly representative of what's out there waiting for you.

It is my list, compiled by my eyes, my nose, my mouth, my brain. It is not your list (although you're welcome to it), because you may hate the wine I loved and love the wine I hated.

 Remember: Wines can change
I have rated each of these wines on the basis of my 14-point eye-ear-nose-brain system. If your evaluation turns out different from mine, don't immediately assume our tastes are different. Instead, remember, as I pointed out in the closing paragraphs of the last chap-

ter, wines do change. They can change from year to
year, from shipment to shipment, from bottle to bottle in the same case. It is possible that if I were sitting
in your kitchen, taste-testing with you, evaluating a
wine I had previously given a high score, I might at
this later time find it just as deficient as you do. (On
the other hand, let's hope we'd both find it terrific!)

Symbols to help you find your way
To help you find the higher-rated wines easily, I have
identified them with wineglass symbols, as follows:

This number of wineglasses in the Index . . .	. . . means this rating on the 14-point scale:
	14
ŸŸŸŸŸ	13+
	13
	12+
ŸŸŸŸ	12
	11+
	11
ŸŸŸ	10+
	10
ŸŸ	9+
	9
Ÿ	8+
	8

Distribution key . . .
You'll also find that each listing has a reference to
distribution, a letter—A, B, C, or X—that will give

you a rough idea of whether you're likely to find the wine in your city. Here's the key:

A = Available in most major cities, and in many stores in those cities.

B = Available in many cities, but you may have to search to find a store that carries it.

C = Limited distribution, both as to number of cities and number of stores. But still worth a try.

X = Distribution so meager you'll probably never find it. A phenomenon, a freak, a miracle.

Incidentally, the letters refer to the distribution of the *brand* of wine—for example, Paul Masson—and not necessarily to that particular wine within the brand—for example, Paul Masson California Chenin Blanc 1980. At best, wine distribution is chancy and unpredictable, so it's just not possible to pinpoint the distribution of each individual wine. Still, if you can find the brand, maybe you can persuade the store-keeper to try to get hold of the particular wine you want to try.

 The full name is important

Each wine in the Index carries its full name, and the name and location of the company that puts it on the market. It's important to keep the full name in mind, because one vintner may put out several different Burgundies. One may be labeled "Jones Brothers California Burgundy," another at a slightly higher price "Jones Brothers North Coast Counties Burgundy," and a third at a still higher price "Jones Brothers Vintage Burgundy 1973." Chances are, all three will fall within our $5.00-a-bottle guidelines, but it still pays to know precisely which wine you're buying.

"Made by" vs. "Produced by"
Each listing also states that the wine was "produced and bottled by," or "made and bottled by," or "cellared and bottled by" a particular vintner. In the case of California wines, this is a very rough guide to how much of the wine in the bottle was actually fermented and finished by the company that put it into the bottle.

If the label states "produced and bottled by," then at least 75 percent of the wine was fermented and finished by that winery. If the label says "made and bottled by," then only 10 percent of the wine need have been produced by the winery, and the other 90 percent or some portion of it may have been bought from another source and blended into the final product. If the label says anything else—"cellared," "vinted," "bottled," "perfected," or any long and glorious combination of these words, then none of the wine in the bottle need have been produced by that winery.

The fact that the label says simply "Bottled by Jones Brothers Winery" doesn't mean the wine is no good, however. It may be excellent. Its goodness will simply depend on the ability of the Jones Brothers to *buy* good wine, rather than on their ability to make it. This may mean that Jones Brothers wines will be subject to more variation from year to year or from batch to batch, but if the Jones Brothers are smart, careful, and normally lucky, quality variation may not be a problem.

All about price . . .

Finally, some words about price. First, the prices in the Index don't include tax. Second, prices vary from city to city, from state to state, from coast to coast. California wines are generally—but not always—cheaper in California than in New York or Washington, D.C. Wines imported from Europe frequently—but not always—cost less in the East than they do in the West. And so on.

In the Index, therefore, I've shown not just a price, but a price *range* for each wine listed. This range is an amalgam of the most recent prices observed at the shelf in major U.S. cities at the time the Wine Index went to press. The prices won't tell you to-the-penny how much a particular wine is going to cost you, but they will let you know whether the wine you're interested in is in the $1.99 or $2.99 or $4.99 price area. Actually, they'll probably give you a closer idea than that, but that's a start, anyhow.

More about price . . .

A word of warning. I know, just as sure as I'm sitting here typing this into my word processor, that you're going to read about a wine the Index says you should be able to buy for $3.99 to $4.99, and immediately thereafter find it selling for $8.00. It's bound to happen.

When this occurs, please don't assume the price list is totally cockeyed. Instead, remember that the heart of the system for finding great wines at low, low prices lies in shopping around . . . a lot! I can't stress this too much.

If, however, it happens too many times and shopping around doesn't seem to help, wet your finger and hold it in the air to see how the winds of inflation are blowing. Although, as this Second Edition goes to press, the outlook for continued low prices appears excellent, nobody can predict the future with absolute accuracy. At some time, inflation *could* afflict the wine business again.

Should this happen, your self-help tools for finding and judging wines will be even more valuable than before. Your eyes, nose, mouth, and brain should be able to lead you to bargains in any kind of economic situation.

A word about language and wine snobbery
A next-to-last word—about language. Talking about wine can be as much of a game as "where'd-you-go-to-school-and-who-do-you-know." I've choked over hearing someone describe a wine as "a feisty, truculent little red," and, believe it or not, I've heard people say, "The bouquet reminds me of violets soaked in prune juice." Was that *wine* they were talking about?

Well, I'm sure I've made some similarly stupid comments in the Wine Index you're about to explore. If so, please remember that I've been seriously exposed to this malady for a good many years, and it would be a miracle if I didn't contract the disease now and again. Nevertheless, I've tried to avoid jargon and use the English language to give you some idea of which wines are dry, sweet, fruity, tart, and so forth, and if I get carried away from time to time in my descriptions, just draw a line through the offensive word or phrase, and read on.

Finally, let me say to you, dear reader, and to retailers, wholesalers, and to the winemakers themselves, I know I've probably omitted some brand or some type of wine that you desperately want included in this Index. Please believe me, I'm sorry. Maybe I can cover them some other time.

 Let's go!
So, now, without further qualification or disclaimer, here they are. They're listed in three categories: Reds, Whites, and Pinks. Happy tasting—I hope you have a wonderful time!

7

Red Wines

𝖸𝖸𝖸𝖸𝖸 ADRIATICA CABERNET SAUVIGNON 1978 Produced & bottled by Adriatica, Istria, Yugoslavia. Rating: 13. Distribution: C. Adriatica continues to be a star performer in the low-cost red-wine sweepstakes. The color is a russet cherry. The masculine nose is quite accessible, ripe and round and spicy, well-proportioned, full of fruit, and moderately complex. The taste is dry, light-bodied, and has a rich, juicy flavor that delivers everything the nose promised—the fruit, the spice, the good, solid feeling of life and energy. A lot of value for the dollar, friends! Price range: 750 ml, $2.99–4.99.

𝖸𝖸𝖸𝖸𝖸 ALMADÉN VINEYARDS MONTEREY BURGUNDY Produced & bottled by Almadén Vineyards, San Jose, California. Rating: 14. Distribution: A. Score one for Alamadén's Monterey Burgundy, a sensuous, velvety wine full of dignity and character! The color is a royal purple. The bouquet is beautifully, powerfully feminine, a handsome fusion of developed fruit aromas and vanilla extract. The taste is rich, dry, and smooth, with an excellent finish. It has all the grace and charm of a lovely, mature woman, and I urge you to try it at once! Price range: 750 ml, $2.54–4.99.

ΨΨ ALMADÉN CALIFORNIA MOUNTAIN RED BUR-GUNDY Vinted & bottled by Almadén Vineyards, San Jose, California. Rating: 9. Distribution: A. This is a nice, straightforward wine, deep crimson in color, with a simple, sturdy, respectable nose. The taste is dry and lively, with lots of ripe, clean fruit, and while it may not have the style that will make you want to serve it for company dinner, I think you'll like its honesty and directness, and find it's just great to go with Thursday's spaghetti and meatballs. Price range: 750 ml, $2.25–4.49.

ΨΨΨΨΨ ALMADÉN MONTEREY CABERNET SAUVIGNON 1979 Produced & bottled by Almadén Vineyards, San Jose, California. Rating: 13. Distribution: A. You'll find a lot of value in this Cabernet, especially if you buy it in the 1.5–liter bottle. It's a handsome ruby color, and the nose is clean, upright, and displays its Cabernet backbone very nicely. The taste is dry, full of juice and youthful vigor, yet it has an air of maturity and refinement, a feeling of control that gives it strength and character. Shop around, find it at the right price in the right-size bottle, and then make your buy! Price range: 1.5 l, $5.76–8.50.

ALMADÉN CALIFORNIA MOUNTAIN RED CHIANTI
Vinted & bottled by Almadén Vineyards, San Jose,
California. Rating: 7+. Distribution: A. This is a decent, unremarkable wine, a lovely cardinal red, with
a dignified if somewhat stuffy nose. It shows mature
fruit, but it's mature almost to the point of being
elderly. It has a good balance, and it gives hints that
it comes from a good family, but it doesn't display
much charm. Price range: 750 ml, $2.25–4.49.

Ŷ ALMADÉN CALIFORNIA MOUNTAIN RED CLARET
Vinted & bottled by Almadén Vineyards, San Jose,
California. Rating: 8. Distribution: A. The color is a
clear, churchy red. The nose, when you coax it up, is
decent, mannerly, and unspectacular. The taste is dry
and convivial, simple, fruity, and supported by a
good acid balance. Nothing fancy, just decent and
honest. Price range: 750 ml, $2.25–4.49.

ŶŶŶ ALMADÉN SAN BENITO GAMAY BEAUJOLAIS 1980
Produced & bottled by Almadén Vineyards, San Jose,
California. Rating: 10. Distribution: A. This Gamay is
a lovely red-orange, and has a lively, fruity nose. In
the mouth it's semidry with lots of fruit, nicely balanced, youthful but not quite as ingenuous as some
Gamays. This one shows the beginnings of character.
Price range: 750 ml, $2.99–5.50.

ŶŶŶ ALMADÉN MONTEREY ZINFANDEL 1979 Produced
& bottled by Almadén Vineyards, San Jose, California. Rating: 11. Distribution: A. If you like blackberry
jam, you'll like this Zinfandel from Almadén, be-

cause that's what comes through strongly in the taste. It's a moderately dry wine of no tremendous complexity, juicy, refreshing, and full of fruit. The nose is round and sedate, rather matronly, but quite respectable nevertheless. The color is a light vermilion. Price range: 750 ml, $3.15–5.50.

ᵀᵀᵀ ANDEAN CABERNET SAUVIGNON 1975 Produced & bottled by Andean Vineyards, Mendoza, Argentina. Rating: 10. Distribution: C. This wine from Argentina has obvious quality, but it may be too stern and spare for you. It's a rich churchy-red color, and the forthright nose has a sort of berry-jam bouquet, round and fruity, with quite a bit of oak. In the background lurks a faint, stalky component, but it's minor. The taste is exceedingly restrained, dry, oaky— more oak than I like, but there are some palates that thrive on it. The fruit is there, the quality is there, and a very austere approach to winemaking is there, too. Price range: 750 ml, $4.19–6.75.

ᵀᵀᵀᵀᵀ BAROSSA VALLEY CABERNET SAUVIGNON 1979 Vintaged & bottled by Barossa Co-operative Winery, Ltd., Nuriootpa, South Australia. Rating: 13. Distribution: C. The Aussies have sent us a big (13 percent), brilliant, orangey-red Cabernet with an exotic charm and an oaky, seductive nose that exudes cedar, spice, the rare perfumes of the Orient, and God knows what else! The taste is dry and elegant, with an array of oak and complex fruit flavors ranging from currants to raspberry jam. It's a wine of real quality, a broad-gauge wine with a fine finish, and

I'm sure you'll enjoy it. Price range: 750 ml, $2.88–4.50.

ǴǴǴǴ BEAULIEU NAPA VALLEY BURGUNDY 1978 Produced & bottled by Beaulieu Vineyard, Rutherford, California. Rating: 11+. Distribution: A. The color is dark cherry, the nose is pleasing and serious, an aristocratic, masculine bouquet of some breadth. In the mouth you'll find it smooth, rich, and velvety, displaying a lovely, oaky mixture of nicely developed fruit flavors. It's a wine that shows both breeding and care, a wine you can count on to deliver lots of quality. Price range: 750 ml, $3.65–5.99.

ǴǴǴǴ BERINGER NAPA VALLEY BURGUNDY Produced & bottled by Beringer Vineyards, St. Helena, California. Rating: 12+. Distribution: B. This royal-purple wine has a rich, round, velvety nose, rather solemn and masculine, with a varied bouquet of blackberry jam and dried fruits. There's a feeling of power and expansiveness in the taste, which is big and juicy, with a mouthful of the same berry jam and other complexities signaled by the nose. It's an excellent, well-made wine, and I'd award it five glasses if it weren't a bit more tannic than I wish it were. Nonetheless, we can all still enjoy it a lot, and also enjoy knowing we're drinking a big bargain. Price range: 750 ml, $2.55–4.50.

ǴǴǴǴǴ BERINGER NAPA VALLEY ZINFANDEL 1979 Produced & bottled by Beringer Vineyards, St. Helena, California. Rating: 13+. Distribution: B. This scarlet

Zinfandel has a volatile, assertive nose of some complexity—fruit, spice, a dash of pepper, and above all, life and vigor. In the mouth you'll find it a wine with a backbone, juicy, nervy, full of style and energy. It's dry, has medium body, and a good, long finish. Beringer aged it in redwood, so it will give you a chance to make comparisons with the more customary oak-finished wines. But don't get academic about it—just enjoy it! Price range: 750 ml, $3.83–5.50.

🍷🍷🍷 BOLLA BARDOLINO 1979 Bottled by Casa Vinicola Frabo, S.P.A., Verona, Italy. Rating: 10+. Distribution: A. This brilliant light vermilion wine has a congenial, pleasing nose, clean, fresh, and attractively fruity. The taste is also clean and fresh, a well-made wine of charming simplicity, full of fruit, sunshine, and the verve of youth. Price range: 750 ml, $2.99–5.50.

🍷🍷 BOLLA VALPOLICELLA Produced & bottled by Casa Vinicola Frabo, S.P.A., Verona, Italy. Rating: 9+. Distribution: A. The color is a charming light red, the nose, though thin, shows some decent fruit, and the taste is dry, pleasantly simple, and just a trace astringent as though the grapes were picked before they had completely matured. Great with the pizza you just sent out for. Price range: 750 ml, $2.99–5.50.

🍷🍷🍷🍷 BROLIO CHIANTI CLASSICO 1978 Bottled by Barone Ricasoli, Firenze, Italy. Rating: 11+. Distribution: B. Here's a brilliant, Titian wine with the energy of an Olympic athlete! The nose is lively and assertive, full of fruit—ripe black currants and a touch of spice—and the taste is dry, light-bodied, brash, zesty, full of life. In fact, you may overlook the subtle complexity of this wine in its frantic call for activity— dancing, jokes, romance, adventure. Shop around, the price varies a lot. Price range: 750 ml, $2.99–6.00.

♥♥♥♥♥ BUENA VISTA SONOMA COUNTY BURGUNDY 1979 Produced & bottled by Buena Vista Winery, Sonoma, California. Rating: 13. Distribution: C. Here are my tasting notes, verbatim: "Crimson, 12.9 percent, pleasing, serious nose, energy, backbone, developed fruit, sinewy, dependable. Taste: Big, dry, smooth, juicy, nice breadth of flavors—plum jam, blackberry jam—cultivated, supple, drinkable, mouth-filling, everything under control of the oak." You may gather I find this an outstanding wine. I do. Price range: 750 ml, $3.68–5.75.

♥♥♥ BULLY HILL 100% NEW YORK STATE OLD BARNYARD RED WINE Produced & bottled by Bully Hill Vineyards, Hammondsport, New York. Rating: 10+. Distribution: X. Bully Hill Wines are the product of a very capable and slightly eccentric winemaker, and I'm afraid only Eastern readers will be able to find his wines very easily. This one is a medium red with a nose that is quietly assertive, and offers a genial, modestly complex blending of wine flavors. The taste is moderately dry and supple, with a modest elegance. It's a harmonious blending of the fruits of the vine. Price range: 750 ml, $3.49–5.69.

♥♥♥ CAMBIASO 1852 HOUSE CALIFORNIA BURGUNDY Produced & bottled by Cambiaso Vineyards, Healdsburg, California. Rating: 10+. Distribution: C. This rich crimson wine is a serious wine with a serious nose and a serious taste. The nose is deep and mature, full of meat and sinew, with plenty of mature fruit. The taste is dry, big and brawny, mouth-filling, well balanced, and full of solid refreshment. It's not a member of the nobility, but it's a sturdy knight who lives in the palace and serves as bodyguard to the prince. Price range: 750 ml, $1.99–3.00.

ȲȲȲȲ CAMBIASO SONOMA COUNTY CABERNET SAUVIGNON 1978   Produced & bottled by Cambiaso Winery, Healdsburg, California. Rating: 12. Distribution: C. The color is a deep red-purple. The nose is deep, full, masculine, a serious, powerful, authoritative nose that's full of mature fruit. The taste? Well, forget delicacy, this is power time. The taste is all meat and sinew and powerful fruit flavors, a bit rough and tannic, but still quite a treat. In a few more years, it may be even more so. Price range: 750 ml, $3.60–5.99.

ȲȲ CARMEL ISRAEL CABERNET SAUVIGNON 1979   Produced & bottled by Societe Coop. Vigneronne des Grandes Caves, Richon Le Zion & Zichron Jacob, Israel. Rating: 9+. Distribution: B. The bouquet of this medium red wine is rounded, mature, and dignified, and the taste is dry, pleasing, with lots of fruit and spice. It's not a whole lot of fun to drink right now, however, because it is quite tart and tannic, qualities that mean it will probably drink better in about ten years. If you can afford to wait, lay some down. If you can't, look elsewhere. Price range: 750 ml, $2.67–5.25.

CASA DE ROJAS CABERNET SAUVIGNON DE CHILE   Produced & bottled by Vina Tarapaca, Santiago, Chile. Rating: 6. Distribution: C. Chile makes some very fine wines, but this scarlet number is not one of them. The nose has both fruit and vigor, but it also has a brash, vegetable pungency that's not very nice. This same veggie characteristic also appears in the taste, and I can't imagine you liking it very much. Price range: 750 ml, $3.99–5.15.

CHRISTIAN BROTHERS CALIFORNIA BURGUNDY   Produced & bottled by The Christian Brothers, Napa, California. Rating: 7+. Distribution: A. There's really nothing wrong with this Burgundy, so I wonder why I can't get more excited about it. I guess it's the nose—it seems somewhat baked. The taste is good, though, lively and fruity, and on balance it's an acceptable, middle-of-the-road wine. Price range: 750 ml, $1.99–4.25.

ΨΨΨΨΨ CHRISTIAN BROTHERS NAPA VALLEY CABERNET SAUVIGNON   Produced & bottled by The Christian Brothers, Napa, California. Rating: 13. Distribution: A. The color: Grenadier scarlet. The nose: easily accessible and full of Cabernet varietal character, upright, structured, with a lot of vigor and a nicely developed berry-jam bouquet. The taste also displays its varietal character as well as the lovely jam flavors, and it has lots of sap and vigor. It's a sound, honest wine with spine, power, and dignity. I think you'll like it. Price range: 750 ml, $3.77–6.75.

ΨΨ CHRISTIAN BROTHERS NAPA VALLEY ZINFANDEL Produced & bottled by The Christian Brothers, Napa,

California. Rating: 9. Distribution: A. With the exception of its scarlet color, there is an air of restraint about this Zinfandel. The taste is pleasant enough, suitably fruity though limited in its flavor range, but the nose is a bit closed in, and there's a dank note lurking in the background. On balance, it's a pleasant, dry wine without great pretension. Price range: 750 ml, $3.55–5.99.

ŶŶ COLONY CALIFORNIA CLASSIC BURGUNDY Vinted & bottled by Colony Wines, San Francisco. Rating: 9+. Distribution: A. The color is scarlet, heading for purple. The nose has a pleasant country simplicity, fruity, with a faint spiciness. The taste is moderately dry, with a pleasant juiciness and good acid, and the whole feeling is one of natural structure, open fields, sunshine, and a gratifying, native honesty. Price range: 1.5 l, $2.99–4.75.

ŶŶŶ COLONY CLASSIC CABERNET SAUVIGNON OF CALIFORNIA Vinted & bottled by Colony Wines, San Francisco. Rating: 11. Distribution: A. The nose of this purply-red Cabernet displays the Cabernet character very nicely. You can sense the structure of the wine in its developing fruit bouquet. The taste is dry, the fruit is plentiful but muted, and I have the feeling this wine has not yet reached the peak of its flavor development. Lay a couple of bottles on the floor of your closet, and try them in a year or two. (In case of emergency, you can always abbreviate the aging period.) Price range: 1.5 l, $3.18–5.25.

COLONY CLASSIC ZINFANDEL OF CALIFORNIA Vinted & bottled by Colony Wines, San Francisco, California.

Rating: 7+. Distribution: A. This vermilion Zinfandel has a pleasant nose, fruity and rounded, but gives a flat, lackluster performance in the mouth. Not a bad wine, just less than I'd hoped for. Price range: 750 ml, $2.45–4.50.

♆ CONCANNON CALIFORNIA BURGUNDY 1980   Made & bottled by Concannon Vineyards, Livermore, California. Rating: 8. Distribution: B. The wine is a lovely cherry color, the nose comes forward with a pleasing bouquet of fruit, and the taste, if not spectacular, is warm and amiable. Could use a touch more acid, but why quibble? Price range: 750 ml, $2.77–4.99.

♆♆♆ CONCHA Y TORO CABERNET SAUVIGNON 1976 Produced & bottled by Viña Concha y Toro, Maipo, Chile. Rating: 10. Distribution: C. This is a slightly restrained, somber wine, orangey-red in color, with a proper, respectable, sedate—perhaps even stuffy— nose. In the mouth, however, you'll find it dry, mild, and pleasingly fruity, with a good acid balance. It's a quiet wine, serious, rather mellow, and very drinkable. Price range: 750 ml, $3.69–5.99.

CORBANS CABERNET-PINOTAGE 1978 Produced & bottled by The Corban Estate, Henderson Valley, New Zealand. Rating: 5+. Distribution: C. This wine has a light, clear, red-orange color and a smell and taste that won't make many friends for it. Both have a stalky, vegetable quality that is quite unpleasant. Too bad. Price range: 750 ml, $3.99–5.99.

♆ CRESTA BLANCA MENDOCINO BURGUNDY   Produced & bottled by Cresta Blanca Vineyards, Ukiah, California. Rating: 8+. Distribution: B. The color is scarlet, the nose is shy, clean, and unpretentious. The taste is sprightly and pleasing, with good acid, plenty of fruit, and some hints of spice to make it interesting. Price range: 750 ml, $2.68–4.99.

☗ CRESTA BLANCA MENDOCINO CABERNET SAUVIGNON 1977 Produced & bottled by Cresta Blanca Vineyards, Ukiah, California. Rating: 8. Distribution: B. This Cabernet has a lovely nose, assertive and fresh, with a developing fruit bouquet that includes a pleasing mint component. In the mouth you'll find lots of fruit and acid, but it is so astringent I find it hard to enjoy. With such a wonderful bouquet, maybe all it needs is aging, in which case it might be a darned good Cabernet to drink five years from now. Price range: 750 ml, $3.95–6.50.

☗ CRESTA BLANCA MENDOCINO GAMAY BEAUJOLAIS 1978 Produced & bottled by Cresta Blanca Vineyards, Ukiah, California. Rating: 8+. Distribution: B. This wine is a lovely auburn red, and has a deep, robust, peasant strength to its bouquet. In the mouth it shows lots of fruit and youthful vigor, with more character than the average Gamay. Price range: 750 ml, $2.77–5.50.

☗☗☗ CRESTA BLANCA MENDOCINO PETITE SIRAH 1978 Produced & bottled by Cresta Blanca Vineyards, Ukiah, California. Rating: 10. Distribution: B. The nose of this deep-purple wine is quite decent, but somewhat restrained. The taste, however, belies the nose and is surprisingly pleasant and refreshing. It's dry, medium-bodied, and has a clean, rich flavor that will make you think of mixed-fruit jams. It also has a slight, pleasing tartness, and an overall character of nice, crisp dignity. Price range: 750 ml, $2.77–5.50.

ꔫꔫꔫꔫ CRESTA BLANCA CALIFORNIA PINOT NOIR 1975 Produced & bottled by Cresta Blanca Vineyards, Ukiah, California. Rating: 11+. Distribution: B. This Pinot Noir is built along classic lines. The color is a clear, brilliant red-orange. The nose is quiet, tasteful, polite, with a modest yet pleasing bouquet development—you can tell it comes from a good family. The taste is dry, medium-bodied, generous and assertive, full of fruit and fruit-jam flavors, with everything pulled together nicely in a clean and refreshing way. I think you'll like it. Price range: 750 ml, $3.37–6.50.

ꔫ CRESTA BLANCA MENDOCINO ZINFANDEL 1979 Produced & bottled by Cresta Blanca Vineyards, Ukiah, California. Rating: 8+. Distribution: B. This crimson Zinfandel is on the light side, both in the nose and in the mouth. The nose is restrained, even a little cooked, but the mouth sensations are dry and lively, with a slender range of flavors. It's refreshing all the same. Price range: 750 ml, $2.77–5.50.

CRIBARI CALIFORNIA MELLO BURGUNDY Made & bottled by Cribari & Sons, Lodi, California. Rating: 7+. Distribution: A. This is a simple, decent, forgettable wine. That's not really a negative comment. It's simply a recognition that this kind of wine—"mellow," or as in the present case, "mello," is almost always the same. Usually clean, fruity, and low in acid. Often rather sweet, although this one is medium dry. Generally a pleasant accompaniment to a hearty meal. And in almost every case, simple, decent, forgettable. Price range: 1.5 l, $2.99–4.75.

CRIBARI CALIFORNIA MENDOCINO BURGUNDY Made & bottled by Cribari & Sons, Lodi, California. Rating: 6+. Distribution: A. Although the wine has adequate fruit, it lacks acid and has a slightly baked character both in the nose and the mouth. It's not terrible, however, it's just there and I wish it weren't. Price range: 1.5 l, $2.99–4.75.

CRIBARI CALIFORNIA MOUNTAIN BURGUNDY Made & bottled by Cribari & Sons, Lodi, California. Rating: 7+. Distribution: A. This is another simple, serviceable wine. It's maroon in color, with a slightly reticent nose that shows respectable fruit. The taste is decent, a bit earthy, with good fruit and acid. It's a hardworking wine, good for lots of simple mealtime purposes, but not a wine you'd spend much time talking about. Price range: 1.5 l, $2.99–4.75.

🍷🍷🍷 CRIBARI CALIFORNIA CABERNET SAUVIGNON Made & bottled by Cribari & Sons, Lodi, California. Rating: 10. Distribution: A. This vermilion Cabernet has a decent, unpretentious nose, somewhat austere and displaying a Cabernet weediness. The taste is dry, serious, medium-bodied, and the varietal characteristics come through quite clearly. It has a rather attractive dried fruit quality, a feeling of restraint, and a simple country dignity. Price range: 750 ml, $3.29–4.99.

♥ CRIBARI CALIFORNIA ZINFANDEL   Made & bottled by Cribari & Sons, Lodi, California. Rating: 8. Distribution: A. The color is scarlet with purple glints, the nose is fruity, although rather lacking in Zinfandel character. The Zinfandel shows in the mouth, however, somewhat masked, and if the wine had a better acid balance it would earn a better rating. As it is, it's a bit flat. Price range: 750 ml, $2.99–4.75.

♥♥♥♥ DEMESTICA   Produced & bottled by Achaia-Clauss Wine Co., S.A., Patras, Greece. Rating: 11+. Distribution: B. Would you like a quick trip to Greece? Open a bottle of this orangey-red wine and inhale the robust aromas of fruit, spice, and briers. Then taste it: dry, athletic, full of ripe grapes, brambles, and boundless Greek vitality. You won't want to drink it every night, because you might start dancing and break every dish in the kitchen, but for an occasional treat, and a very pleasant foreign experience, put a few bottles in your cellar. Price range: 750 ml, $2.83–4.99.

♥ EGRI BIKAVER 1978 Produced & bottled in Hungary, exported by Monimpex, Budapest, Hungary. Rating: 8. Distribution: B. This crimson wine has an attractively fruity nose that displays an air of quiet maturity and refinement. The taste is pleasant in regard to fruit and acid, but it's a bit too astringent to achieve a higher score. An interesting wine, nevertheless. Price range: 750 ml, $3.63–5.59.

♥♥♥♥ FETZER LAKE COUNTY CABERNET SAUVIGNON 1980   Produced & bottled by Fetzer Vineyards, Redwood Valley, California. Rating: 12+. Distribution: B. There is something aristocratic about this dry, cranberry-colored Cabernet. You find it first in the nose—the feeling of backbone, the hints of vanilla, the beginnings of complexity in the fruit bouquet. You confirm it in the mouth when you experience its richness and breadth, the ongoing melding of its fruit flavors, its modest oakiness. And even after you've swallowed your mouthful, it lingers on in a lovely finish. Try a bottle. Price range: 750 ml, $4.14–6.99.

🍷 FETZER MENDOCINO GAMAY BEAUJOLAIS 1981 Produced & bottled by Fetzer Vineyards, Redwood Valley, California. Rating: 8+. Distribution: B. The color is deep red with purple tones. The nose is youthful and light-hearted, with lots of fruit. The taste is similarly young and simple, dry, pleasing, one-dimensional, slightly astringent, but offering loads of juicy fruit. Price range: 750 ml, $3.25–5.75.

🍷🍷🍷 FETZER MENDOCINO PETITE SYRAH 1980 Produced & bottled by Fetzer Vineyards, Redwood Valley, California. Rating: 11. Distribution: B. Here's a wine—deep, rich purple in color—that's just bursting with juice. It has a sturdy, forthright, generous nose, full of youthful energy and showing the beginnings of refinement. The taste: well, it's big (13 percent), full, dry, wholesome, and it "*tastes* purple." It's a bit tannic, it has touches of spiciness, it's lovely and outdoorsy, and the fruit just won't stop. I suggest you give it a try. Price range: 750 ml, $4.25–6.49.

🍷🍷🍷🍷🍷 FETZER MENDOCINO PINOT NOIR 1980 Produced & bottled by Fetzer Vineyards, Redwood Val-

ley, California. Rating: 13. Distribution: B. Force and
vigor are the key words here. The color is a clear,
clean scarlet, and the nose is handsome, a good, clean
example of the Pinot's varietal character, with a bouquet that has substance, power, and developing complexity. The taste is dry, oaky, spicy, full and textured, profuse in its energy, exuding good breeding.
It's a winner, folks; don't pass it by. Price range: 750
ml, $4.25–6.99.

FETZER MENDOCINO PREMIUM RED   Produced & bottled by Fetzer Vineyards, Redwood Valley, California. Rating: 7+. Distribution: B. The nose of this
handsome, scarlet wine is fruity enough, but it's off-
set by a touch of cellar stuffiness. In the mouth it's
pleasant—dry, fruity, tart—but there's just enough
reminder of the nose in the taste to keep it from scoring higher. Price range: 750 ml, $2.48–4.25.

ŸŸŸ FETZER LAKE COUNTY ZINFANDEL 1980   Produced
& bottled by Fetzer Vineyards, Redwood Valley, California. Rating: 10+. Distribution: B. The color is medium red heading toward purple. The nose is decent,
assertive, somewhat matronly, and reveals a developing compound of mature fruits. The taste is dry, full-
bodied, and full of serenity and assurance. It's not
showy, but it does have a lot of lovely fruit, which it
presents in a calm, unhurried way. Price range: 750
ml, $3.45–5.99.

ŸŸŸŸŸ FETZER MENDOCINO COUNTY ZINFANDEL 1979
Produced & bottled by Fetzer Vineyards, Redwood
Valley, California. Rating: 13+. Distribution: B. Pull

the cork on this crimson Zinfandel and you're in for a fine experience! It's a big wine—13.1 percent alcohol—a powerful wine, and a wine that displays the kind of soundness and quality that we all keep searching for. The nose is round and rich and has a charming berry-jam bouquet. The taste delivers more power and more berries—blackberries, raspberries, currants—plus a pleasing tart edge. The finish is long and satisfying. What more could you ask? Price range: 750 ml, $3.68–6.99.

ŸŸŸ FOLONARI BARDOLINO   Bottled by SPAL, Pastrengo, Italy. Rating: 10. Distribution: B. The color is a very light orange-red. The nose has plenty of fruit, and the approach is serious rather than jolly, with the nose a bit closed-in. The taste is dry and refreshing, full of strength and life, but it's a somber, hardy, pensive life with very little fun and games. The fruit seems considerably sobered by the cooperage, but it's a nice wine all the same, and perhaps just right for those occasions when you feel thoughtful and thirsty at the same time. Price range: 1.5 l, $2.99–5.95.

ŸŸŸŸ FOLONARI VALPOLICELLA   Bottled by SPAL, Pastrengo, Italy. Rating: 11+. Distribution: B. If Folonari's Bardolino seems somber, its Valpolicella is just the opposite. Its color is a light, clear vermilion, and the nose is clean, sunny, charming, light-hearted, dashing. It's not complex, but it's lavish in its fruit and flowers and general feeling of youth. The taste is the same—dry, light-bodied, athletic, tasting of grapes and ripe cherries. It's not a big wine, and it's not an important, demanding wine. It's just a lot of good, clean, refreshing fun. Try it. Price range: 750 ml, 1.5 l, $2.99–5.95.

♀ FRANCISCAN CALIFORNIA BURGUNDY CASK 319 Produced & bottled by Franciscan Vineyards, Rutherford, California. Rating: 8+. Distribution: B. This lively red wine has a pleasing, forthright nose with hints of herbs in it. It's not a biggie, but it's a comfortable wine, fruity, mellow, and well balanced. You could do lots worse. Price range: 750 ml, $2.29–4.25.

♀♀ FRANCISCAN VINEYARDS CASK 320 CALIFORNIA RED DINNER WINE Produced & bottled by Franciscan Vineyards, Rutherford, California. Rating: 9. Distribution: B. This bricky, red-orange wine has a respectable, easily approachable nose, not a blockbuster, but filled with ripe, mature fruit. The taste is dry, pleasant, accommodating, with slightly restrained fruit flavors and good acid. In fact, it's just the thing for a good many different kinds of midweek dinners, while saving your weekend for something a mite more exciting. Price range: 750 ml, $2.48–4.49.

FRANZIA CALIFORNIA BURGUNDY Made & bottled by Franzia Brothers Winemakers, San Francisco, California. Rating: 6+. Distribution: B. The color is a deep blood-red. The nose has a faint vegetable whiff that, while not absolutely awful, won't heighten your enjoyment of the wine. The same veggie note comes through in the taste, so it's my guess you won't find the wine too enticing. Price range: 1.5 l, $2.49–4.25.

ΨΨ **FRANZIA CALIFORNIA CABERNET SAUVIGNON** Bottled by Franzia Brothers Winemakers, San Francisco. Rating: 9. Distribution: B. Simplicity is the key word for this wine. The nose has a slightly intrusive edge that displays a lot of ripe fruit, but very little complexity. The taste is dry, straightforward, and loaded with fruit. Everything's pretty much on the surface, however, in a style that's simple and not terribly imaginative, but it's a pleasant wine nevertheless. Price range: 1.5 l, $2.49–4.99.

FRATELLI LAMBRUSCO Bottled by F.A.C.V., Dosimo, Italy. Rating: 7+. Distribution: B. Alexis Lichine describes Lambruscos as "sweetish, semi-sparkling wines of little virtue," and I go along with Alexis. This purply-red example, however, is a little better than most. Effervescent, as they all are, sweet, as they all are, but with a trifle less of the hot-weather nose and taste that seem a general characteristic of the species. I still don't recommend it, although I suppose you do have to try a Lambrusco once. If so, try this one. Price range: 750 ml, $2.29–4.25.

GALLO BURGUNDY OF CALIFORNIA Made & bottled by Gallo Vineyards, Modesto, California. Rating: 7+. Distribution: A. This is "no frills" wine, friends— plain, fruity, simple. That goes for the nose, that goes for the taste: hardworking, honest, straightforward, with little complexity or style. Price range: 1.5 l, $2.49–4.49.

ΨΨ **GALLO HEARTY BURGUNDY OF CALIFORNIA** Made & bottled by the Gallo Vineyards, Modesto, California. Rating: 9+. Distribution: A. Over the years a lot of writers have said this wine is a good value. Well, friends, it is. It's hardly a complicated wine, but it's good and it's reliable. The color is crimson with hints of purple, the nose is fruity and mellow, and the taste is simple, amiable, and well balanced. Price range: 1.5 l, $2.99–4.49.

▼▼▼▼ ERNEST & JULIO GALLO CABERNET SAUVIGNON OF CALIFORNIA Vinted & cellared & bottled by Ernest & Julio Gallo, Modesto, California. Rating: 12. Distribution: A. Gallo's Cabernet has a lot of class, friends, and you would do well to give it a try. The color is a deep crimson, and the nose has a stately fragrance, a strong, erect backbone supporting a nicely developing bouquet. The taste is dry, medium-bodied, and has a kind of austere majesty. It's a sober and authoritative wine, with a harmonious balance of fruit and oak. A good, solid, well-made wine. Price range: 750 ml, $3.68–6.00.

GALLO CHIANTI OF CALIFORNIA Made & bottled by Gallo Vineyards, Modesto, California. Rating: 7+. Distribution: A. This wine, red as a Cardinal's hat, is a simple, "mellow," plain-Jane wine, one of the crowd, one of the "smooshed fruit" wines, decent, unexciting, and serviceable. The nose and taste are clean, acceptable, and simplistic. I can think of worse things to say about a wine! Price range: 1.5 l, $2.99–4.49.

GEYSER PEAK CALIFORNIA BURGUNDY 1977 Produced & bottled by Geyser Peak Winery, Geyserville, California. Rating: 6. Distribution: B. This is one of those wines you can swig down on a jolly picnic and have a very good time. At your dinner table, however, sniffing the aroma will make you lift your eyebrows, and the flavor will seem ordinary and not terribly appealing. Sorry. Price range: 750 ml, $2.49–4.25.

ͳͳͳͳ GEYSER PEAK CALIFORNIA PINOT NOIR 1976 Produced & bottled by Geyser Peak Winery, Geyserville, California. Rating: 12+. Distribution: B. Some people like wine that just sits there in the glass and looks pretty. Others like a little action. This lovely orange-red wine is for the latter type, because it's a real roller coaster of energy and power. The nose is deep, rich, authoritative, easily accessible, and has a developing bouquet of elegant fruit. The taste is dry, a bit tannic, but brimming over with zest and brawn, full of life, full of juicy, ripe fruit, and full of refreshment. Price range: 750 ml, $4.49–7.00.

GIACOBAZZI LAMBRUSCO Produced & bottled by Grandi Vini, Nonantola, Italy. Rating: 7. Distribution: A. This scarlet wine has all the Lambrusco characteristics: ponderous, hot-weather nose, frothy, sweet, baked taste. I don't recommend you drink Lambrusco, but don't feel sorry for the Lambrusco makers, because Lambruscos are the number one wine import into the United States! Shows how much *I* know about it! Price range: 750 ml, $2.34–4.50.

ͳͳ GIUMARRA VINEYARDS BURGUNDY OF CALIFORNIA 1980 Produced & bottled by Giumarra Vineyards,

Edison, California. Rating: 9. Distribution: C. This velvety red wine has a lively, fruity nose with a trace of spice. The taste shows the same slight spiciness, and the whole effect is clean, smooth, and pleasant. Price range: 750 ml, $2.34–4.25.

ΨΨΨ GIUMARRA VINEYARDS CABERNET SAUVIGNON OF CALIFORNIA 1977 FOUNDER'S CHOICE Produced & bottled by Giumarra Vineyards, Edison, California. Rating: 10+. Distribution: C. This orangey-red Cabernet has a very pleasing, generous, jamlike flavor and a moderate oakiness. The fruit bouquet is slightly held back, as though it couldn't decide whether it was going to be aristocratic or stuffy. Aristocracy wins out, however, especially when you view all aspects of the wine as a whole. It's called "Founder's Choice," and while it's a nice wine, if I'd been the founder, *my* choice would have been the next wine on this list. Check it out. Price range: 750 ml, $3.69–6.99.

ΨΨΨΨ GIUMARRA VINEYARDS CABERNET SAUVIGNON OF CALIFORNIA 1980 Produced & bottled by Giumarra Vineyards, Edison, California. Rating: 11+. Distribution: C. This wine is forceful, not subtle, and it will win you over with its sheer power and urgency. The color is a dark bluish red. The nose is aromatic, masculine, straightforward, no kidding around. It's full of ripe, fresh berries, as is the taste, which will fill your mouth with a rich, blackberry-jam flavor. The wine is moderately dry, meaty and full. It's not one of your effete little Cabernets, and I think you'll find it a real treat. Price range: 750 ml, $3.49–6.99.

ΥΥ GIUMARRA VINEYARDS PETITE SIRAH OF CALIFORNIA 1980 Produced & bottled by Giumarra Vineyards, Edison, California. Rating: 9+. Distribution: C. You get a big load of simple, sunshiny fruit in this royal-purple wine. The mildly piquant nose is full of plums and currants, and the taste is moderately dry, juicy, and full of clean, ripe, simplistic fruit flavors. It's not long on complexity; what you taste is what you get, but that ain't bad! Price range: 750 ml, $3.49–6.49.

ΥΥΥΥ GIUMARRA VINEYARDS ZINFANDEL OF CALIFORNIA 1980 Produced & bottled by Giumarra Vineyards, Edison, California. Rating: 12+. Distribution: C. Hey, what a nice experience! A deep, majestic, purply wine with a lovely nose full of fruit, spice, brambles, and lots of zip. The taste? Dry, well structured, with complex flavors of herbs and dried fruits. It makes me think of a tramp through the autumn fields with a dog, starting up woodcocks. What on earth will it make you think of? Price range: 750 ml, $3.49–6.49.

ΥΥ GRAN CONDAL RED RIOJA WINE 1977 Produced & bottled by Bodegas Rioja Santiago, Haro, Spain. Rating: 9+. Distribution: C. Here's a pleasant, unspectacular wine from the Rioja region of Spain, light red with russet tones. The nose is solid upper-middle class, clean and round with mature fruit, but with the oak providing a somber, maybe even dour, note. The taste is dry and refreshing, with just enough gloom mixed in to remind you we're all mortal after all. Price range: 750 ml, $1.69–4.99.

♟ GRAO VASCO DAO 1977 Produced & bottled by Vinicola do Vale do Dao, Lda., Viseu, Portugal. Rating: 8. Distribution: B. The nose of this vermilion wine doesn't have a lot to say, but the taste is dry and decent, nothing to get all stirred up about, but pleasantly full of just-ripe fruit and a good acid balance. Good, not great. Price range: 750 ml, $2.89–5.49.

♟♟♟♟ GUNDLACH-BUNDSCHU SONOMA VALLEY SONOMA RED WINE 1978 Produced & bottled by Gundlach-Bundschu Winery, Vineburg, California. Rating: 11+. Distribution: C. The color is crimson, shading to orange. The nose is aromatic and thought-provoking, with a nicely developed bouquet of old spice, dried flowers, and black-currant jam. The taste is spare and structured, dry, full of vigor, with a pleasant complexity. It has a good finish. If you can find it, I think you'll like it. Price range: 750 ml, $2.99–4.59.

♟♟♟♟ HARDY'S NOTTAGE HILL CLARET 1977 Bottled by Thomas Hardy & Sons, Pty. Ltd., South Australia. Rating: 12. Distribution: C. "Quality, dignity, style." That's what my tasting notes say. Deep scarlet in color, this wine has a nose that is solid, not racy, clean and generously endowed with mature fruit that is developing into a bouquet of jams and pleasant kitchen extracts. In the mouth it's dry, smooth, of medium body, with its fruit in a delicate and harmonious balance with its oak. Made in the classic style, it's well worth hunting for. Price range: 750 ml, $4.39–5.49.

ꬶꬶꬶ INGLENOOK NORTH COAST COUNTIES VINTAGE BURGUNDY 1978 Produced & bottled by Inglenook Vineyards, Rutherford, California. Rating: 12+. Distribution: A. There's a fetching, juicy aroma to this clear, medium-red wine. It's fresh, rounded, an aromatic compound of good fruit and sunshine. There's a smooth, dry, mouth-filling flavor to go along with the nose, a fairly complex mixture of ripe fruits, vanilla, and other lovely tastes. I hope you can find a bottle! Price range: 1.5 l, $4.99–6.49.

ꬶꬶꬶꬶ INGLENOOK NAPA VALLEY PETITE SIRAH 1978 Produced & bottled by Inglenook Vineyards, Rutherford, California. Rating: 13+. Distribution: A. This is a dry, rich, velvety wine, full of quiet elegance. The color is an ecclesiastical purplish red. The bouquet is a strong, serene compound of developed fruit aromas, with a touch of vanilla extract. The taste confirms all the evidence of the nose—the subtle blending of refined fruit flavors, the dignity, the sensuous air of rich repose. Price range: 750 ml, $3.69–5.49.

ꬶꬶꬶ INGLENOOK NAVALLE RUBY CABERNET OF CALIFORNIA Vinted & bottled by Inglenook Vineyards, San Francisco, California. Rating: 11+. Distribution: A. Ruby Cabernets are frequently a little strident, but this one manages to turn that quality into an asset. The nose, loaded with fruit, is somehow shaped and tamed by those weedy tones that sometimes make a Ruby Cabernet less than appealing. The same is true in the taste. It's dry, generously fruity, even powerful, and it owes its success to the Cabernet compo-

nents of its still-developing character. Price range:
1.5 l, $3.66–5.49.

♉♉♉♉ INGLENOOK ESTATE BOTTLED NAPA VALLEY ZIN-
FANDEL 1978   Produced & bottled by Inglenook Vineyards, Rutherford, California. Rating: 12+. Distribution: A. Here's another terrific, low-cost Zinfandel for
you! You'll admire its brilliant orange-red color, and
you'll love the nose—an inviting, ingratiating bouquet of ripe berries and spicy briers. This delightful
experience continues in the mouth, where you'll find
a refreshing range of fruit and herbal flavors, a long,
satisfactory finish, and a staggering 14.5 percent alcohol content! Price range: 750 ml, $3.69–5.99.

♉♉♉♉ LOUIS JADOT BEAUJOLAIS JADOT 1981   Bottled
by Louis Jadot, Beaune, France. Rating: 11+. Distribution: B. The wines of Beaujolais are supposed to be
fresh and light-hearted, and M. Jadot's crimson Beaujolais certainly fits these specifications. Its aroma is
robust, full of ripe fruit. The taste is dry, youthful,
rather light in body, not complex by any means, but
delivering a carload of vigor and sunshiny, mildly
spicy fruit. It makes me think of goatherds chasing
maidens across a French hillside, but that's my problem, not yours, right? Price range: 750 ml, $3.97–5.59.

♉♉♉♉♉ KAISER   STUHL   AUSTRALIAN   CABERNET
SAUVIGNON 1979   Vintaged & bottled by Kaiser Stuhl
Wine Distributors Pty. Ltd., Nuriootpa, South Australia. Rating: 13. Distribution: C. You're going to like
this wine! You'll like it from its lively red-orange

color through its zesty, aromatic nose to its lively, broad-gauge taste. You'll find the nose oaky, full of fruit, spice, brambles, and briers, and you'll find the taste the same—sunshiny, energetic, alive with a lovely spectrum of fruity-spicy flavors. Price range: 750 ml, $3.99–5.59.

TTT CHARLES KRUG NAPA VALLEY BURGUNDY 1977 Produced & bottled by Charles Krug Winery, St. Helena, California. Rating: 10+. Distribution: A. This dry, oaky wine is purply red in color, and has a nose that will make you think of grapes growing in hedgerows, fruit mixing with brambles. The bouquet outlines the dignified, slightly austere structure of the wine, and the taste enlarges on it: dry, vigorous, mature, with nicely developed fruit flavors and good acid. Price range: 750 ml, $2.33–4.15.

TTTT CHARLES KRUG NAPA VALLEY CABERNET SAUVIGNON 1978 Produced & bottled by Charles Krug Winery, St. Helena, California. Rating: 11+. Distribution: A. There is nothing effete about this Cabernet—it's all brawn and power. The nose is pungent, aggressive, full of intensely flavored fruit. The taste is dry, powerful, full of juice, energy, muscle, character. The wine has considerably more power than style, yet it's a very refreshing, enjoyable wine. Ordinarily, you wouldn't find it selling for under $5.00, but since at the moment it is, why don't you jog on out and get a bottle? Price range: 750 ml, $4.39–6.99.

TTT CHARLES KRUG NAPA VALLEY CLARET 1976 Produced & bottled by Charles Krug Winery, St. Helena,

California. Rating: 10+. Distribution: A. Not too many California wineries make wines called "Claret" any more. This one, the color of ripe Bing cherries, has a lively, oaky nose full of fruit, thistles, and subtle earth tones. It's a lovely bouquet that will make you think of fruit extracts in the kitchen cabinets. The taste is dry, clean, formal, complex, refreshing, outdoorsy, and has a good finish. Try it. Price range: 750 ml, $2.33–4.99.

ȲȲȲȲ CHARLES KRUG NAPA VALLEY CLARET 1978 Produced & bottled by Charles Krug Winery, St. Helena, California. Rating: 12+. Distribution: A. There's a certain oaky nobility to this vividly scarlet Claret. The nose is quiet, subtle, refined, with a well-bred, modestly complex fruit bouquet. The taste is dry, rich, spare, elegant. The flavor is full and fresh, and it has lots of power, yet it displays these properties with such assurance and such a quiet air of dignity that it's a complete pleasure to drink it. Price range: 750 ml, $2.33–4.99.

ȲȲȲȲ CHARLES KRUG NAPA VALLEY ZINFANDEL 1979 Produced & bottled by Charles Krug Winery, St. Helena, California. Rating: 11+. Distribution: A. Here's a big (13.2 percent), purple wine that earns its four-glass rating on power alone. Actually, it has more going for it than raw muscle, but it's the kind of wine that's so brawny it wants to wrestle with you. You start with the aggressive nose—honest, masculine, hardworking, handsomely fruity—and move on to the taste: dry, tannic, energetic, with a barrelful of ripe, juicy Zin berries. It's a zesty, refreshing wine with a good finish, and I like it a lot. I have to warn you, however, it's not subtle. Price range: 750 ml, $3.36–5.49.

♟♟♟ LANCERS RUBEO 1979 Produced & bottled by J. M. Da Fonseca, Lisboa, Portugal, Rating: 10+. Distribution: A. Lancers gives us a pleasant surprise with this one: A smooth, sedate, medium-dry wine with many touches of refinement. The color is a light, clear vermilion. The nose is quite accessible, a rather formal fruit aroma with an obliging, quiet dignity. The taste is similarly formal, mouth-filling, with some attractive development of fully mature fruit. I expected something different. I guess the unique shape of the bottle has been misleading me all these years. Price range: 750 ml, $2.99–4.29.

♟♟♟♟ LE FLEURON NAPA VALLEY VIN ROUGE Produced & bottled by Joseph Phelps, St. Helena, California. Rating: 12. Distribution: C. Most Joseph Phelps wines are far beyond our modest price range, but this one isn't. It has a dark cherry color and a straightforward, sturdy nose. The taste is dry, vigorous, juicy, and full of lovely, succulent flavors. It's a manly, energetic wine, obviously made from some very good grapes, and I hope you stumble on a bottle now and then. When you do, buy it and enjoy! Price range: 750 ml, $2.29–5.00.

♟♟♟ L'EPAYRIE DRY FRENCH RED TABLE WINE Bottled by Armand Roux, France. Rating: 10+. Distribution: C. This vivid scarlet import has a somewhat reticent nose that shows a little oak and not much else. The taste, however, goes a long way toward making up for the shortcomings of the nose. It's dry, filled with handsome fruit, and has a feeling of character that, along with its generous helping of outdoorsy, wholesome qualities, make it quite pleasant indeed. Price range: 750 ml, $2.39–4.49.

ŸŸŸŸ LE PIAT D'OR VIN DE TABLE FRANCAIS   Bottled by Piat Père & Fils, Chapelle-de-Guinchay, France. Rating: 11+. Distribution: C. The color is a light crimson, the nose has a youthful sophistication. It's nervy and forthright, with fruit and spice and violets all mixed up together. The taste is off-dry, dashing, medium-bodied, loaded with verve and vigor. I find it a pleasing mixture of fruit, spice, brambles, sunshine, and the joy of living. At the price you can't afford not to try it. Price range: 750 ml, $2.59–4.25.

ŸŸ ALEXIS LICHINE RED TABLE WINE OF FRANCE Shipped by Alexis Lichine & Co., Gironde, France. Rating: 9+. Distribution: C. This bricky-red wine has a decent, presentable nose, with a generous quantity of fruit displayed in a quiet, respectable, middle-class setting. The taste is spare, conservative, slightly tannic, the fruit modestly restrained by the cooperage, and the whole effect is decent, bourgeois, and pleasant. Price range: 750 ml, $1.98–3.49.

ŸŸŸ LOS HERMANOS BURGUNDY FROM CALIFORNIA Produced & bottled by Los Hermanos Vineyards, St. Helena, California. Rating: 10. Distribution: A. Here is a simple, well-made wine you can enjoy quite a bit if you don't demand too much from it. It's cardinal red in color, and the nose is simple, fruity, and youthful. The taste offers the same ingenuous simplicity, dry, simple, and clean, with a lot of fruit and refreshment, and a lot of vigor. It has an admirable, peasant quality, sturdy and confident, and I think it's quite a nice wine. Price range: 1.5 l, $3.59–5.29.

ƎƎƎƎ LOS HERMANOS CALIFORNIA CABERNET SAUVIGNON　Cellared & bottled by Los Hermanos Vineyards, St. Helena, California. Rating: 12. Distribution: A. This handsome scarlet wine has a full, round, refined nose, with a nicely developed fruit bouquet. The taste is dry, well balanced, expansive, mouth-filling, and loaded with fruit. Finally, it has a very nice finish. So what are you waiting for? Price range: 1.5 l, $4.85–6.49.

Ǝ LOS REYES VINTO TINTO　Produced & bottled by Pedro Domecq, Los Reyes, Mexico. Rating: 8. Distribution: C. The nose of this orange-red wine doesn't send out any substantial message, but the taste is dry and zesty, with pleasantly tart fruit and a lot of vigor. Not the world's greatest wine, but you did want to sample a wine from Mexico, didn't you? Price range: 750 ml, $3.49–5.49.

ƎƎƎƎ MARQUÉS DE CACERES RIOJA 1976　Shipped by Union Viti-Vinicola-Vinedos, Cenicero, Spain. Rating: 12. Distribution: C. The color is a light vermilion, the nose is soft, round, and lovely, showing vanilla from the oak and a complexity in its bouquet that has developed in the bottle. The taste is dry, with medium body, a nice balance of fruit, oak, and flavors of dried berries and other fruits. It's a nice way to sample what the Rioja region has to offer. Price range: 750 ml, $3.49–5.99.

♟♟♟♟♟ MARQUÉS DE RISCAL RIOJA LIGHT RED WINE 1978 Produced & bottled by Marqués de Riscal, Elciego, Spain. Rating: 14. Distribution: B. My tasting notes for this wine, unedited, read: "Color: crimson. Nose: handsome, dignified, beautifully developed bouquet, serene & confident, layers of scent to explore. Taste: dry, classic, more dignity, oak, cornucopia of developed fruit—jams, jellies, elegant mysteries, finesse, breeding, nobility. Terrific!" If you get the idea I like this wine a lot and want you to try it, you're absolutely right. Price range: 750 ml, $3.85–6.49.

♟ LOUIS M. MARTINI CALIFORNIA BARBERA 1978 Produced & bottled by Louis M. Martini, St. Helena, California. Rating: 8. Distribution: A. Nobody expects Barberas to exhibit a lot of delicacy, and this one doesn't. It's dry, light-bodied, and puckery, and the nose is rather commonplace, but it has a lot of fruit and a lot of zest, so you might want to pull its cork on the night you send out for anchovy pizza. I guarantee this wine will stand up to the pizza, and I'll give 9-to-5 odds you'll enjoy them both. Price range: 750 ml, $3.18–5.49.

♟♟♟ LOUIS M. MARTINI CALIFORNIA BURGUNDY Prepared & bottled by Louis M. Martini, St. Helena, California. Rating: 10. Distribution: A. You'll find attractive vanilla overtones in the nose of this vermilion

Burgundy, and in the mouth you'll find a straightforward, light, dry wine with modest tannin and lots of fruit. It's not a fancy wine, but there's a solid, sturdy, peasant dignity to it that makes me like it quite a bit. Price range: 750 ml, $2.49–4.49.

ɏɏɏɏɏ LOUIS M. MARTINI CABERNET SAUVIGNON 1978 Produced & bottled by Louis M. Martini, St. Helena, California. Rating: 13+. Distribution: A. If prices hadn't softened recently, you would never have found this wine in the "Under $5.00" category, and even now, most places may still have it at a higher price. Nonetheless, keep your eyes open, because it's a handsome, red wine with a very accessible Cabernet nose, fresh and rich and full and rounded, with a dry, upright taste full of backbone and quality. It's a mouth-filling wine, smooth and vigorous at the same time, sort of an iron hand in a velvet glove. It's also still very youthful, so if you find some at the right price and have a place to lay it down, by all means, do it! Price range: 750 ml, $3.37–7.50.

LOUIS M. MARTINI CALIFORNIA CHIANTI Cellared & bottled by Louis M. Martini, St. Helena, California. Rating: 7+. Distribution: A. This bricky-red wine has a rather reticent, though inoffensive, nose, and a dry, somewhat thin taste. The fruit flavors seem held back, and the decent but prosaic result is not up to Mr. Martini's customary effort. Price range: 750 ml, $2.49–4.49.

ɏɏɏ LOUIS M. MARTINI CALIFORNIA CLARET Prepared & bottled by Louis M. Martini, St. Helena, California. Rating: 10+. Distribution: A. This is a mannerly wine, pleasing but unpretentious, a lobster-red wine with a few modest touches of class. You won't get terribly excited over the nose, although it's decently fruity and free of defects, but I think you'll find the taste quite enjoyable. It's dry, rather light-bodied, and it has a note of cultivation and restraint about it. A nice wine: good fruit, good balance, and as I said, good manners. Price range: 750 ml, $2.49–4.49.

♈♈♈ LOUIS M. MARTINI CALIFORNIA GAMAY BEAUJO-LAIS 1979 Produced & bottled by Louis M. Martini, St. Helena, California. Rating: 10. Distribution: A. The color: red-orange. The nose: young, vigorous, fruity. The taste: dry, juicy, fresh, uncomplicated. It's an appealing, unassuming wine with light acid and tons of fresh, simple fruit. Price range: 750 ml, $3.78–5.25.

♈♈♈ LOUIS M. MARTINI NAPA VALLEY PINOT NOIR 1979 Produced & bottled by Louis M. Martini, St. Helena, California. Rating: 10+. Distribution: A. This wine is a surprise—an extremely light-hearted Pinot Noir, light scarlet in color, with a youthful, fresh, charming nose and a lot of ripe, sunshiny fruit. The taste is dry and cheerful and has medium body and a zesty feeling of simplicity and refreshment. It's simple, but not mindless, a very nice wine, and I think it would taste great on a picnic. Price range: 750 ml, $3.56–6.50.

♈♈♈ LOUIS M. MARTINI CALIFORNIA ZINFANDEL 1979 Produced & bottled by Louis M. Martini, St. Helena,

California. Rating: 11. Distribution: A. The color is a light fire-engine red, and the nose is slightly bashful. Nonetheless, it's very presentable—clean, plenty of decent, ripe fruit, just nothing to get all steamed up over. The taste is dry and medium-bodied, the fruit is ripe and present in generous quantity, and the whole effect is clean, sunshiny, and refreshing. It's the kind of "uncomplex" wine that reminds you that wine is, after all, simply the "juice of grapes." Price range: 750 ml, $3.18–5.49.

MARTINI & ROSSI SANGIOVESE DI ROMAGNA Produced & bottled by L.B., Lugo, Italy. Rating: 7+. Distribution: C. This is a clear-red wine with purple tones, a decent but unexceptional nose, and a taste that is dry, decent, and fruity, but also a bit sedate and simplistic. Price range: 750 ml, $3.59–5.49.

♥♥♥♥ MASI BARDOLINO CLASSICO SUPERIORE 1979 Bottled by Masi Agricola S.P.A., S. Ambrogio di Valpolicella, Italy. Rating: 12. Distribution: B. This clear, lipstick-red wine has an air of nobility about it. The nose is clean and assertive, full of plums, currants, and sunshine. In the mouth it's dry and refreshing, light-bodied, with fruit that has an attractive, earthy spiciness. There's an air of sophistication about this wine, a feeling of charm and elegance, and a zest for living. Price range: 750 ml, $3.71–6.39.

♥♥♥ MASI VALPOLICELLA CLASSICO SUPERIORE 1979 Bottled by Masi Agricola, S.P.A., Valpolicella, Italy. Rating: 11. Distribution: B. The wine is crimson, light in color, and has a slight, not unpleasant mustiness in the nose, along with faint spice components. It has a refreshing taste, tart and lively, as though it were made from fruit just on the edge of ripeness. I think it's a stylish wine, and you should serve it next time the Italian ambassador comes to dinner. Price: 750 ml, $3.71–6.39.

♈ PAUL MASSON RARE PREMIUM CALIFORNIA BURGUNDY   Made & bottled by Paul Masson Vineyards, San Jose, California. Rating: 8. Distribution: A. This Burgundy is an ecclesiastical purple-red, and has a sturdy, straightforward nose. It has a nice country vigor to it, upright and dignified, and the taste is the same: dry, stable, honest, hardworking, and no surprises. Price range: 750 ml, $2.21–4.49.

♈ PAUL MASSON CALIFORNIA ZINFANDEL 1980   Made & bottled by Paul Masson Vineyards, Saratoga, California. Rating: 8+. Distribution: A. There's not a lot of Zinfandel character to this handsome, raspberry-red wine. The nose is small and slightly candied, but the taste is pleasant enough, on the simple, uncomplicated side. If that's your dish, you may enjoy this Masson offering. Price range: 750 ml, $2.28–4.99.

♈♈ MIRASSOU MONTEREY COUNTY BURGUNDY, UNFILTERED, 1977   Produced & bottled by Mirassou Vineyards, San Jose, California. Rating: 9+. Distribution: B. The color is a deep scarlet, and the nose is lively, with a piquant, well-developed bouquet of black-currant jam and spice. The taste is dry, almost thin, with a spare dignity and rather restrained fruit. Price range: 750 ml, $2.73–5.19.

ΤΤΤΤ MOMMESSIN COTES DU RHONE 1979   Bottled by Mommessin, La Grange Saint Pierre, France. Rating: 12+. Distribution: B. The bouquet of this clear, crimson wine has a refined character, balancing between elegarce and sedateness. Elegance wins, however, and you'll enjoy its compound of mature fruit aromas. The taste is dry, medium-bodied, refreshing, and there's a rich succulence to its fruit, and a feeling of backbone in its character. Price range: 750 ml, $3.49–5.69.

ΤΤΤΤΤ MOMMESSIN CUVEE SAINT PIERRE   Bottled by Mommessin, La Grange Saint Pierre, France. Rating: 13. Distribution: B. Here is a stylish, elegant wine. The color: a lovely, light crimson. The nose: the charming, spicy fragrance of maturing fruit. The taste: smooth, well proportioned, a skillful blend of energy and refinement, fruit and briers, simplicity and sophistication. It's a wine that's full of life and verve, and I want you to go get a bottle right away! Price range: 750 ml, $2.99–4.59.

ΤΤΤ CK MONDAVI CALIFORNIA BARBERONE   Made & bottled by C. Mondavi & Sons, St. Helena, California. Rating: 10+. Distribution: A. This crimson wine has a clean, youthful, fruity, slightly reluctant nose, and a dry, quietly powerful taste. It's a "country wine," not as refined as some, not as effete as others. What it has is a truckload of handsome, mature fruit for your mouth to savor, a lot of energy and rough-hewn character, and a lot of enjoyment. Price range: 1.5 l, $2.97–4.59.

CK MONDAVI CALIFORNIA BURGUNDY Made & bottled by C. Mondavi & Sons, St. Helena, California. Rating: 7+. Distribution: A. This is one of those wines about which there isn't all that much to say. It's a lovely color, red with purple tones, the nose doesn't send any particular message, and the taste is pleasant, dry, and unspectacular. It's the kind of wine that will make a perfectly good accompaniment to your next meal. It just won't make you exclaim, "Eureka!" Price range: 1.5 l, $2.97–4.59.

ŸŸŸ CK MONDAVI CALIFORNIA LIGHT BURGUNDY Made & bottled by C. Mondavi & Sons, St. Helena, California. Rating: 11. Distribution: A. This crimson wine is not a "light" wine in the current fashion of the word—that is, low alcohol, low calorie—because it has 12 percent alcohol, and the calories that go with it. It's a nice wine with a fresh, youthful nose that shows lots of uncomplicated fruit. The taste is dry and zesty, full of life and energy. It has a sturdy "country" quality, a simplicity and honesty that is both appealing and very enjoyable. And the price is right. Price range: 1.5 l, $2.97–4.59.

ŸŸŸ CK MONDAVI CALIFORNIA ZINFANDEL Made & bottled by C. Mondavi & Sons, St. Helena, California. Rating: 10+. Distribution: A. This Zinfandel has a rich, churchy-red color and a very proper nose. It's clean, fruity, and I get a slight cigar-box aroma, which, if I haven't said so before, is not necessarily a defect. In fact, in some wines it's considered very classy. In the mouth you'll find it dry and medium-bodied, with engaging berry flavors that have been pleasantly modified by the cooperage, or by time, or by something very benevolent. Price range: 1.5 l, $2.97–4.59.

ᵀᵀᵀ ROBERT MONDAVI RED 1980   Produced & bottled by Robert Mondavi Winery, Oakville, California: Rating: 11. Distribution: A. The color is a brilliant scarlet, the nose is surprisingly shy. What comes through, however, is clean, pleasant, and dignified. Take a sip and you know you're drinking a well-made, well-balanced product. It's not a complex or pretentious wine, there's nothing showy about it, but I think you'll agree it's a wine of admirable character. Price range: 1.5 l, $2.97–6.99.

ᵀᵀᵀᵀᵀ MONTE REAL 1975   Produced & bottled by Bodegas Riojanas, Cenicero, Spain. Rating: 13. Distribution: C. Another big winner. An orange-red wine from the Rioja region of Spain, with a rich, round, aromatic nose that will remind you of crushed flowers and old velvet. It's a deep, layered bouquet, a real pleasure to smell even if you never got around to tasting the wine. However, since it be a real sin not to taste it, let me tell you that it is opulent—dry, full, rich, smooth, with lovely, complex flavors of berry jams, jellies, and exotic perfumes. It's an elegant wine, and a real value at its price. Price range: 750 ml, $3.99–5.99.

ᵀᵀᵀᵀ MONTEREY VINEYARD CLASSIC CALIFORNIA RED 1979   Produced & bottled by The Monterey Vineyard, Gonzales, California. Rating: 11+. Distribution:

B. I believe you will like this dark, cherry-colored wine. The nicely developed and rather aromatic nose has a silky refinement that speaks of dried flowers and almond and vanilla extracts. The taste is dry and has an engaging delicacy—I detect fruit jams, flower petals, all kinds of sweet and lovely things. All in all, it's a charming wine and a great value. Price range: 750 ml, $2.98–4.99.

ȲȲȲȲȲ MOREAU ROUGE Bottled by J. Moreau & Fils, France. Rating: 13. Distribution: C. This scarlet import has a rather complex nose with a somewhat ponderous majesty, very pleasant and approachable, but on the somber, dignified side. The taste is dry, rich, round, full, with a sense of power and elegance. It has vigor and style, it has jam and berry flavors, it has a good finish, and it has a good price. What could be a nicer combination? Price range: 750 ml, $3.28–4.99.

ȲȲȲ NORTH COAST CELLARS APPELLATION NORTH COAST CABERNET SAUVIGNON Produced & bottled by North Coast Cellars, Geyserville, California. Rating: 10. Distribution: C. Deep raspberry color, nice, cheerful berry nose. As for taste, it's dry, somewhat light in body, well balanced, and refreshing. It doesn't have a lot of complexity, but it's sturdy and straightforward and, all in all, a rather pleasing wine. Price range: 750 ml, $2.49–4.99.

NORTH COAST CELLARS APPELLATION NORTH COAST NAPA GAMAY Produced & bottled by North Coast Cellars, Geyserville, California. Rating: 7+. Distribution: C. This purple wine has a rather dense, fruity nose with hints of spice. The spice and fruit are also very much in evidence in the mouth, but the wine is so astringent that it's hard to settle down and enjoy it. Too bad, because it starts out so well. Price range: 750 ml, $2.29–4.49.

ŸŸ NORTH COAST CELLARS APPELLATION NORTH COAST PINOT NOIR   Produced & bottled by North Coast Cellars, Geyserville, California. Rating: 9+. Distribution: C. This crimson Pinot has an approachable nose that shows a developing fruit bouquet that is quietly sedate, yet solid and straightforward. The taste is dry, oaky, reserved, pleasantly fruity, a bit astringent. It's a decent, upright wine with some nice quality overtones. Price range: 750 ml, $1.99–4.49.

ŸŸ NORTH COAST CELLARS APPELLATION NORTH COAST ZINFANDEL   Produced & bottled by North Coast Cellars, Geyserville, California. Rating: 9. Distribution: C. The color is cardinal red. The nose is easily accessible and shows some complexity, including a not unpleasant whiff of the cigar box. The taste is dry, a bit astringent, and a bit limited in its spectrum of fruit flavors. Still, what's there is quite clean and refreshing, and it's a good bit better than middle of the road. Price range: 750 ml, $2.29–4.49.

ŸŸŸŸ OLARRA RIOJA RED TABLE WINE 1975   Produced & bottled by Bodegas Olarra, Logroño, Spain. Rating: 11+. Distribution: B. The best wines from the Rioja region have a nose and a distinctive flavor that I like quite a bit. This russet wine definitely has those qualities. Its complex fruit bouquet rushes toward you effortlessly, crisp, piquant, and stylish. In the mouth it's dry, racy, energetic, with an attractive spiciness. In part, my notes read: "Life! Energy! Youth! Beautiful, red-haired women competing in the Olympics. . . ." *The Olympics!* Please don't suggest therapy. Just try the wine. Price range: 750 ml, $3.00–5.49.

♈♈♈♈ OLD DOG RED TABLEWINE Produced & bottled by David Bruce Winery, Los Gatos, California. Rating: 11+. Distribution: C. Despite its whimsical name there is nothing whimsical about this big (13 percent), carefully crafted wine. Its red color shades to purple, its nose shows lots of lovely, fully ripe fruit that is developing into a serious, dignified bouquet. The taste, similarly, shows a great deal of breeding and care and a complex texture of flavors. You'll pay some hefty prices for David Bruce's Chardonnays and Cabernets, but for this day-to-day wine from the same maker—if you can find it—you won't pay much, and you'll get a whale of a lot of value. Price range: 750 ml, $3.38–4.99.

♈♈♈♈ PAGLIARESE CHIANTI CLASSICO 1979 Produced & bottled by Fattoria Dei Pagliaresi di Alma Biasotto, San Gusme, Italy. Rating: 11+. Distribution: C. This charming import has a light, smoky-red color and a fresh, youthful, berrylike nose. The taste is crisp and racy, dry, clean, and well balanced. You'll find spice and briers in its fruit, and a touch of casual elegance in its energy. It will grace your fettucini or your veal piccata, or any number of other dishes, no matter

which country they come from. Price range: 750 ml,
$2.99–5.49.

♟♟♟♟♟ ANGELO PAPAGNI CALIFORNIA BARBERA 1973
Cellared & bottled by Papagni Vineyards, Madera,
California. Rating: 13+. Distribution: B. What a Barbera! Big, lovely, full of juice, bursting with flavor!
The color: medium scarlet. The nose: pointed, intense, forceful, full of berries and dried fruits, a nose
that telegraphs the fact the mouth has plenty to look
forward to. The taste: dry, full-bodied, full of blackberry jam, energy, hardy rustic power, refreshment,
life! What a Barbera! Worth searching for. Price
range: 750 ml, $4.10–6.29.

♟♟♟♟ PAPAGNI VINEYARDS CALIFORNIA RED WINE
Produced & bottled by Papagni Vineyards, Madera,
California. Rating: 11+. Distribution: B. If you can
find it, it's a good value. The color: deep vermilion,
shading to orange. The nose: assertive, clean, with a
sedate late-summer ripeness. The taste: just off dry,
enough acid to guarantee refreshment, a harmonious
blending of mature fruits. Price range: 750 ml, $2.99–
4.49.

♟♟♟♟♟ ANGELO PAPAGNI CALIFORNIA ZINFANDEL
1978 Produced & bottled by Papagni Vineyards,
Madera, California. Rating: 13. Distribution: B. Another good one. A deep blood-red Zinfandel with a
clean, fruity, inviting nose that shows a touch of
class. In the mouth you'll find an oaky dignity and
austerity, and a generous display of developing fruit
flavors. It's a broad-gauge wine; it keeps unfolding.

It gives you something to think about, and I'm certain you'll like it. Price range: 750 ml, $4.10–6.29.

ŶŶŶŶ PARDUCCI MENDOCINO COUNTY BARBERA 1977 Produced & bottled by Parducci Wine Cellars, Ukiah, California. Rating: 12+. Distribution: B. Here's a cardinal-red wine that mixes style with brawn, and we're the lucky winners. The nose is round and genteel, showing mature fruit that has developed a quietly complex bouquet. It's not showy, but it's solid. The taste is dry, full, rich, juicy, with lovely bottle flavors emerging from the harmonious balance between fruit and oak. It's a quiet, dignified wine, yet it has a lot of style and power, and an overall feeling of quality. Price range: 750 ml, $3.53–6.29.

ŶŶŶŶŶ PARDUCCI MENDOCINO COUNTY BURGUNDY 1978 Produced & bottled by Parducci Wine Cellars, Ukiah, California. Rating: 13. Distribution: B. The wine is the color of dark cherries. The nose is assertive and vigorous, a bit oaky, sober, thoughtful, developing. The taste is dry, serious, structured, with both vigor and dignity, and full of interesting flavors— black-currant jam, berry jams, dried fruit. It's a lovely, sophisticated wine, a wine of great quality, and the price is right. Go for it. Price range: 750 ml, $2.98–4.49.

ŶŶŶ PARDUCCI MENDOCINO COUNTY GAMAY BEAJO-LAIS 1981 Produced & bottled by Parducci Wine Cellars, Ukiah, California. Rating: 10. Distribution: B. There's a charming simplicity about this wine that starts with its clear vermilion color. The nose is forthright and ingenuous, youthful and full of fruit. The taste is similarly fruity, medium-dry, clean, sound, and refreshing. It's a wine of no great pretensions, but it's a lovely wine all the same, a wine for sharing on a lazy summer afternoon. Price range: 750 ml, $3.44–4.99.

♥♥♥ PARDUCCI VINTAGE RED 1980 Produced & bottled by Parducci Wine Cellars, Ukiah, California. Rating: 10+. Distribution: B. The color: bright scarlet. The nose: full, mature, lots of fruit, together with a slight, somber, oaky note. The taste: dry, vigorous, full of life and strength, with lots of healthy, ripe fruit held quietly under control. It's a wine with sturdy, "country" qualities, in the best sense of the word. Price range: 1.5 l, $4.38–5.99.

♥♥♥ PARTAGER VIN ROUGE Bottled by Barton & Guestier, Blanquefort, France. Rating: 10. Distribution: B. This is not a spectacular wine, but a very nice one all the same. The color is a brilliant ruby, the nose is suitably fruity and respectable without being showy, something like the quiet visitor who has good manners but doesn't talk too much. The taste is generous and dry, with rounded, mature, and altogether likable flavors. Price range: 750 ml, $2.03–4.49.

♥ J. PEDRONCELLI SONOMA COUNTY GAMAY BEAUJOLAIS 1981 Produced & bottled by J. Pedroncelli Winery, Geyserville, California. Rating: 8+. Distribution: B. This Gamay has a rich, deep purple color, and a nose and taste that are both pleasantly simple, clean, and juicy. It's a simple, undemanding wine, full of fruit, a bit astringent, with a feeling of freshness throughout. Price range: 750 ml, $2.99–4.69.

ᵀᵀᵀ J. PEDRONCELLI SONOMA COUNTY PINOT NOIR 1979 Produced & bottled by J. Pedroncelli Winery, Geyserville, California. Rating: 10+. Distribution: B. This is a dignified, severe Pinot Noir, stern and ramrod-straight. The color: cardinal red. The nose: manly and assertive, with an interesting texture of clean, straightforward fruit aromas. The taste: very dry, slightly astringent, a no-nonsense wine with an air of nobility. It's a somewhat unyielding wine, but it's well made, a wine of quality. Just don't expect velvet. Price range: 750 ml, $3.39–5.99.

ᵀ J. PEDRONCELLI SONOMA RED WINE Produced & bottled by J. Pedroncelli Winery, Geyserville, California. Rating: 8. Distribution: B. The color is a majestic purply red, the nose is a bit on the sedate, stuffy side, but still better than middle-of-the-road. In the mouth the wine has good acid and good fruit. There's also a modest astringency, however, and an echo of the stuffy nose. Price range: 750 ml, $1.99–3.49.

ᵀ J. PEDRONCELLI SONOMA COUNTY ZINFANDEL 1979 Produced & bottled by J. Pedroncelli Winery, Geyserville, California. Rating: 8. Distribution: B. This scarlet Zinfandel—I almost said Pimpernel—has a nose that is mature almost to the point of being middle-aged. The taste is similar—the fruit is there, but it's so mature and so lacking in acid that the wine, while pleasant, seems flat and matronly. Price range: 750 ml, $3.44–5.99.

ŸŸŸŸŸ PÉRE PATRIARCHE ROUGE Bottled by Patriarche Pére & Fils, Meursanges, France. Rating: 13. Distribution: C. The color is a light scarlet. The nose is fresh, lively, attractive, and has a feminine charm and an obliging bouquet that displays a modest amount of fruit development. The taste is lively, spicy, juicy, full of berries and brambles, youth and vigor. It has charm, it has sophistication, it has an enjoyable flavor complexity, but most of all it has a feeling of life and energy and sunshine. I like it a lot, and hope you try it. Price range: 750 ml, $2.66–5.49.

Ÿ PINOT NERO 1975   Produced & bottled by Cantina Viticoltori, Ponte di Piave, Italy. Rating: 8. Distribution: B. There's a world of energy in Italian wines, but many of them need food to make that energy come off. This is one of them, a wine rich red-orange in color, with a slightly matronly nose, and a dry, fruity, zingy, zesty taste so tart that if you don't have some spaghetti carbonaro handy, you may find it just too rough to handle! Price range: 750 ml, $3.59–5.49.

ŸŸŸŸ PORTO PALO VINO DA TAVOLA ROSSO   Produced & bottled by Cantina Settesoli, Menfi, Italy. Rating: 12. Distribution: C. Under the right circumstances an outstanding country wine can be just as satisfying as something much more noble. This is such a wine. The color is reddish purple, and the nose is both pleasant and serious, mature in a dashing way, with a slight touch of spiciness. The taste is dry, crisp, fresh, medium-bodied, with a congenial tart edge to keep you from losing interest. It's full of fruit, of course, an interesting collection of Sicilian flavors, and you could pay a lot more money and get a lot less quality than you'll find here. Do look for it. Price range: 1.5 l, $2.89–5.00.

ŸŸŸ PREMIAT CABERNET SAUVIGNON Produced & bottled in Romania. Imported by Monsieur Henri, New York, New York. Rating: 11. Distribution: B. The color is light red, shading toward orange. The nose is pleasantly weedy, and the taste is rather dashing— dry, nervy, slightly tart, well balanced, and very refreshing. The price is right because it never occurs to anyone the Romanians know how to make wine. But they do! Price range: 750 ml, $1.88–4.59.

ŸŸŸ PREMIAT PINOT NOIR 1977 Produced & bottled in Romania. Imported by Monsieur Henri, New York, New York. Rating: 10. Distribution: B. Cigar boxes and fruit don't usually spring to mind as a pleasing combination, but this vermilion Pinot demonstrates it can be so. The nose, while not overwhelming, does indeed have a cigar-box component, nicely complementing the fruit aromas, and this quality appears again in the taste, which is clean, dry, and refreshing. The wine doesn't have a wide spectrum of flavor, but it's well made, and I think you'll find it a very congenial accompaniment to a rather highly flavored meal. Price range: 750 ml, $1.88–4.59.

ŸŸŸŸ PRINCIPATO MERLOT DEL TRENTINO 1979 Produced & bottled by Nuova Organizzazione Enologica Soc. Coop., Ravina, Italy. Rating: 11+. Distribution: C. This raspberry-colored import has a sturdy, enduring peasant dignity that makes it very appealing. The nose doesn't offer any fireworks, but is somewhat reserved, sedate, and very proper. The taste has a lot of refreshing fruit with congenial overtones of herbs and hedgerows, good acid, and a respectable finish. It's not a noble wine, and it doesn't try to be. It is what it is: honest, well made, hardworking, and I think, extremely enjoyable. Price range: 1.5 l, $4.00–7.49.

ȲȲȲȲȲ PRIVILEGIO DEL REY SANCHO RESERVA 1976 Produced & bottled by Sogeviñas Elciego, Alava, Spain. Rating: 13. Distribution: C. Nice! *Very* nice! Red-orange in color. An enchanting nose, beautifully rounded, a complex mixture of fruits. Strawberries? Raspberries? Currants? You tell me. The taste is elegant, round and supple, an artful orchestration of complex flavors. If you have trouble finding a bottle, keep looking. It's worth it! Price range: 750 ml, $3.49–6.49.

RIUNITE LAMBRUSCO   Produced & bottled by Cantine Coop. Riunite, Reggio Emilia, Italy. Rating: 7+. Distribution: A. This frothy, raspberry-colored wine is the single, largest-selling imported brand of wine in the United States today—one out of every three bottles of foreign wine entering the country is labeled Riunite. So who cares if the nose and mouth make you think of grapes ripening under the hot sun until they scorch? Certainly not the millions who blithely buy it by the shipload! Well, more power to them. I have other plans. Price range: 750 ml, $2.34–3.99.

♟♟ RIVERSIDE FARMS PREMIUM DRY RED Made & bottled by L. Foppiano Wine Company, Healdsburg, California. Rating: 9+. Distribution: B. This is a clean, well-scrubbed wine with a wholesome teen-age charm: buoyant and nubile. The color is bluish red, the easily approached nose is sunny, ingenuous, and attractively simple. There's a hint of spice in the nose, and when you sample its refreshing taste, you'll wallow in tons of juicy, uncomplicated fruit. Price range: 750 ml, $2.19–3.99.

♟♟♟ RIVERSIDE FARMS NORTHERN CALIFORNIA ZIN-FANDEL 1980 Made & bottled by L. Foppiano Wine Company, Healdsburg, California. Rating: 10. Distribution: B. There's a nice, solid, country simplicity about this wine. The taste is dry, there's a lot of luscious berry flavor, and there's also a pleasing balance between its freshness and energy, and the slight feeling of country dignity and reserve. The color is a deep ruby, the nose is civil and mannerly, and the bottom line is you will probably like it. Price range: 750 ml, $2.77–4.29.

♟♟♟♟ RUFFINO CHIANTI CLASSICO 1980 Bottled by Chianti Ruffino S.P.A., Pontassiere, Italy. Rating: 11+. Distribution: B. You'll find an air of quiet authority in this well-bred import. Its classic fruit bouquet is easily accessible—I detected raspberry and plum aromas—yet it has a lot of dignity and reserve. The taste has this same feeling of elegance and proportion. The wine is dry and smooth, well balanced, and the fruit flavors have developed handsomely. I think you'll like it—what say we split a bottle? Price range: 750 ml, $3.06–5.49.

♈♈ SAN MARTIN CALIFORNIA BURGUNDY 1978   Produced & bottled by San Martin Winery, San Martin, California. Rating: 9. Distribution: B. The color is a darkish red, the nose is surprisingly herbaceous, grassy and weedy. That may not sound too promising, but don't go away, because it's really a very pleasant and unusual wine, sprightly and appealing, and it could be just the thing to go with one of your spicy, sprightly dinners. Price range: 750 ml, $2.78–4.29.

♈♈ SAN MARTIN CALIFORNIA RED TABLE WINE   Produced & bottled by San Martin Winery, San Martin, California. Rating: 9. Distribution: B. This wine is a pleasant surprise. It's really a "jug" wine, but it has a touch of class. The color is orangey-red, the nose is brash and spicy, with a touch of brambles thrown in. In the mouth it's pleasantly dry, tart, and refreshing. You wouldn't want to drink it every night, but I think you'll find it interesting enough to enjoy now and then between whatever else you're drinking. Price range: 1.5 l, $3.39–5.19.

♈ SAN MARTIN SOFT GAMAY BEAUJOLAIS 1981   Produced & bottled by San Martin Winery, San Martin, California. Rating: 8. Distribution: B. This wine is so light and transparent it looks more like a rosé than a red wine. Nevertheless, it still manages to put forth a fruity, aggressive, young nose, and to provide a taste that is all juice and sunshine and fruit sugar. It's not really a sweet wine, but it's not all that dry, either. It's just something nice to quaff on a hot summer afternoon. Price range: 750 ml, $3.98–5.49.

ΨΨΨΨΨ SEBASTIANI CALIFORNIA BARBERA 1979 Produced & Bottled by Sebastiani Vineyards, Sonoma, California. Rating: 13. Distribution: A. My notes read: "Rich, smooth, good finish, I love this wine!" The color is dark, a church-robe red. The nose is oaky, racy, authoritative, and you sense the power of its developing fruit bouquet. The taste is big, dry, juicy, broad-gauge. It's a rich, smooth, mouth-filling wine. Few Barberas show so much structure, so much personality, so much class. I suggest you run right down to the store and get a bottle. I'll get out the glasses! Price range: 750 ml, $3.99–5.99.

ΨΨΨ AUGUST SEBASTIANI CALIFORNIA MOUNTAIN BURGUNDY Vinted & bottled by Sebastiani Vineyards, Sonoma, California. Rating: 10+. Distribution: A. This is a clear, crimson wine with a pleasant, uncomplicated, fruity nose and a taste to match. It has plenty of fruit, a good acid balance, and a simple, friendly appeal. Price range: 750 ml, $1.98–3.49.

ΨΨΨ SEBASTIANI NORTHERN CALIFORNIA BURGUNDY 1978 Produced & bottled by Sebastiani Vineyards, Sonoma, California. Rating: 11. Distribution: A. There's a distinctive brier-patch scent mixed into the aroma of this dark cherry-colored wine. It's a pleasant sensation, and it lends dignity and character to the nose. The taste replicates the nose, zesty, full of ripe fruit and briers, and I think you'll find this a good wine to go along with a richly seasoned meal. Try it, see if I'm right. Price range: 750 ml, $2.35–4.19.

ΨΨΨΨΨ AUGUST SEBASTIANI COUNTRY CABERNET SAUVIGNON   Vinted & bottled by Sebastiani Vineyards, Sonoma, California. Rating: 13. Distribution: A. You'll admire this wine's fiery orange-red color, but even more you'll admire its bouquet and taste. The nose is forthright and generous, and shows breadth in its fruit, spice, and bramble character, and refinement in their union. The taste is similarly complex—the bouquet made liquid—and you'll find it dry, developed, well balanced, and full of health and energy. Price range: 1.5 l, $4.69–7.99.

ΨΨ SEBASTIANI NORTH COAST COUNTIES GAMAY BEAU-JOLAIS 1980   Produced & bottled by Sebastiani Vineyards, Sonoma, California. Rating: 9. Distribution: A. This scarlet wine has an ingenuous nose, a quiet uncomplicated offering of fresh, juicy fruit. Like the nose, the taste is fruity, dry, simple, succulent, almost tart. It's not the kind of wine that's studded with character. Think of it as a charming and mannerly adolescent. Price range: 750 ml, $3.29–4.99.

ΨΨΨΨ AUGUST SEBASTIANI COUNTRY PINOT NOIR 1979 Produced & bottled by Sebastiani Vineyards, Sonoma, California. Rating: 11+. Distribution: A. Some wines are like lace. Others—like this one—are all nerve and sinew. The nose is masculine and athletic, youthful, sturdy, intense. The taste is dry, robust, and manly, bursting with juice. It's a well-structured wine, supple and refreshing, open-handed in its generosity. All this, and a good finish, too! Price range: 1.5 l, $3.74–7.49.

ŸŸŸŸŸ AUGUST SEBASTIANI COUNTRY ZINFANDEL Vinted & bottled by Sebastiani Vineyards, Sonoma, California. Rating: 13. Distribution: A. Sebastiani does it again with this handsome, crimson Zinfandel. It's the classic formula in both the nose and mouth: good fruit, skillfully fused to produce complex smells and tastes. The nose has an authoritative air, a nicely developed bouquet of fruit and oak, seductive in a classy, dignified way. The taste has the same synthesis of complex flavors, dry and refined. It's the kind of wine you can sit around the table and discuss, because it gives you a lot to talk about. Price range: 1.5 l, $3.74–7.49.

ŸŸŸŸŸ SEBASTIANI NORTHERN CALIFORNIA ZINFANDEL 1978 Produced & bottled by Sebastiani Vineyards, Sonoma, California. Rating: 13. Distribution: A. We've hit pay dirt again, friends! This big (13.8 percent alcohol), orange-red Zinfandel has a nose that is assertive, and a pleasantly weedy bouquet that will make you think of dignified old men clad in black, sitting in the sun outside a *bodega*. The taste has this same peasant strength and honesty. You'll find it full of character, full of vigor, and full of Zin berries that have matured into a broad spectrum of delightful flavors. Price range: 750 ml, $3.29–4.99.

Ÿ SIDI BRAHIM RED SUPERIOR TABLE WINE Produced in Algeria; bottled in France by Les Vins Vigna, Chalon-sur-Saône. Rating: 8. Distribution: C. The color is a deep Valentine red. The nose is quiet, not much to say. The taste is medium dry, with honest fruit and good acid, a simple, unexceptional, but thoroughly respectable wine. You did want to try a wine from Algeria, didn't you? Price range: 750 ml, $3.19–4.99.

🍷🍷🍷 SIMI ALEXANDER VALLEY GAMAY BEAUJOLAIS 1980 Produced & bottled by Simi Winery, Healdsburg, California. Rating: 10. Distribution: B. This fiery orange wine has a nose that is just as racy and energetic as its color. There's a slight spiciness in it that carries over into the taste. The taste is not complex, nor would you expect it in a Gamay, but it is very juicy and fresh, loaded with fruit, a little light on the acid, but altogether a simple, friendly, downhome wine that you won't have to put yourself out to enjoy! Price range: 750 ml, $3.88–5.49.

🍷🍷🍷 SIMPATICO EUROPEAN RED WINE Blended & bottled by Alfred Franzen, Germany. Rating: 10. Distribution: C. Okay, so 86 percent of the grapes in this wine came from Italy, 14 percent from France, and it was blended and bottled in Germany. So is it any good? The answer is yes. It's an honest, vigorous, hard-working, country wine that offers a lot of enjoyment per dollar. The color is a light, clear scarlet, the nose is fresh, simple, and upbeat. It has lots of clean, ripe fruit, and it's lively and outdoorsy. The taste mirrors the nose—dry and fruity, with lots of attractive, country vitality. It won't put the Cabernets out of business, but it *will* deliver a lot of solid value and satisfaction. Price range: $2.49–4.50.

ŸŸŸŸ SONOMA VINEYARDS RED TABLE WINE Produced & bottled by Sonoma Vineyards, Windsor, California. Rating: 11+. Distribution: B. The vintner tells you right on the label what went into this wine: 36 percent Ruby Cabernet, 30 percent Pinot Noir, 19 percent Zinfandel, 15 percent Cabernet Sauvignon. What it all adds up to is this: a brilliant scarlet wine with a forthcoming, full, upright nose that offers a lot of wholesome, ripe fruit. The taste is pleasingly dry, crisp, clean, and youthful. It's a well-mannered wine, refined but not complicated, with lots of tasty fruit flavors and lots of verve. Price range: 1.5 l, $3.99–5.99.

ŸŸŸ SOUVERAIN APPELLATION NORTH COAST BURGUNDY 1979 Produced & bottled by Souverain, Geyserville, California. Rating: 10+. Distribution: B. This darkish ruby wine has a modest touch of dignity in its fruity nose, and a decent helping of fruit in the mouth. The acid balance is good, and the result is very pleasing. Price range: 750 ml, $2.99–4.29.

SOUVERAIN APPELATION NORTH COAST GAMAY BEAUJOLAIS 1981 Produced & bottled by Souverain, Geyserville, California. Rating: 7+. Distribution: B. How can a wine be such a beautiful cardinal red and taste so middle-of-the-road? The nose and taste both seem slightly candied, and although there's adequate fruit and good acid, it doesn't quite come off. There's a bit too much astringency, too. Price range: 750 ml, $3.69–5.39.

ΨΨΨ SOUVERAIN CALIFORNIA RED TABLE WINE   Cellared & bottled by Souverain, Geyserville, California. Rating: 10+. Distribution: B. This lovely purple wine doesn't have much of a nose, but what's there is free of defects. The taste is the payoff, however, and turns out to be spicy and lively and full of fruit, a few briers, and lots of sunshine. It's not a sophisticated wine by any means. It's a "country" wine, and a very enjoyable one. Price range: 1.5 l, $4.19–6.49.

ΨΨ SOUVERAIN APPELLATION NORTH COAST ZINFANDEL 1979   Produced & bottled by Souverain, Geyserville, California. Rating: 9+. Distribution: B. This is a very decent, upper-middle-class wine, medium red in color, with a clean, fruity, respectable, if not terribly exciting nose. The taste is dry, medium-bodied, slightly astringent, with lots of nice, ripe Zinfandel berries doing their bit. Not a whole lot of complexity, but a nice wine all the same. Price range: 750 ml, $3.77–5.49.

ΨΨΨΨ SPANNA DEL PIEMONTE 1980   Bottled by Luigi Ferrando e Figlio, Ivrea-Corso Cavour, Italy. Rating: 11+. Distribution: C. This is a velvety, dry, well-bred wine, brilliant scarlet in color, with the kind of nose you can sit and think about for quite a while. It's serious, has considerable breadth and texture, plus a handsome, oaky bouquet that has developed far beyond simple fruit aromas. The taste is dry, smooth, cultivated, generously fruity, a lovely synthesis of refreshment and genteel reserve. It's obviously a wine of quality, and I think you will enjoy drinking it. Price range: 750 ml, $4.39–6.49.

SUMMIT PREMIUM CALIFORNIA BURGUNDY Prepared & bottled by Geyser Peak Winery, Geyserville, California. Rating: 7+. Distribution: A. This wine has a rich red color and a slightly austere, "dried fruit" nose. The flavor is decent, even somewhat dignified, but the wine is a little flat. It's okay wine, just not great. Price range: 4 l, $3.99–5.39.

Ⓨ TAYLOR CALIFORNIA CELLARS BURGUNDY OF CALIFORNIA Cellared & bottled by Taylor California Cellars, Gonzales, California. Rating: 8+. Distribution: A. This is a wine that could have gone in the direction of "mellow" but chose to have some character instead. The color is medium red, heading toward purple. The nose is amiable, ripe, clean, a sturdy, honest workman who knows what he is doing. The taste has the same peasant respectability—dry, direct, and upright, with pleasing fruit and fairly good acid. Price range: 1.5 l, $3.59–4.99.

ⓎⓎⓎⓎ TAYLOR CALIFORNIA CELLARS CABERNET SAUVIGNON OF CALIFORNIA Cellared & bottled by Taylor California Cellars, Gonzales, California. Rating: 11+. Distribution: A. This medium-red Cabernet has a forthcoming nose with some depth of character. There are overtones of richness. The fruit is mature. The bouquet is developing. In the mouth you'll find a feeling of wealth and breeding, and you'll observe how the power of the fruit has been restrained and modified by the oak. Like old money, it has quality if not zest, and I think you should give it a try. Price range: 1.5 l, $4.79–6.49.

ŶŶ TAYLOR CALIFORNIA CELLARS PREMIUM CALIFORNIA DRY RED WINE   Cellared & bottled by Taylor California Cellars, Gonzales, California. Rating: 9. Distribution: A. You'll find bluish tones in Taylor's Dry Red, and you'll find maturity in its clean, deep, uncomplicated nose. The taste is dry, simple, direct, with plenty of pleasing fruit flavor, plus a minimum of complexity. Solid, an honest workman. Price range: 1.5 l, $3.59–4.99.

ŶŶŶŶ TAYLOR CALIFORNIA CELLARS ZINFANDEL OF CALIFORNIA   Cellared & bottled by Taylor California Cellars, Gonzales, California. Rating: 11+. Distribution: A. The color is cherry red, the nose is aromatic, assertive, and displays a nice complexity. The taste is pleasingly dry, generously fruity, and has a refreshing amount of acidity. The finish is good. So what are you waiting for? Price range: 1.5 l, $3.99–5.49.

ŶŶŶŶŶ TORRES CORONAS 1979   Produced & bottled by Miguel Torres, Vilafranca del Penedēs, Spain. Rating: 14. Distribution: B. This is an elegant, almost voluptuous wine, with a deep, purple-red color and a rich, aromatic nose that is both subtle and complex. The bouquet displays character and breeding, plus a generous quantity of beautifully developed fruit and some oaky, vanilla overtones. In the mouth you'll find the same lovely message—a wine that's dry, velvety, refined, full of finesse. The price has remained astonishingly low since the first edition of this book came out, but you'd better hurry—that could change! Price range: 750 ml, $2.99–5.49.

ŸŸŸ TORRES SANGRE DE TORO 1978 Produced & bottled by Miguel Torres, Vilafranca del Penedēs, Spain. Rating: 11. Distribution: B. This wine has a deep scarlet hue and a nose that shows some complexity, a pleasant blend of developed fruit aromas. The taste is dry, clean, and stylish. The fruit has a charming spiciness, and I think you'll find the total effect one of good structure and enjoyment. Price range: 750 ml, $2.99–5.49.

ŸŸŸŸ TORRES GRAN SANGRE DE TORO 1977 Produced & bottled by Miguel Torres, Vilafranca del Penedēs, Spain. Rating: 11+. Distribution: B. The churchy, purple-red color of this wine is only a prelude to its intriguing bouquet. It's the kind of bouquet you just want to keep on smelling—full of handsome, mature fruit, stylish and rewarding. The taste is dry and energetic, with a broad range of flavors from the fruit and oak, and a nice, tart edge. It's a wine that has been carefully crafted and well tended, and the results are well worth the effort. Price range: 750 ml, $4.18–6.19.

ŸŸŸŸŸ TORRES VIGNA SANTA DIGNA 1977 Produced & bottled by Miguel Torres, Vilafranca del Penedēs, Spain. Rating: 14. Distribution: B. This rich, crimson wine has a bouquet that is full, rounded, velvety, and has an air of nobility. It offers the nose crushed violets, berry jams, all kinds of treats. The taste has similar treats—flowers, jams, berries—all fused into a pattern of complex flavors. The finish is lovely. It's a wine to talk about as much as to drink, a wine of breeding and elegance. When you try it, I'll bet money you love it. Price range: 750 ml, $4.85–6.49.

♈♈♈ TRAKIA CABERNET SAUVIGNON 1977   Produced & bottled by Vinimpex, Sofia, Bulgaria. Rating: 11. Distribution: C. This wine has a clean, masculine nose, slightly reticent, with fruit flavors that are honest and mature, and if I'm not mistaken, a touch of gorse. (Do they have gorse in Bulgaria?) The taste is charming, clean, well-bred, with some complexity. The Bulgarians are doing very well with their entry into the United States wine market, and this wine is one reason why. Price range: 750 ml, $1.89–4.99.

♈♈♈♈ TRAKIA MERLOT Produced & bottled by Vinimpex, Sofia, Bulgaria. Rating: 12. Distribution: C. I don't know why it should come as a surprise that the Bulgarians know how to make wine, but let me tell you, they do! Take this fiery orange-red Merlot, for example. The nose is brash and lively, full of spicy fruit. Taste it, and you'll find it fresh, dry, nervy, zesty, and generous with the fruits and spices the nose told you about. Trakia hasn't been in this country very long, so at the moment the price is right. You'd better buy some while it's still a bargain! Price range: 750 ml, $1.89–4.49.

♈♈♈ TRAPICHE ARGENTINE CABERNET SAUVIGNON 1975   Produced & bottled by Establecimiento A Exp. 01019, Mendoza, Argentina. Rating: 10+. Distribution: C. This dark, cherry-colored Cabernet has an agreeable, settled, unostentatious nose that displays neither defects nor fireworks. The taste is dry, juicy, and conservative, with a considerable quantity of mature fruit that appears to have been "oaked" into submission. Some nice flavors have developed, however, rather reserved and formal. You'll find it a wine that offers a great deal of quiet quality without offering a whole lot of excitement. Price range: 750 ml, $4.26–6.49.

ᵀᵀᵀᵀᵀ TRAPICHE ARGENTINE MALBEC 1975　Produced & bottled by Establecimiento A Exp. 01019, Mendoza, Argentina. Rating: 13. Distribution: C. The color is a gorgeous Titian red. The nose is broad-gauge, mature, rich and refined, with a lovely, developed bouquet and a feeling of nobility. The taste is mouth-filling, expansive, full of complex jam and berry flavors, smooth, velvety, aristocratic. It's a great demonstration of the wonders that can be accomplished when good wine spends time in the bottle. I hope you can find this wine in your city—it's worth a lot of looking! Price range: 750 ml, $4.19–5.99.

ᵀᵀᵀ VALBON RED TABLE WINE　Produced & bottled by Bouchard Père & Fils, France. Here's a dry, honest, unpretentious red wine that offers a lot of value for a very decent price. The color is crimson, the nose is quiet, solid, fruity, pleasant. The taste is dry and out-doorsy, and there's a slight bramble spiciness in the fruit. The duke and duchess probably don't drink this wine, but the people who do are getting a lot of genial flavor and satisfaction, and if they go over budget next month, this wine won't be to blame. Price range: 1.5 l, $4.49–6.75.

ᵀᵀᵀ VERDILLAC BORDEAUX SUPERIEUR 1979   Shipped
by Armand Roux, France. Rating: 10. Distribution: C.
This reddish-purple wine is very single-minded—it
does one thing and it does it well. It has a fresh,
penetrating, very decent nose that really has only one
tone, but it has a lot of it. The taste is the same: dry,
clean, simple but not simple-minded, with lots of
blunt energy and fruit. If you're looking for a wide,
sophisticated flavor spectrum, you've come to the
wrong place. If you're looking for a good, honest
wine to add pleasure to a good honest meal, walk
right in and pick up a bottle. Price range: 750 ml,
$3.99–5.99.

ᵀᵀᵀᵀᵀ VILLA ANTINORI CHIANTI CLASSICO RISERVA
1978 Produced & bottled by Marchesi Antinori,
S.P.A., Firenze, Italy. Rating: 13. Distribution: C.
There are no sharp corners in this handsome red-orange wine. Everything has been shaped, rounded,
sandpapered. The nose is smooth, graceful, seductive, complex, scented with quality. The taste is dry,
harmonious, classic, full of the same lovely fruits
your nose admired, energetic yet elegant. It's a wine
with nobility and character, a handsome example of
what a winemaker can do when he puts his mind to
it. Price range: 750 ml, $4.39–6.19.

ᵀᵀᵀᵀ VILLA BANFI BARDOLINO CLASSICO SUPERIORE
1980 Bottled by Cav. P. Sartori, S.P.A., Negrar, Italy. Rating: 12. Distribution: C. This is a clean, zesty,
refreshing wine with a certain nobility about it. It's
the nobility of a prince, however, not a king—a king
wouldn't have this much energy. The color is a

bright, clear scarlet. The nose is racy, crisp, stylish, light-hearted. Along with the fruit there's a touch of tweed and brier. The taste is dry, with a quiet, sunshiny energy that reveals a lot of fruit and a lot of class. I like it a lot. Maybe you will, too. Price range: 750 ml, $3.99–5.99.

♈♈♈ WEIBEL BURGUNDY Produced & bottled by Weibel Champagne Vineyards, Mission San Jose, California. Rating: 10. Distribution: B. The color: dark scarlet with flashes of orange. The nose: assertive, spicy, peppery, with structure, a developed bouquet, and a bit of class. The taste: dry, lively, with the tastes of fruit, spice, and brambles. A nice wine and a good value. Price range: 750 ml, $2.49–4.29.

♈♈♈ WEIBEL NORTH COAST GAMAY BEAUJOLAIS 1979 Produced & bottled by Weibel Vineyards, Mission San Jose, California. Rating: 10. Distribution: B. This aromatic, purply-red wine has a rich, fruity, spicy nose, and the spice and fruit carry over pleasantly into the taste. It's nice and dry, and has more character than you generally expect in a Gamay. Don't get me wrong—like most Gamays it's a slender wine, but it's one of the nicer ones. Price range: 750 ml, $3.68–5.49.

♈♈♈ WEIBEL NORTH COAST MENDOCINO PETITE SIRAH 1978 Produced & bottled by Weibel Vineyards, Mission San Jose, California. Rating: 10. Distribution: B. Weibel's Petite Sirah is a pleasant wine, a bit on the thin side, but very decent nevertheless. It has a rich, ruby color, and a handsome, assertive nose in which you can perceive the bouquet developing into something much more serious than simple fruit aromas. The taste is dry, pleasantly fruity, with a nice oakiness. There's somewhat less flavor than you might hope for, plus a touch of astringency. Still, it's a nice wine for lots of occasions, but just not a top winner. Price range: 750 ml, $3.59–5.49.

TTT WEIBEL NORTH COAST PINOT NOIR 1975 Produced & bottled by Weibel Vineyards, Mission San Jose, California. Rating: 11. Distribution: B. Here's a vibrant, cherry-colored Pinot you will enjoy. It has a lovely textured nose that displays a lot of charm and character and offers a complex bouquet of fruity treats. The taste is dry, medium-bodied, with a nice feeling of structure and a pleasing, oaky development of the fruit flavors. Price range: 750 ml, $3.98–5.99.

TT WEIBEL MENDOCINO COUNTY ZINFANDEL 1980 Produced & bottled by Weibel Vineyards, Mission San Jose, California. Rating: 9+. Distribution: B. This lobster-red wine is one of the "light" Zinfandels, not light in terms of calories or alcohol content, but light and energetic in style. The nose is delicate, rounded, a pleasing bouquet of ripe berries, and the taste is light, fruity, zesty, and altogether pleasant. The other kind of Zinfandel—dark, heavy, brooding—is nice, too, but this one definitely isn't of that breed. Price range: 750 ml, $3.79–5.99.

WENTE BROTHERS CALIFORNIA GAMAY BEAUJOLAIS 1980 Produced & bottled by Wente Brothers, Livermore, California. Rating: 7+. Distribution: A. The color is scarlet, the nose shows a lot of fruit, but it also has a dour quality that seems out of place. The taste tries to make up for the nose by projecting character, not just reckless youth, and while it has good acid and lots of fruit, it's still just a middle-of-the-road wine. Price range: 750 ml, $3.10–5.49.

♼♼♼♼ WENTE BROTHERS MONTEREY PINOT NOIR 1979 Produced & bottled by Wente Brothers, Livermore, California. Rating: 11+. Distribution: A. How to describe this wine? How about: ripe, young, fruity, brash, aggressive, joyously refreshing? It's a wine with much more vigor than style. But what's wrong with a lusty, youthful wine that has a dash of spice thrown in? It's well balanced, zesty, and juicy as all get out. It makes a fine drink for young satyrs, whether they pursue maidens through forest glades or down concrete canyons. If you're a satyr, buy a bottle immediately! Price range: 750 ml, $3.63–5.99.

♼♼♼♼ WENTE BROTHERS CALIFORNIA ZINFANDEL 1980 Produced & bottled by Wente Brothers, Livermore, California. Rating: 11+. Distribution: A. This clear, clean, strawberry-colored wine has an unusual, aggressive nose, a fairly sturdy and complex bouquet that indicates there's a lot still developing inside the bottle. The taste is lively, well balanced, full of honest fruit. It's another example of the light, upbeat style of making Zinfandels, not as inky and thoughty as many others, and it's a style I think you'll enjoy a lot. Price range: 750 ml, $3.49–5.99.

8

White Wines

🍷 ADRIATICA RIZLING 1979 Produced & bottled by Adriatica, Yugoslavia. Rating: 8. Distribution: C. This Riesling from Yugoslavia is definitely a foreign experience. There's more to it than meets the eye, but I doubt it will win a big following. The color is a lovely lemon-gold. The nose is aggressively aromatic and has a riverbank greenness, as though the grapes had grown up among reeds and cattails. The taste is off-dry, full-bodied, and has lots of exotic, honeyed fruit mingled with its basic reediness. It's interesting to see what a Yugoslavian Riesling tastes like, but I don't think you'll drink this one too often. Price range: 750 ml, $3.49–4.99.

ALMADÉN CALIFORNIA MOUNTAIN WHITE CHABLIS Vinted & bottled by Almadén Vineyards, San Jose, California. Rating: 7. Distribution: A. I have finally learned not to be too disappointed when a wine is merely drinkable without being wonderful. Case in point: this Chablis, which has a nice light barley color, but whose nose and mouth are merely acceptable—both a little middle-aged, with a faint mustiness in the nose and a bitter element in the taste. Still, well chilled on a picnic, it would probably slide down the old gullet without any problem at all! Price range: 750 ml, $2.25–3.49.

ALMADÉN VINEYARDS MONTEREY CHABLIS Produced & bottled by Almadén Vineyards, San Jose, California. Rating: 7. Distribution: A. Color: parchment yellow. Nose: no come-hither, a touch of something acrid. The mouth: fruit and reasonable acid, plus a faint, dank cellar note that makes it score right near the middle of our 0–14 scale. Price range: 750 ml, $2.58–3.99.

℣ ALMADÉN LIGHT CHABLIS Vinted & bottled by Almadén Vineyards, San Jose, California: Rating: 8+. Distribution: A. It looks more like water than wine, but it has a small, innocent nose that displays some fresh, uncomplicated fruit, so it can't be water. There's a slight effervescence in the mouth, along with light body and a lot of simple fruit. It's a wine to help you stay thin—only 48 calories per 100 ml ("regular" wine has about 75 calories)—and it tastes a little thin, too. Price range: 1.5 l, $3.57–4.99.

℣℣℣ ALMADÉN SAN BENITO CHARDONNAY 1981 Produced & bottled by Almadén Vineyards, San Jose, California. Rating: 10. Distribution: A. This pale, blond Chardonnay has a clean, respectable, fruity nose with a slight grassiness. The taste is off-dry with touches of sweetness. It's decent, settled, sedate, solid to the point of being a trifle ponderous, but it's full of clean, mature fruit, and finishes quite pleasantly. Price range: 1.5 l, $2.77–5.99.

ỸỸỸ ALMADÉN MONTEREY CHENIN BLANC 1981 Produced & bottled by Almadén Vineyards, San Jose, California. Rating: 10. Distribution: A. A common problem with many California white wines is lack of acid, but it's no problem for this one! The color is a pale, delicate gold, and the nose is mild and unpretentious. The big performance goes on in the mouth, where you'll find it's semidry, loaded with lots of clean, forthright fruit, and, because of the excellent acid balance, zesty and extremely refreshing. Price range: 750 ml, $2.77–5.19.

ỸỸ ALMADÉN CALIFORNIA FRENCH COLOMBARD Vinted & bottled by Almadén Vineyards, San Jose, California. Rating: 9. Distribution: A. This parchment-yellow wine has an innocent fragrance, simple and fruity, with no overwhelming character. Its taste is a perfect match—modestly sweet, genial, relaxed, relatively low acid, full of unassuming fruit flavors. A nice white wine for those times when all you want is a pleasant glass of something that tastes good. Price range: 750 ml, $3.15–4.99.

ỸỸỸ ALMADÉN SAN BENITO GEWURZTRAMINER 1981 Produced & bottled by Almadén Vineyards, San Jose, California. Rating: 11. Distribution: A. This is a lovely wine, light barley in color, with a lusciously fruity nose, quiet and mature. The taste is charmingly sweet, a basket of beautifully ripe fruit, rich and supple, with a touch of spice in the background. I wish it had a little bit more acid, but you can't have everything, so let's just be thankful for what we've got. Price range: 750 ml, $3.88–5.25.

℥ ALMADÉN LIGHT RHINE Vinted & bottled by Almadén Vineyards, San Jose, California. Rating: 8+. Distribution: A. When a wine looks like a glass of water, you expect it to smell and taste like water as well. Almadén's Light Rhine, however, has a fragrant, delicate nose that is velvety and full of ripe fruits. The taste has a slight effervescence, lots of simple fruit and sweetness, and it's all very pleasant, if somewhat one-dimensional. For dieters, of course, the payoff is an alcohol content of only 7 percent, and 54 calories per 100 milliliters. Just make sure you don't drink two glasses of "light" where you used to drink one of "regular"! Price range: 1.5 l, $3.57–4.99.

℥℥℥ ALMADÉN CALIFORNIA GREY RIESLING 1978 Produced & bottled by Almadén Vineyards, San Jose, California. Rating: 11. Distribution: A. This wine is a handsome greenish gold, and has a nose that is fresh, forthright, clean, and invitingly fruity. In the mouth you'll find it moderately dry, with medium body and rather low acid. There's plenty of fruit showing in this wine, the flavors are expansive and harmoniously blended, and there's a good finish. All in all, an attractive, well-made wine. Price range: 750 ml, $3.15–5.49.

♉♉ ALMADÉN CALIFORNIA MOUNTAIN WHITE SAU-TERNE Vinted & bottled by Almadén Vineyards, San Jose, California. Rating: 9. Distribution: A. This is a very decent wine, slightly sedate in its approach to life, but pleasant and refreshing nevertheless. The color is very pale, and has a greenish cast. The nose is forthcoming and ripe, pungent and full of fruit, but there's a faint stuffiness in the background. The taste is dry and medium-bodied with plenty of attractive fruit flavors, and it has a good acid balance. It's not one of your jolly fun-and-games wines, however. It's a serious wine, and you would do well to remember that in matching it up with food. Price range: 750 ml, $2.25–4.49.

♉♉♉♉♉ ALMADÉN MONTEREY SAUVIGNON BLANC 1980 Produced & bottled by Almadén Vineyards, San Jose, California. Rating: 13. Distribution: A. Here's a dry, crisp, mouth-filling wine I think you'll like a lot, provided you enjoy the varietal grassiness found in the nose and taste of many Sauvignon Blancs. I like it, so I find this wine delightful. The color is parchment-yellow. The nose has a fresh, nervy, outdoorsy quality that is very sensuous, maybe even sensual. The taste is full of verve and life, with plenty of clean, ripe fruit, and, of course, the Sauvignon Blanc grassiness. For me, it calls up fauns and fair maids and ribald goings-on behind trees and along riverbanks. Try a bottle and see what it calls up for you. Price range: 750 ml, $3.88–5.49.

♉♉♉♉ ANDEAN VINEYARDS CHARDONNAY 1980 Produced & bottled by Andean Vineyards, Mendoza,

Argentina. Rating: 12. Distribution: C. This is a charming, innocent Chardonnay, pale, almost watery in color, with a nose that breathes sunshine and flowers and has lots of fruit with a dash of honey thrown in. Despite a similar wealth of comely fruit and honey in the taste, it's a moderately dry wine, and it has good body and good balance. Argentina makes a lot of very handsome wines, but not many get to the United States, so you'd better grab this one while you have the chance. Price range: 750 ml, $2.99–5.99.

ΨΨΨ ANTINORI EST! EST!! EST!!! DI MONTEFIASCONE 1981 Bottled by Marchesi L.e.P. Antinori, Firenze, Italy. Rating: 10+. Distribution: C. The wine is good, but the story is even better. In the year 1111 a touring bishop sent his servant ahead to scout inns where the wine was good, and to mark their entrances with the Latin word *est* ("it is"). At one inn the servant was so impressed with the wine he scrawled *est* on the doorpost three times. This greenish gold beverage is alleged to be that wine. It is witheringly dry, spare, lean, and herbal. It's a wine of some considerable character, formal and monklike, a wine for "dry" freaks, and while some will like it a lot, others will think I'm crazy to give it three *est*'s—that is to say, three glasses. Price range: 750 ml, $4.59–6.49.

ΨΨΨΨ ANTINORI ORVIETO CLASSICO 1980 Bottled by Marchesi L.e.P. Antinori, Firenze, Italy. Rating: 11+. Distribution: C. Some people like their wines dry, lean, spare, and dignified, and for those people let me recommend this Orvieto. The color is a pale amber-gold, and the nose, which is very forthright and accessible, has a penetrating forest pungency. The taste is somewhat unusual—dry, crisp, and lively, but in a rather formal way. You get a feeling of energy from the refreshing acid balance, but you also get a feeling of reserve, restraint, and dignity. Price range: 750 ml, $4.49–6.49.

� ANTINORI SOAVE 1980 Bottled by Marchesi L.e.P. Antinori, Firenze, Italy. Rating: 11. Distribution: C. There's a streak of mischief in this dry, crisp import. You move past the bottle, shaped like a fish, and the color, pale as lemon juice, into a nose that is green and lively and full of fruit and saucy herbs. Not surprisingly, the slightly tart taste mirrors the nose— herbs, mischief, and all—and I get a feeling of energy, refreshment, and shaggy goat-men, bottles in hand, sunning themselves on sunny Italian hillsides, thinking up mildly vulgar adventures. Price range: 750 ml, $4.49–6.29.

♥♥♥ BAROSSA VALLEY JOHANNISBERG RIESLING 1980 Vintaged & bottled by Barossa Cooperative Winery, Ltd., Nuriootpa, South Australia. Rating: 10+. Distribution: C. Color: wheat, tinged with green. Nose: fruit held back, restrained, formal. Taste: plenty of fruit, dry, refreshingly balanced, but with a stiffness, a ramrod up the back, and an air of moderately stuffy aristocracy. Not necessarily a defect, however, just a bit unusual, and a very pleasant wine to boot. Price range: 750 ml, $2.88–4.79.

♥♥♥ BEAULIEU VINEYARDS NAPA VALLEY CHABLIS 1981 Produced & bottled by Beaulieu Vineyards, Rutherford, California. Rating: 11. Distribution: A.

The color is pale and wan, the nose is a delicate, innocent, fruit-and-tea compound. In the mouth it's big
(13 percent), smooth, mouth-filling, and moderately
dry, with a pleasant blending of some fairly diverse
fruit flavors. Herb Caen, columnist for the San Francisco *Chronicle*, says Legh Knowles (head of Beaulieu)
thinks there are only four kinds of wine: good, bad,
red, and white. If so, classify this one as white and
good. Price range: 750 ml, $3.65–5.49.

♈♈♈ BERINGER NORTH COAST CHABLIS 1981   Vinted &
bottled by Beringer Vineyards, St. Helena, California.
Rating: 10. Distribution: A. This very pleasant golden
wine has greenish glints at its edge. The bouquet has
an unassuming, cheerfully fruity personality. The
taste is light and dry, with a zesty balance as though
it were made from slightly underripe fruit. It's a
good, well-made wine. Price range: 750 ml, $2.55–
4.49.

♈♈ BERINGER NAPA VALLEY CHENIN BLANC 1981   Produced & bottled by Beringer Vineyards, St. Helena,
California. Rating: 9+. Distribution: A. This pale,
barley-colored wine has an assertive nose that is
fresh, jaunty, and slightly underripe. The taste is just
off-dry, with lots and lots of honeyed fruit—peaches,
apricots, and let us not forget grapes—and the only
drawback is there's not quite enough acid to keep the
whole thing from being kind of flat. Price range: 750
ml, $3.69–5.49.

♈♈♈♈ BERINGER NAPA VALLEY DRY FRENCH COLOM-
BARD 1981 Produced & bottled by Beringer Vineyards, St. Helena, California. Rating: 11+. Distribu-

tion: A. Here's an outstanding French Colombard! Pale wheat in color, it has a captivating, honeyed nose that is clear, clean, and full of peaches and nectarines. The taste is fairly dry, a sort of supple, light nectar bursting with voluptuous fruit. The acid is decent, and the whole thing comes off as a first-class production. Price range: 750 ml, $3.88–5.29.

♈♈♈ BLACK TOWER LIEBFRAUMILCH 1981 Bottled by H. Kendermann Weinkellerei, Bingen, Germany. Rating: 11. Distribution: B. This is a very pleasant, undemanding wine for Liebfraumilch lovers, or anyone else who enjoys a well-made, light-acid wine of moderate sweetness. The color of parchment, this wine has a clean, mannerly nose that shows a dignified fusion of fruit and honey, and a taste that further projects this supple union of fruit, flowers, and modest, natural sweetness. Don't let the funny black bottle fool you, it's a comely, pleasing, feminine wine. Price range: 750 ml, $3.68–4.99.

♈♈ BLASON DE MAUCAILLOU 1979 Bottled by Dourthe Fréres, Gironde, France. Rating: 9+. Distribution: C. This wine has a silvery, pale straw color and a cool, slightly grassy nose. The taste is quite dry, pleasantly tart, and the fruit, while zesty, has a restrained, unripe quality. It's a dignified wine, and if you like your wines crisp, crackling, and dry, you ought to rush out and start looking for this one. Price range, 750 ml, $3.79–5.99.

♈ BLUE NUN LIEBFRAUMILCH 1981 Bottled & shipped by H. Sichel Sohne, Mainz, Germany. Rating: 8. Distribution: A. This famous wine, the color of pale barley, has a nose that is fruity but slightly stuffy and sedate. The taste is decent, relatively sweet, and rather routine. It shows a fair quantity of fruit, plus fair acid, but the nasal stuffiness carries over into the taste and keeps it from scoring higher. That doesn't keep Sichel from selling a million-plus cases in the United States each year, however, so maybe you'll side with the hordes who buy it rather than with me. Price range: 750 ml, $3.29–5.25.

ΤΤΤ BOLLA SOAVE 1980 Produced & bottled by Frabo, S.P.A., Verona, Italy. Rating: 11. Distribution: A. This Soave is an ingratiating, pale gold wine with a greenish cast. The nose is youthful and fruity, and the taste reflects that same lively spirit. It's a fairly dry wine, with lots of ripe fruit in the taste, good acid, and a pleasant, energetic personality throughout. Price range: 750 ml, $2.99–4.49.

ΤΤΤΤ BOLLINI CHARDONNAY DI MEZZOCORONA 1981 Bottled by Cascom, Mezzocorona, Italy. Rating: 11+. Distribution: C. This is a fairly new entry in the field of low-cost white varietals, and it's my guess it won't stay low-cost long. So, hurry up and try it. Here's what you'll find: A wine the color of very dry Sherry. A nose that's ripe and clean, slightly formal, with a bouquet of fully mature fruit. A taste that is dry and crisp, medium-bodied, with lots of obliging fruit, and flashes of elegance and richness. It's a quality wine, and as presently priced, a great value. Price range: 750 ml, $3.50–5.99.

ỶỶỶỶỶ **BOLLINI PINOT GRIGIO VALDADIGE 1981**   Bottled by Cascom, Mezzocorona, Italy. Rating: 13. Distribution: C. The companion piece to Bollini's United States market entry is even better than the Chardonnay. The color is pale gold, the nose is forthright, fresh, and full of life and energy. There's a new-mown grass quality to the taste, which is pleasantly dry and spirited, and has lots of clean, wholesome fruit. It fills the mouth, has good acid, good body, and an overall feeling of quality. It's the kind of wine Pope Julius II might have shared with Michelangelo before he told him to get cracking on the Sistine Chapel. Price range: 750 ml, $3.55–5.99.

BROLIO BIANCO 1980   Bottled by Casa Vinicola Barone Ricasoli, Firenze, Italy. Rating: 7. Distribution: B. The wine is the color of clover honey. The nose has a middle-of-the-road respectability marred by a slight pungency, and the taste is dry, slightly baked, not terrible, but nothing to write home about, either. Price range: 750 ml, $2.99–4.49.

ỶỶỶỶ **BUENA VISTA NORTH COAST CHABLIS 1978**   Produced & bottled by Buena Vista Winery, Sonoma, California. Rating: 11+. Distribution: B. This is a mature, serious wine, well-made and enjoyable. In color, it's a rich, viridescent gold. The nose is easily accessible, full of ripe fruit, and has a racy, greenish character that is quite attractive. The taste is mouth-filling—dry, round, full, and loaded with clean, fully ripe fruit. It has good body, good acid, and a good finish. Next time you happen upon a bottle, pick it up. Price range: 750 ml, $3.68–4.99.

♼ CAMBIASO 1852 HOUSE CALIFORNIA CHABLIS   Produced & bottled by Cambiaso Vineyards, Healdsburg, California. Rating: 9+. Distribution: C. Cambiaso's Chablis is pale lemon in color, and has a brash, racy nose with a piquant riverbank grassiness. The taste is dry, pleasantly tart and lively, with lots of fruit just at the edge of ripeness. It's a pleasant, refreshing wine with good acid, and a good price. Price range: $1.99–3.49.

CAMBIASO NORTHERN CALIFORNIA CHENIN BLANC 1980 Produced by Cambiaso Vineyards, Healdsburg, California. Rating: 6. Distribution: C. The color is a deep lemon-gold. Unfortunately, the nose has an unattractive vegetable quality, and the taste, which is semidry, with good body, good acid, and lots of fruit, suffers from an echo of the nose. Price range: 750 ml, $2.35–3.99.

CARMEL CHATEAU RICHON 1979   Produced & bottled by Carmel Wine Growers Cooperative, Richon le Zion & Zichron Jacob, Israel. Rating: 5+. Distribution: B. Carmel needs a new copywriter, because the label on this wine declares it is semidry, when actually it's syrupy enough to pour on waffles. It's a light honey color, the nose is aggressive and reedy, and the taste is baked. If I still haven't driven you away, the price range is: 750 ml, $3.38–4.99.

CASA DE ROJAS SAUVIGNON BLANC DE CHILE   Produced & bottled by Viña Tarapaca, Santiago, Chile. Rating: 6+. Distribution: C. Such a handsome gold color, such a lovely label, such a disappointing wine!

The nose is stuffy, closed-in, and rather cooked. The taste is not bad, just commonplace. It has lots of fruit, also somewhat cooked and somewhat bitter. But what a terrific label! Price range: 750 ml, $3.99–4.99.

CHATEAU DES TOURTES, COTE DE BLAYE 1979   Bottled by Philippe Raguenot, Saint Caprais de Blaye, France. Rating: 4. Distribution: C. Unfortunate. A lovely lemon-gold wine with a pungent, tannic nose and a bitter, medicinal flavor. Price range: 750 ml, $3.79–5.49.

♆♆♆ CHRISTIAN BROTHERS CALIFORNIA CHABLIS   Produced & bottled by The Christian Brothers, Napa, California. Rating: 10. Distribution: A. This barley-colored wine has a piquant, racy nose that is fruity, has a trace of spice, and gives a supple, clean performance in the mouth. It's a nice wine, refined and gentle, not quite dry, with moderate acid and some pleasing floral tones. I think you'll like it. Price range: 750 ml, $1.99–4.19.

♆♆ CHRISTIAN BROTHERS CHATEAU LA SALLE   Produced & bottled by The Christian Brothers, Napa, California. Rating: 9+. Distribution: A. This wine is a long-time favorite with many people as a dessert wine. It has a buttery, golden color, and its nose shows lots of fresh, aromatic fruit, sunny but tempered by a feeling of maturity. In the mouth you'll find it very sweet, full-bodied, almost thick, and full of fruit and fruit sugars, albeit in a fairly narrow flavor spectrum. Price range: 750 ml, $2.77–4.49.

▼▼▼ CHRISTIAN BROTHERS NAPA VALLEY CHENIN BLANC Produced & bottled by The Christian Brothers, Napa, California. Rating: 11. Distribution: A. There is a dignity and reserve in the nose of this pale, lemon-colored wine. In the mouth, however, the reserve disappears, and the taste is juicy, full, bursting with fruit, and pleasantly balanced. It's a nice, sunshiny wine, generous and outdoorsy. Price range: 750 ml, $3.72–5.49.

▼▼ CHRISTIAN BROTHERS CALIFORNIA RHINE WINE Produced & bottled by The Christian Brothers, Napa, California. Rating: 9. Distribution: A. Well, The Christian Brothers may call this pale, lemon-colored wine a Rhine, but to me it's more like a French Chablis. That is, the nose has that austere, gun-metal character, and the taste is dry and formal, the kind of wine that would do well with the fish course. If you like that particular style of Chablis, and many people do, don't buy a Chablis. Instead, run out and buy a bottle of Christian Brothers Rhine Wine! Price range: 750 ml, $1.99–4.19.

▼ CHRISTIAN BROTHERS CALIFORNIA RIESLING Produced & bottled by The Christian Brothers, Napa, California. Rating: 8+. Distribution: A. When I blind-tasted this handsome green-gold wine with other Rieslings, I couldn't believe it was a Riesling at all. The nose was too stiff, almost stuffy, the taste was bone-dry, extremely austere, and like the Rhine mentioned above, had an almost bitter, gunmetal character. I would have given it a very low mark as a Riesling, so I graded it as a Chablis, and still found it a bit too tough and unyielding to score very high. Price range: 750 ml, $2.97–4.49.

℗ CHRISTIAN BROTHERS SELECT CALIFORNIA SAUTERNE   Produced & bottled by The Christian Brothers, Napa, California. Rating: 8+. Distribution: A. The color is deep, gold, lemony. The nose is unusual—aromatic, heavy, almost syrupy, and slightly cooked. The taste is off-dry, with some sweetness, lots of slightly syrupy fruit, and a modest acid balance. Despite its defects, which are real, there is still an air of quality about this wine, which is how it beat—just barely—a middle-of-the-road rating. Price range: 750 ml, $2.09–4.29.

COLLI DI CATONE FRASCATI 1980   Produced & bottled by Cantine Colli di Catone, S.P.A., Monte Porzio Catone, Italy. Rating: 7+. Distribution: C. No two Frascatis are the same, and this is a reedy, grassy one. That goes for both the nose and the taste. The wine is dry, tart, and has fruit, but the fruit gets lost in the reediness in both the aroma and the flavor. Some people will like this, just as some people like an overload of oak or retsina, but for me it's a little much. Price range: 750 ml, $3.79–5.99.

℗℗℗ COLONY CALIFORNIA CLASSIC CHABLIS   Vinted & bottled by Colony Wines, San Francisco. Rating: 10. Distribution: A. This engaging, upbeat wine could use some acid to give it more zip, but if you'll forgive it that, it has some nice things to offer. First, there's a nose full of flowers and fruit, and second, there's a sunny, lively taste of apricots, tea, and would you believe mandarin oranges? (You wouldn't? Why not?) It's not a dry wine, it has some sweetness, but if that's what you like, you should give this one a try. Price range: 1.5 l, $2.99–4.99.

Ⴘ COLONY CLASSIC CHENIN BLANC OF CALIFORNIA Vinted & bottled by Colony Wines, San Francisco. Rating: 8+. Distribution: A. This is a simple, light-hearted wine, full of ripe fruit and innocence, semi-dry, and low on acid. The nose is clean, ripe, and approachable. The color is a medium gold. A pleasant, low-energy wine. Price range: 1.5 l, $3.18–4.99.

ႵႵ COLONY CLASSIC FRENCH COLOMBARD OF CALIFORNIA Vinted & bottled by Colony Wines, San Francisco. Rating: 9+. Distribution: A. French Colombards are all over the lot in sweetness, acid, and the style of making them. This is a simple one with a sunny, golden color and an uncomplicated, slightly mature, and very accessible nose. The taste is also uncomplicated, but that's all right. It's lively, clean, and filled with lots of ripe fruit. Nothing sophisticated, just a good, honest, workaday wine. Price range: 1.5 l, $3.18–4.99.

Ⴘ COLONY CALIFORNIA CLASSIC RHINE Vinted & bottled by Colony Wines, San Francisco. Rating: 8. Distribution: A. This Rhine has a pale blond color and a fragrant, cheerful, fruity nose. The taste is also cheerful, sweet, fruity, and, because of the customary lack of acid in California Rhines, rather flat. Still, well iced, it could bring a lot of sunshine to a picnic! Price range: 1.5 l, $2.99–4.99.

🍷 CONCANNON CALIFORNIA CHABLIS 1981 Produced & bottled by Concannon Vineyard, Livermore, California. Rating: 8+. Distribution: B. This pale yellow wine has a mild, rounded, faintly floral aroma of crushed fruit, and a light-hearted, fruit-bloom taste. But it lacks the energy that an adequate acid balance would give it. Too bad; it's nice, but it could be so much nicer! Price range: 750 ml, $2.77–4.99.

🍷 CONCANNON CALIFORNIA CHENIN BLANC 1981 Produced & bottled by Concannon Vineyards, Livermore, California. Rating: 8. Distribution: B. This is one of those basically good wines that would be a lot "gooder" if it weren't so lacking in acid. It's the color of light clover honey, and the nose has some diffident charm—a few touches of fruit bloom, that sort of thing. In the mouth it's very pleasant, clean, fruity, juicy, and . . . sorry, rather flat. But it's still nice. Price range: 750 ml, $3.80–5.49.

🍷 CONCHA Y TORO CHILEAN CHABLIS 1979 Produced & bottled by Viña Concha y Toro, Maipo, Chile. Rating: 8+. Distribution: C. Concha y Toro's Chablis has a deep golden hue in the glass, and a kind of goaty aggressiveness in the nose. If that sounds bad, and I'm sure it does, let me say it's not terrible. It's really a sort of amiable weediness, and it's inside the bounds of acceptability, even if not very far inside. The taste is much better than the nose—dry, tart, lively, with lots of barely ripe fruit and (you guessed it) some slight weediness. Price range: 750 ml, $2.88–4.49.

ᵱᵱ CONCHA Y TORO SAUVIGNON BLANC 1979 Produced & bottled by Viña Concha y Toro, Maipo, Chile. Rating: 9+. Distribution: B. The color is intermingled gold and green. The nose is dry, unspectacular, with a slight woody note. The taste is pleasantly dry and crisp, rather light, with an abundance of underripe fruit and good acid. All in all, an enjoyable little dry wine. Price range: 750 ml, $3.44–5.49.

ᵱᵱᵱᵱ CORBAN'S SYLVANER RIESLING 1980 Vinted & bottled by The Corban Estate, Henderson Valley, New Zealand. Rating: 12. Distribution: C. You didn't know they made wine in New Zealand, but they do, and some of it is very good. This Sylvaner Riesling from Corban's is a good example, with its clean, clear, straw color, and its demure, dignified, yet very approachable, floral nose. Although the taste is medium dry, it has lots of lovely nectar flavors, and is generally rich, smooth, and honeyed. It has good body and a good acid balance, and an air of casual elegance. If you can find a bottle, check it out. Price range: 750 ml, $4.39–6.39.

ᵱᵱᵱ CRESTA BLANCA BLANC DE BLANC Produced & bottled by Cresta Blanca Vineyards, Ukiah, California. Rating: 10. Distribution: B. This Blanc de Blanc has a medium gold color and a clean, pleasant, moderately fruity nose. Taste it, and you'll find a comely, sunshiny wine of modest sweetness, showing lots of luscious fruit, generous, well proportioned, and finishing clean. Price range: 750 ml, $2.68–4.49.

℈ CRESTA BLANCA MENDOCINO CHABLIS 1980 Produced & bottled by Cresta Blanca Vineyards, Ukiah, California. Rating: 8. Distribution: B. You could call this wine affable. It has a pleasant, mouth-filling taste, generous fruit, a decent if unexceptional nose, and a lovely golden color. It's a bit short on acid, but it's a very drinkable wine nevertheless. Price range: 750 ml, $2.68–4.49.

℈ CRESTA BLANCA SANTA MARIA VALLEY CHENIN BLANC 1981 Produced & bottled by Cresta Blanca Vineyards, Ukiah, California. Rating: 8+. Distribution: B. This sunny blond wine has an assertive nose that bespeaks dignity as well as the grapes from which it comes. The taste is attractively fruity, slightly reserved, and if it had just a bit more acid it would score a little higher. Nice nonetheless. Price range: 750 ml, $2.77–5.29.

℈ CRESTA BLANCA MENDOCINO FRENCH COLOMBARD 1980 Produced & bottled by Cresta Blanca Vineyards, Ukiah, California. Rating: 8. Distribution: B. This golden-blond French Colombard has a fairly undemonstrative nose—no defects especially, but no merit badges, either. It tastes surprisingly good, however, and I think you'll find it honest, decent, dry, and a trifle sedate, but eminently drinkable. Price range, 750 ml, $2.77–5.29.

℈℈℈ CRESTA BLANCA SAN LUIS OBISPO GEWURZTRAMINER 1979 Produced & bottled by Cresta Blanca Vineyards, Ukiah, California. Rating:

10. Distribution: B. This Gewürztraminer is a pale saffron color, and has a nose that is almost, but not quite, dignified. The taste is semidry, clean, masculine, liquorous, with good acid and lots of ripe fruit. It shows the beginnings of complexity and character—just the beginnings—and all in all, it's a nice wine. Price range: 750 ml, $3.37–5.99.

ΤΤΤ CRESTA BLANCA CALIFORNIA RHINE   Produced & bottled by Cresta Blanca Vineyards, Ukiah, California. Rating: 10. Distribution: B. First, you admire the vibrant, deep gold color of this wine. Then you sniff: pleasant, straightforward, respectable, a *masculine* wine, no Rhine maidens in sight. You taste: on the sweet side, fruity, full of peaches and apricots, and as with most California Rhines, short on acid. But you can overlook that, can't you, when the rest of the picture is so beautiful? Price range: 750 ml, $2.68–4.49.

Τ CRESTA BLANCA CALIFORNIA GREY RIESLING 1980 Produced & bottled by Cresta Blanca Vineyards, Ukiah, California. Rating: 8. Distribution: B. Some wines, while unspectacular, are still very accommodating and perfectly acceptable. This Grey Riesling is one. Pale parchment in color, it has a decent nose with muted fruit and a faint musky overtone. The taste, while not exciting, is civil, mannerly, and provides a nice level of refreshment. Don't expect to be knocked off your chair, but do expect a seemly, better-than-average wine. Price range: 750 ml, $2.77–5.29.

CRESTA BLANCA SANTA MARIA VALLEY JOHANNISBERG
RIESLING 1981   Produced & bottled by Cresta Blanca
Vineyards, Ukiah, California. Rating: 7+. Distribution: B. The middle of the road: That's where this
Riesling can be found. It's greenish gold in color, and
the nose is acceptable, fruity, and unsophisticated.
The taste is slightly sweet, with decent fruit and acid,
but there's a slight bitterness that keeps it where it is,
squarely in the middle of the road. Price range: 750
ml, $3.97–5.99.

CRIBARI CALIFORNIA CHABLIS BLANC   Made & bottled
by Cribari & Sons, Lodi, California. Rating: 6. Distribution: B. The wine is very pale, almost transparent,
and the nose is hardly there at all. The taste is simple
and routine. It's not a bad wine, it's just nothing to
get excited about. Price range: 1.5 l, $2.99–4.49.

CRIBARI CALIFORNIA LIGHT MOUNTAIN CHABLIS
Made & bottled by Cribari & Sons, Lodi, California.
Rating: 6. Distribution: B. Cribari's entry in the
"light" white-wine sweepstakes has only 47 calories
per 100 milliliters, but I doubt that dieters will find
the trade-off very attractive. The color is just slightly
darker than water, the nose is aggressive and reedy,
and the taste echoes the nose. Price range: 1.5 l,
$2.99–4.49.

Ƭ CRIBARI CALIFORNIA MOUNTAIN CHABLIS   Made &
bottled by Cribari & Sons, Lodi, California. Rating:
8. Distribution: B. Clean, straw color, decent nose
with moderate fruit. In the mouth, a just-off-dry
sweetness that is better than middle-of-the-road,

with a fair balance and lots of unspecified fruit. Price range: 1.5 l, $2.99–4.49.

CRIBARI CALIFORNIA CHENIN BLANC   Made & bottled by Cribari & Sons, Lodi, California. Rating: 7. Distribution: B. The color: pale gold. The nose: civil, a bit closed-in, a trifle stuffy. The taste: unremarkable, sedate, somewhat lacking in life. The ingredients are all there, and it's not a bad wine, it's just not going to be your favorite. Price range: 1.5 l, $3.29–4.99.

CRIBARI CALIFORNIA FRENCH COLOMBARD   Made & bottled by Cribari & Sons, Lodi, California. Rating: 5. Distribution: B. The color: pale and washed out. The nose: dry, withered, little fruit showing. The taste: semidry, restrained, musty. My advice: Forget it. Price range: 1.5 l, $3.29–4.99.

CRIBARI CALIFORNIA PINOT CHARDONNAY   Made & bottled by Cribari & Sons, Lodi, California. Rating: 7. Distribution: B. The color is light straw, the nose is shy, almost speechless. The taste is dry, thin, and unimpressive, and there's a faint bitter note that detracts from the fruit flavors. Price range: 750 ml, $3.29–5.99.

♉ CRIBARI CALIFORNIA MOUNTAIN RHINE   Made & bottled by Cribari & Sons, Lodi, California. Rating: 8. Distribution: B. This Rhine is the color of ripe barley, and has a civil, sedate, undistinguished, but acceptable nose. It also has a civil, sedate, not terribly distinguished, but acceptable, taste that is very low on acid. How do you drink it? You chill it and gulp it. Any other questions? Price range: 1.5 l, $2.99–4.49.

ȲȲȲ DEINHARD GREEN LABEL MOSELLE 1980 Produced & bottled by Deinhard & Company, Koblenz, Germany. Rating: 11. Distribution: C. If you expect fruit and flowers from Moselle wines (or Mosels, if you come from Koblenz, as this wine does), prepare to be surprised. This pale flax-colored wine appears to have no grapes at all in the nose, and instead presents bark, spice, and herbs, almost like a May Wine. If that sounds terrible, it isn't. It's just an unusual wine, medium dry, with a refreshing and somewhat exotic flavor. Woodsy, you might say, and every now and then a little woodsiness can be a refreshing change. Price range: 750 ml, $4.40–6.19.

ȲȲȲ DEMESTICA Produced & bottled by Achaia-Claus Wine Company, Patras, Greece. Rating: 11. Distribution: B. You'll be struck by the deep, brilliant, lemony-gold color of this wine. The nose has an air of attractive maturity—amiable, accessible, full of spice. The taste is dry, round, spicy, full of fruit and brambles, and it has a charming, almost mysterious character, as though it were a wine drunk by glamorous female spies. It has good acid, and I commend it to you not as an every-night drink, but as a very pleasant foreign experience in which to indulge every now and again. Price range: 750 ml, $2.83–4.79.

ȲȲȲȲȲ FAZI-BATAGLIA VERDICCHIO DEI CASTELLI DI JESI 1980   Bottled by Casa Vinicola Fazi Bataglia Titulus, Castelplanio, Italy. Rating: 13. Distribution: B. Here's a pale green-gold wine with a clean, fresh, light-hearted nose full of ripe grapes, sunshine, and a zest for living. The taste is dry, crisp, and lively, packed full of just-ripe fruit and offering a nice acid balance. The finish is charming and lingers long enough to give you time to think about sunny Italian hillsides with goats grazing peacefully and castles in the distance. Price range: 750 ml, $3.76–5.99.

🍷🍷🍷🍷 FETZER MENDOCINO BLANC DE BLANCS 1981 Produced & bottled by Fetzer Vineyards, Redwood Valley, California. Rating: 12. Distribution: B. This is a wine that gives a lot. It's the color of pale parchment, and has a pleasant, genteel nose full of clean, ripe fruit, a dash of tea, and some attractive touches of class. The taste is dry, crisp, refreshing, self-assured, and modestly complex with a pleasant range of fruit flavors. It has a vigor and a sophistication I think you will appreciate as much as I do, but there's only one way to find out! Price range: 750 ml, $3.19–5.29.

🍷🍷🍷 FETZER CALIFORNIA CHENIN BLANC 1981 Produced & bottled by Fetzer Vineyards, Redwood Valley, California. Rating: 11. Distribution: B. This is a lovely wine to look at in the glass, pale straw with a golden rim. The nose is nice, too—rounded, fruity, with iced-tea overtones. The taste is honeyed, full of ripe fruit and more tea. Its only problem is a slight acid deficiency, but it's a nice wine all the same. Price range: 750 ml, $4.21–5.99.

🍷🍷🍷 FETZER MENDOCINO FRENCH COLOMBARD 1981 Produced & bottled by Fetzer Vineyards, Redwood Valley, California. Rating: 10+. Distribution: B. This tawny-gold wine has an uncomplicated nose that is fetching and easily approachable. It's full of simple aromas of fruit and iced tea, and the semisweet taste mirrors the nose. Your palate will find it mild, nectarlike, rather low on acid, but very charming nevertheless. Price range: 750 ml, $3.25–5.99.

♟♟♟ FETZER PREMIUM WHITE   Made & bottled by Fetzer Vineyards, Redwood Valley, California. Rating: 11. Distribution: B. Here's a nice, clean, fruity wine that has a lot of charm and zest. It's a very pale olive in color, with an unostentatious but very decent nose that shows both fruit and flowers. The taste is dry, almost tart, and seems energized by the verve of its just-ripe fruit. It's a wine with a lot of athletic charm and the beginnings of character. I think you'll like it. Price range: 750 ml, $2.48–4.99.

♟♟♟ FOLONARI SOAVE   Bottled by SPAL, Pastrengo, Italy. Rating: 10+. Distribution: A. If you like your wines on the dry, crisp, austere side, this wine is for you. The color is pale barley, and the nose has musky, tweedy overtones with very little fruit showing. The taste is very dry, rather severe, almost flinty. Lots of people like a wine like this with a delicately flavored dish because it won't overpower the food. If you're one of those people, here's your wine. Price range: 750 ml, $2.12–4.49.

♟♟♟ FOLONARI VERONA WHITE   Bottled by Fratelli Folonari Antica Casa Vinicola, Persico Dosimo, Italy. Rating: 11. Distribution: B. This wine is the color of pure clover honey. The nose is conservative, quiet, and rather musky, with the fruit hidden. The taste is dry, crisp, and refreshing, dignified and rather steely, with good acid and an overall feeling of character. It's a bit like a French Chablis, having plenty of upright vigor along with a measure of elegance and austerity. Price range: 3 l, $4.99–7.49.

♈♈ FONTANA CANDIDA FRASCATI 1981   Bottled by Vini di Fontana Candida, S.P.A., Frascati, Italy. Rating: 9+. Distribution: B. This pale, nearly transparent wine has a shy nose that shows only the most modest hints of fruitiness. In the mouth the fruit is similarly held back, but the taste is still very dry, breezy, clean, and enjoyable. It's a wine for adults, none of your juvenile hearts-and-flowers stuff, and I think you'll find it pleasant, simple, and refreshing. Price range: 750 ml, $2.59–4.49.

♈♈♈ LOUIS J. FOPPIANO NORTHERN CALIFORNIA DRY CHENIN BLANC 1980   Produced & bottled by Foppiano Winery, Healdsburg, California. Rating: 10. Distribution: B. This nice, zesty wine is simple and uncomplicated, but it certainly isn't simple-minded! It's a golden straw color, and the nose is direct, clean, fresh, and full of fruit. The taste is crisp and fairly dry, full of sunshine and energy, and it has excellent acid, which, of course, is what pulls it all together and makes it so refreshing! Price range: 750 ml, $3.98–5.49.

♈♈♈♈ CHARLES FOURNIER PERSONAL SELECTION DRY RIESLING 1981   Produced by Gold Seal Vineyards, Hammondsport, New York. Rating: 11+. Distribution: C. If you want to one-up your friends who are California-wine buffs, slip this Riesling into a blind test and see what they have to say. Here's what they *should* say: "Color: Pale lemon. Nose: graceful aroma of ripe, rounded, mature fruit. Taste: medium dry, with good body and some residual sweetness. Definitely a broad-gauge wine, mouth-filling and moderately formal. The acid balance is good, as is the finish. It's a thoughtful, masculine white with good manners and a quiet charm all its own." Naturally, if your friends *do* say that, you're entitled to arrest them for practicing pretentious wine-writing without a license! Price range: 750 ml, $3.99–5.99.

ᵀᵀᵀ FRANCISCAN VINEYARDS PREMIUM CALIFORNIA DRY WHITE WINE Produced & bottled by Franciscan Vineyards, Rutherford, California. Rating: 11. Distribution: B. If this wine had just a little more acid, it would get a rating of four or five glasses. Even so, it's a delightful, lemon-colored wine with a lovely, full, fruit-and-flower bouquet, rich, scented, and wholesome. The taste is also extremely handsome and dry, with a perfume-laden cornucopia of fruit that has developed some nice flavor complexity. It's a nice wine, not quite as zippy as you might wish, but quite enjoyable nevertheless. Price range: 750 ml, $2.69–4.49.

ᵀ FRANZIA MOUNTAIN CHABLIS BLANC OF CALIFORNIA Made & bottled by Franzia Brothers Winemakers, San Francisco, California. Rating: 8. Distribution: A. There's a tea-and-fruit motif running through this wine that I like, both in the nose and in the mouth. The fruit is a little hard to identify, but it's pleasant and sunshiny, and overcomes the points the wine loses because of its lack of acid. It's a genial, low-energy wine with nice flavors, kind of a charming loafer you wish would exert himself more, but whom you have to enjoy just as he is. Price range: 750 ml, $2.39–3.99.

🍷 FRANZIA CALIFORNIA LIGHT CHABLIS Made & bottled by Franzia Brothers Winemakers, San Francisco, California. Rating: 8+. Distribution: A. Only 7.5 percent alcohol, 57 calories per 100 milliliters. All this, and it's still a presentable, somewhat better-than-average "light" white wine. The color is straw, the nose is fruity and presentable without having a lot to say. The taste has a moderate sweetness, good body, good acid, and decent if rather conventional fruit flavors. Not bad for a "light." Price range: 750 ml, $2.39–3.99.

🍷🍷 FRANZIA CALIFORNIA CHENIN BLANC Made & bottled by Franzia Brothers Winemakers, San Francisco, California. Rating: 9+. Distribution: A. This pale lemon-colored wine has a youthful, demure nose that is clean and light-hearted. The taste is lightly sweet, a captivating, fluid-nectar collection of ripe fruit flavors, and the only shortcoming is in the acid balance. Price range: 750 ml, $2.49–4.39.

🍷🍷 FRANZIA CALIFORNIA FRENCH COLOMBARD Made & bottled by Franzia Brothers Winemakers, San Francisco, California. Rating: 9. Distribution: A. This light-straw-colored wine has a bashful, unassuming nose that, when you track it down, turns out to be clean and modestly fruity. The taste is semidry, with a light sweetness, lots of fruit, and fair acid. it's not exactly a world-class wine, but it's pleasant and summery and well made. Also, you won't go broke buying a bottle. Price range: 750 ml, $2.49–4.39.

FRATELLI BIANCO   Bottled by S.V.I., Dosimo, Italy. Rating: 7+. Distribution: B. The color is a deep, smoky orange. The nose is full, ripe, masculine, aggressive, and, unfortunately, slightly baked. In the mouth you'll find it effervescent, sweet, simplistic, and stuffed with hot weather characteristics. Of its kind—a sort of white Lambrusco—it's not too bad, but the whole category seems too close to soda pop for me to recommend you try it. Price range: 750 ml, $2.99–4.29.

♈♈♈ FU JIN   Prepared & bottled by Papagni Vineyards, Madera, California. Rating: 10+. Distribution: B. You'll have to make up your own mind whether this wine is the perfect accompaniment for an Oriental dinner. Papagni obviously thinks so. All I'm going to tell you is that it's a lovely, fruity wine, clear and golden, with a pleasingly honeyed nose and a rounded, opulent taste. It has a charming sweetness, it's full of sunshine and fruit in bloom, and I think it would make a good apéritif, or a good wine to serve with dessert. Price range: 750 ml, $3.45–5.49.

♈♈ GALLO CHABLIS BLANC OF CALIFORNIA   Made & bottled by the Gallo Vineyards, Modesto, California. Rating: 9+. Distribution: A. This Chablis is hard to beat for value. It looks a bit wan and watery, but the nose is clean, fruity, approachable, and the taste is full of sunshine and ripe grapes. It's just off-dry, and it comes up a bit short on acid, but who cares? Chill it well and take it on your next picnic! Price range: 1.5 l, $2.99–4.59.

🍷🍷🍷🍷 ERNEST & JULIO GALLO CHARDONNAY OF CALIFORNIA Vinted & cellared & bottled by Ernest & Julio Gallo, Modesto, California. Rating: 11+. Distribution: A. The Brothers Gallo have done themselves proud with this one, but I have to warn you that it's a serious Chardonnay and not one of the hearts-and-flowers variety. The color is rich and golden, and the nose is expansive, elegant, and oaky. The taste is similarly masculine and restrained, and has a lot of lean, dry dignity. If you don't like the flavor that oak-aging imparts, you won't like this wine. I think it's much more likely, however, that you'll like it as much as I do, and agree it represents excellent value. Price range: 750 ml, $4.59–6.49.

🍷🍷 ERNEST & JULIO GALLO CHENIN BLANC OF CALIFORNIA Vinted & cellared & bottled by Ernest & Julio Gallo, Modesto, California. Rating: 9+. Distribution: A. This is a brilliantly clear wine the color of ripe barley. The nose is congenial, not complex, with a pleasing fruit nectar scent, but it's in the mouth that it comes alive with lots of flowers and fruit. I wish it had more acid, but I wish many Chenin Blancs had more acid, so why not just chill a bottle of this one and enjoy it. Price range: 750 ml, $2.48–3.99.

🍷 ERNEST & JULIO GALLO FRENCH COLOMBARD OF CALIFORNIA Vinted & cellared & bottled by Ernest & Julio Gallo, Modesto, California. Rating: 8. Distribution: A. This wine is pale and watery looking, but the nose is pleasant—deep, fruity, and clean, with a touch of iced tea in it. The taste is decorous and satisfactory, a simple, semisweet fruit nectar with rather low acid. Not great, just pleasant. Price range: 750 ml, $2.48–3.99.

▼▼▼ ERNEST & JULIO GALLO GEWURTZTRAMINER OF CALIFORNIA   Vinted & cellared & bottled by Ernest & Julio Gallo, Modesto, California. Rating: 10. Distribution: A. This is very pale wine, almost wan. It has a graceful, apricot-nectar nose full of flowers and mature fruit, and the taste is rich, ripe, and round, a regular fruit salad. It's a little flat, though, due to low acid, but it's still liquid gold. Price range: 750 ml, $2.99–4.49.

▼▼▼ ERNEST & JULIO GALLO JOHANNISBERG RIESLING OF CALIFORNIA   Vinted & cellared & bottled by Ernest & Julio Gallo, Modesto, California. Rating: 10+. Distribution: A. The color is pale wheat, and the nose is diffident, delicate, and filled with summery fruit. The taste offers a lovely fusion of fruit flavors, and a modest sweetness. Predictably, it's a bit short on acid, but it's still a highly enjoyable wine that says, "Drink and enjoy, tomorrow will take care of itself!" Price range: 750 ml, $2.62–4.49.

▼▼▼ GALLO RHINE WINE OF CALIFORNIA   Made & bottled by the Gallo Vineyards, Modesto, California. Rating: 10+. Distribution: A. The color of this wine is so light you'll think you're drinking a glass of water. When you sniff its bouquet, however, you'll know otherwise, because it's fresh and has the fragrance of fresh peaches. In the mouth it's a charming, light nectar, sweet of course, and tasting of peaches and pomegranates, long summers, warm evenings. Price range: 1.5 l, $2.99–4.59.

TTTT ERNEST & JULIO GALLO SAUVIGNON BLANC OF CALIFORNIA   Vinted & cellared & bottled by Ernest & Julio Gallo, Modesto, California. Rating: 11+. Distribution: A. The brothers Gallo have given us a dry, stylish Sauvignon Blanc (same thing as Fumé Blanc, in case you wondered) that is wholesome and well made. It's pale and wan with a greenish cast, and the nose is sleek, grassy, and sophisticated. It's a healthy, outdoorsy wine, musky and tweedy, with some nice complexities. The taste is dry, luscious, full of fruit, and it gives me a nice feeling of fields, woods, and crisp autumn days. Price range: 750 ml, $2.62–4.49.

TTT GEYSER PEAK CALIFORNIA CHABLIS 1980   Produced & bottled by Geyser Peak Winery, Geyserville, California. Rating: 10+. Distribution: B. Warning! This is a Chablis in the French style, so if you're looking for flowers and honey, you'd better look elsewhere. On the other hand, if you want a dignified Chablis to serve with the salmon trout, this light lemony-colored Chablis may be the ticket. The nose is oaky and austere, and the taste is dry, straightforward, with restrained fruit and good acid. If you've never tried a Chablis like this, now's the time! Price range: 1.5 l, $4.49–6.49.

GIACOBAZZI BIANCO   Produced & bottled by Giacobazzi Grandi Vini, S.p.A., Nonantola, Italy Rating:

7. Distribution: A. Italian wines of this general type—sweet and effervescent—have swept the United States, and in one way it's not hard to see why. Young quaffers like the sweetness and that *spritzig* mouth-feel. However, they're drinking them up so fast they don't notice that the aroma is common and deficient in fruit, and the taste, once the bubbles are gone, is dank and depressing. But why should I try to dissuade anyone? If you like it, drink it! Price range: 750 ml, $2.99–4.99.

GIUMARRA VINEYARDS CHABLIS OF CALIFORNIA Produced & bottled by Giumarra Vineyards, Edison, California. Rating: 7+. Distribution: C. This Chablis has a pale, lemony color and a somewhat bashful, middle-of-the-road nose. It also has a decent flavor, but I get a somewhat elderly feeling from it. Drinkable, but no zip. Price range: 750 ml, $2.49–3.99.

GIUMARRA CHABLIS BLANC OF CALIFORNIA 1980 Produced & bottled by Giumarra Vineyards, Edison, California. Rating: 7. Distribution: B. This wine is a lovely golden color with flashes of green. The nose has a pleasing hint of lemon, but the taste is restrained and stiff, and relatively sweet. It's certainly not a bad wine by any means, but it's not a lot to get worked up about, either. Price range: 750 ml, $2.49–3.99.

GIUMARRA VINEYARDS CHARDONNAY OF CALIFORNIA 1980 Produced & bottled by Giumarra Vineyards, Edison, California. Rating: 7. Distribution: B. The color is a handsome, pale gold, but the nose has a pungent component that seems strident and un-lovely. The taste is slightly sweet, contains fruit, is somewhat light on acid, and without having any-thing terribly wrong, isn't very fetching, either. Price range: 750 ml, $3.59–4.99.

GIUMARRA VINEYARDS FRENCH COLOMBARD OF CALI-FORNIA Produced & bottled by Giumarra Vine-yards, Edison, California. Rating: 7+. Distribution: B. Unfortunately, the nose of this greenish gold wine is somewhat baked, which tends to limit the perfor-mance of what would otherwise be perfectly respect-able fruit. The semidry taste has lots of fruit, but it's put at something of a disadvantage by a slight bitter-ness. Price range: 750 ml, $2.69–4.49.

GIUMARRA VINEYARDS GREEN HUNGARIAN OF CALI-FORNIA 1980 Produced & bottled by Giumarra Vine-yards, Edison, California. Rating: 7+ Distribution: B. The color is pale saffron. The nose has a pungent reedy-grassy quality that hides the fruit. The taste is dry and fruity, with good acid, but it still has a hot-weather character that keeps it from scoring. Price range: 750 ml, $3.29–4.99.

⟐⟐ GIUMARRA VINEYARDS JOHANNISBERG RIESLING OF CALIFORNIA 1981 Produced & bottled by Giumarra Vineyards, Edison, California. Rating: 9+. Distribu-tion: B. There's a faint tawny cast to this golden wine, and it has a delightful nose, warm and summery, quite direct, and full of round, ripe fruit. Taste it, and you'll find it supple, drinkable, and somewhat sweet, with a modest complexity of fruit flavors. Price range: 750 ml, $3.49–5.25.

▼▼ GRAN CONDAL 1981   Produced & bottled by Bodegas Rioja Santiago, Haro, Spain. Rating: 9. Distribution: C. This Spanish white is a trifle reserved, a parchment-yellow wine with a quiet, conventional nose and a somber, semidry taste that somehow seems thoughty and dignified. There's fruit and a touch of sweetness in the taste, and the acid balance is good. You won't jump up and down when you encounter it, yet it's a nice wine for "sometime." Price range: 750 ml, $1.69–4.49.

▼ GRÃO VASCO DÃO 1980   Produced & bottled by Vinicola do Vale do Dão, Lda., Viseu, Portugal. Rating: 8+. Distribution: C. A lovely color: sunny, greenish gold. An unexceptional nose: decently fruity, but nothing special. A modestly dignified taste: dry, with fruit present but restrained. Not an amazing wine, but an acceptable one that is a notch better than average. Price range: 750 ml, $3.48–5.49.

▼▼▼ HARDY'S JOHANNISBERG RIESLING 1981   Produced & bottled by Thomas Hardy & Sons, Pty. Ltd., of South Australia. Rating: 10+. Distribution: C. There's an air of propriety about this wine; a number of disparate qualities seem to be held in a pleasant balance. The taste is generously fruity and has a decent, refreshing balance, yet it's dry and somewhat formal. The nose is guilty of a slight stuffiness, but it shows its fruit acceptably and is pleasant enough when chilled. Sum it all up, and you've got a very nice—and very proper—wine. Price range: 750 ml, $3.99–5.49.

♆ INGLENOOK NORTH COAST COUNTIES VINTAGE CHA-
BLIS 1980   Produced & bottled by Inglenook Vineyards, Rutherford, California. Rating: 8+. Distribution: A. This sunny, golden wine has a charming
pollen-and-flowers bouquet, and a moderate dryness
with some pleasing fruit. But it's flabby and lacks the
energy that a better acid balance would give it. Nice,
nevertheless. Price range: 1.5 l, $4.99–6.49.

♆♆♆♆ INGLENOOK NORTH COAST COUNTIES VINTAGE
CHARDONNAY 1981   Produced & bottled by Inglenook
Vineyards, Rutherford, California. Rating: 11+. Distribution: A. This Chardonnay is a pale, greenish
gold, and has a full, round, quietly fruity nose. In the
mouth you'll find it charming, generous, and full of
mixed fruit flavors—grapes, peaches, nectarines. It
could use a touch more acid, but when a wine is this
nice, why quibble? Price range: 750 ml, $3.99–6.99.

♆ INGLENOOK NAPA VALLEY CHENIN BLANC 1981   Produced & bottled by Inglenook Vineyards, Rutherford,
California. Rating: 8+. Distribution: A. This is a
pale, straw-colored wine with a nose that is nearly
mute. The taste, however, comes through pleasantly
enough as crisp and dry, and it's a wine with somewhat underripe fruit and a fair acid balance. Price
range: 750 ml, $3.96–5.99.

♆ INGLENOOK NAVALLE FRENCH COLOMBARD OF CALI-
FORNIA   Vinted & bottled by Inglenook Vineyards,
San Francisco, California. Rating: 8+. Distribution:
A. A decent wine, pale as winter butter, one notch

better than middle-of-the-road. The nose is fairly conventional, no surprises, and the taste is quite presentable, if unamazing. It's semidry, and shows a fair quantity of ripe, healthy fruit. Price range: 1.5 l, $3.66–5.49.

INGLENOOK NAVALLE RHINE OF CALIFORNIA   Vinted & bottled by Inglenook Vineyards, San Francisco, California. Rating: 7+. Distribution: A. This is one of those middle-of-the-road, conventional wines. Acceptable, of course. Exciting, forget it. It has a light honey color, some fruit in the nose, and an almost complete absence of character in the taste—sweet, flat, undefined. Still, no need to throw the bottle away. Join CIGI instead: Chill-It-Gulp-It. Price range: 1.5 l, $3.49–5.49.

♈♈♈♈ INGLENOOK NORTH COAST COUNTIES VINTAGE RHINE 1979   Produced & bottled by Inglenook Vineyards, Rutherford, California. Rating: 11+. Distribution: A. Aha! A medium gold wine with a piquant nose that exudes the fragrance of ripe nectarines! Very nice! When you taste it, you'll feel that Inglenook has raided a fruit stand, because the light, slightly sweet taste is loaded with luscious fruit flavors. Low in acid, naturally, but who cares? Price range: 750 ml, $3.96–5.99.

♈♈♈♈ INGLENOOK NAPA VALLEY GREY RIESLING 1981 Produced & bottled by Inglenook Vineyards, Rutherford, California. Rating: 12. Distribution: A. It's very pleasant to drink white wines that are charming and inconsequential, but it's also very nice to encounter one where "there's something there." Take this pale tawny Grey Riesling. For starters, it has a fetching, delicately feminine fruit bouquet. The taste is medium dry, with touches of sweetness, low but adequate acid, and it has a smooth, sunshiny mélange of charming fruit flavors. It's not a mindless white. There *is* something there, something very nice, something to think about as you sniff, drink, and enjoy it. Price range: 750 ml, $3.96–5.99.

ΨΨΨ INGLENOOK NAVALLE RIESLING OF CALIFORNIA Vinted & bottled by Inglenook Vineyards, Rutherford, California. Rating: 11. Distribution: A. This tawny-gold wine has a clean, mildly aromatic, mildly serious, fruit-and-flower nose. In the mouth it has a light, summery, honeyed, low-acid sweetness. It's sweet enough, in fact, to be a dessert wine. Or you could drink it, chilled and nectarlike, as you lie in your hammock on a summer afternoon, hoping the phone won't ring. Price range: 1.5 l, $3.66–5.29.

Ψ JACARÉ CRYSTAL BLANC Vinted & bottled by Jacaré Wine Merchants, San Francisco, California. Rating: 8. Distribution: A. Another pleasant, unamazing wine. A flaxen wine with an unamazing nose with an unamazing amount of fruit in it. The taste is somewhat sweet and modestly fruity, with relatively low acid. It's better than the chill 'n' gulpers, but that doesn't keep it from being just another pleasant, unamazing wine. But who needs to be amazed all the time? Price range: 750 ml, $2.27–3.99.

🍷🍷 KAIZER-STULE AUSTRALIAN JOHANNISBERG RIES-
LING 1980   Vintaged & bottled by Kaiser-Stuhl Wine
Distributors Pty. Ltd., Nuriootpa, South Australia.
Rating: 9. Distribution: C. From "down under"
comes a lemon-colored Riesling that's a lot more like
a Chablis than a Riesling. The nose has fruit, but at
the same time is quite formal, with the Chablis gun-
metal quality. The taste is also austere; dry and fruity
with moderate acid. It's a structured wine to go with
the fish course, not a wine full of Australian jollity,
but sedate and serious instead. Price range: 750 ml,
$3.99–5.79.

🍷🍷 KAYSER PIESPORTER MICHELSBERG 1980   Produced
& bottled by Julius Kayser, Traben-Trarbach, Germany. Rating: 9. Distribution: B. Be warned: This is
a wine with a definite personality. The color is very
pale, with a greenish cast, but it's in the nose and
mouth that the wine's individuality shows up. The
nose has a musky, unripe weediness that is not unpleasant, but at the same time may not be for
everyone. The taste is dry, reserved, serious, weedy.
It's formal, austere, definitely not a fun-and-games
kind of wine, but still very pleasant. Price range: 750
ml, $4.39–6.49.

KAYSER ZELLER SCHWARZE KATZ 1981   Produced & bottled by Julius Kayser, Traben-Trarbach, Germany.
Rating: 7+. Distribution: B. The color is pale lemon-
gold. The nose is fruity, but has a faint, stuffy, closed-
in component. The taste is sedate and somewhat oldish, with a faint reediness in among the fruit. It's not

a great wine, but at least you can't say it's faceless! Price range: 750 ml, $3.99–5.79.

♀ CHARLES KRUG CALIFORNIA CHABLIS Made & bottled by Charles Krug Winery, St. Helena, California. Rating: 8+. Distribution: A. Awarding this wine one glass means that it's better than middle-of-the-road, but still not into the big time. The color is fine— medium gold—the nose is acceptable, with no particular pros or cons, and the taste is moderately dry, with adequate fruit and a not unpleasing tartness. Add it all up, and you have a wine that's nice, just not terribly distinguished. Price range: 750 ml, $2.33– 4.49.

♀♀♀ CHARLES KRUG CALIFORNIA CHENIN BLANC 1981 Produced & bottled by Charles Krug Winery, St. Helena, California. Rating: 10+. Distribution: A. The color is a pale, tawny gold. The nose, somewhat reluctant, has a mild apple scent. The taste is moderately dry with medium body, good acid, a wealth of grapes and apples, and a feeling of a healthy, handsome maturity. It has a good finish as well, and it's a nice, well-proportioned wine well worth your trying. Price range: 750 ml, $3.79–5.50.

♀♀♀♀ CHARLES KRUG CALIFORNIA GREY RIESLING 1981 Produced & bottled by Charles Krug Winery, St. Helena, California. Rating: 11+. Distribution: A. This pale-gold Grey Riesling has a youthful, clean, fresh nose that shows lots of ripe fruit as well as a modest and attractive grassiness. The taste is dry and supple, with some breadth to the fruit flavors. It's charming, smooth, and refreshing, and has an air of refinement about it. I think you'll find it a superior wine. Price range: 750 ml, $3.36–5.25.

♥♥ LANCERS VINHO BRANCO 1981   Bottled by J. M. Da Fonseca, Lisbon, Portugal. Rating: 9+. Distribution: A. Lancers has been around a long time, and a lot of people swear by it. They like its effervescent quality, its amiable sweetness, its mild, clean, pleasant but unspectacular nose. To me it's a couple of cuts above the Lambruscos, the Italian chill 'n' gulpers, but nevertheless, it's still a rather simple, unpretentious white wine suitable principally for, well, chilling and gulping on a hot afternoon. Price range: 750 ml, $2.99–4.99.

LANGENBACH LIEBFRAUMILCH 1981 Bottled & shipped by Langenbach & Company, Worms, Germany. Rating: 7+. Distribution: B. There's a faint clothes-closet component in the otherwise fruity nose of this lemon-gold wine, and the taste shares some of this closed-in, slightly bitter quality. It's not a bad wine by any means; it has a good bit of fruit, but the stuffiness keeps it from being all the things you wish a wine would be. Price range: 750 ml, $3.49–5.49.

♥♥ LANGENBACH MOSELBLUMCHEN 1980 Bottled & shipped by Langenbach, Worms, Germany. Rating: 9. Distribution: B. This parchment-yellow wine has a very decent, fruity, unpretentious nose, with a slight muskiness. The taste is modestly dry and dignified, structured, serious, with the same slight musky quality. Price range: 750 ml, $3.59–5.49.

🍷🍷🍷 L'EPAYRIE BLANC DE BLANCS Bottled by Armand Roux, France. Rating: 10. Distribution: C. You'll like this tawny-gold wine if your taste in wines runs to the conservative. The nose is calm, settled, sedate, dignified, with the fruit muted by the cooperage. The taste is similarly restrained. It's dry and pleasant and has a good acid balance, but it's all terribly tailored, sophisticated, and no-nonsense. Does that sound like you? Price range: 750 ml, $2.79–4.49.

🍷🍷🍷 LE PIAT D'OR VIN DE TABLE FRANCAIS Bottled by Piat Père & Fils, Chapelle-de-Guinchay, France. Rating: 11. Distribution: C. This is a very conservative, adult wine, built along formal lines. The color is a tawny gold, the nose has lots of pleasantly exotic fruit which it displays in a dignified, slightly closed-in manner. The taste is dry, refined, sedate, with a slight oakiness and a refreshing balance. It's a serious wine, nothing racy about it, just the right kind of wine for those times when a little seriousness is called for. Price range: 750 ml, $2.59–4.39.

🍷🍷🍷🍷 ALEXIS LICHINE WHITE TABLE WINE OF FRANCE Bottled by Alexis Lichine & Co., Gironde, France. Rating: 11+. Distribution: C. This sunny, golden import has a wholesome, clean, manly nose, lithe and serious and oaky. The taste is dry and crisp, and it's a straightforward, conservative wine, vigorous and pleasantly adult. It has a feeling of solidity and good workmanship, like clothing that has style without being flashy, and is made from good fabric. It's a wine you can drink a long time without getting tired of it, and without going broke. Price range: 750 ml, $1.98–3.99.

🍷 LOS HERMANOS CHABLIS   Cellared & bottled by Los Hermanos Vineyards, St. Helena, California. Rating: 8. Distribution: A. This pale straw-colored wine throws off attractive greenish glints as you turn it in the glass and sniff its mild, clean, moderately fruity bouquet. When you taste it, you find it just off-dry, refreshing in spite of its low acidity, respectably fruity, and eminently drinkable. Price range: 1.5 l, $3.33–4.99.

LOS HERMANOS CALIFORNIA CHENIN BLANC   Cellared & bottled by Los Hermanos Vineyards, St. Helena, California. Rating: 7+. Distribution: A. The color is a greenish gold. The nose is rather commonplace and has a pungent, reedy component—not terrible, just not terrific. The taste is moderately dry, with fruit showing, but it seems baked, and the whole effect is pretty sedate and unspectacular. Price range: 1.5 l, $3.49–4.99.

🍷🍷 LOS HERMANOS LIGHT CHENIN BLANC   Cellared & bottled by Los Hermanos Vineyards, St. Helena, California. Rating: 9+. Distribution: A. When you drink this wine you are not really aware you are drinking a "light" wine. Of course, its 9 percent alcohol content is not too far from the 11 percent that many non-"light" wines contain. The color is a pale parchment, and the nose is light and clean, an uncomplicated mixture of pleasant fruit and flowers. The taste is on the dividing line between dry and sweet, with lots of clean, simple fruit and rather low acid. It's a straightforward, unpretentious wine that manages a little charm while only offering 62 calories for every 100 milliliters you drink. Price range: 1.5 l, $2.50–4.49.

▼▼ LOS HERMANOS LIGHT FRENCH COLOMBARD Cellared & bottled by Los Hermanos Vineyards, St. Helena, California. Rating: 9+. Distribution: A. Here's another 9–percenter, a decent better-than-middle-of-the-roader that offers only 61 calories per 100 milliliters. It's the color of pale straw, with a nose that shows some fruit, but has a stuffy-closet side to it, too. The taste is quite pleasant, medium-dry, with lots of respectable fruit, a bit staid perhaps, but at the same time very obliging and refreshing. Price range: 1.5 l, $2.50–4.49.

▼▼ LOS REYES VINO BLANCO Produced & bottled by Pedro Domecq, Los Reyes, Mexico. Rating: 9+. Distribution: C. Look at the rich, golden color of this wine, then sniff its delicate, modestly complex fruit-and-flower bouquet. Finally, taste its fruity, fresh, feminine flavor. It's fairly dry, and in spite of having relatively low acid, is a very pleasant offering from "South of the Border." Price range: 750 ml, $2.99–4.49.

▼▼ MARQUÉS DE CACERES RIOJA 1979 Shipped by Union Viti-Vinicola Viñedos en Cenicero, Spain. Rating: 10. Distribution: B. A buttercup-yellow wine with a forthright, somewhat pungent nose, full of just-ripe grapes and with a slight touch of grassiness. The taste: dry, sedate, punctilious, orderly, formal, precise. It has plenty of fruit, however. It's a nice wine, but I've always felt the Rioja region shouldn't try to make white wines when it makes so many good reds. Price range: 750 ml, $3.25–5.99.

ŸŸŸ MARQUÉS DE RISCAL WHITE WINE 1979   Bottled by Vinos Blancos de Castilla, S.A., Rueda, Spain. Rating: 10+. Distribution: B. If you like oak, this is your wine; it has more oak than grapes. It's a very serious, stern, no-nonsense dry wine, and long exposure to an oak barrel is what made it that way. The color is a lively greenish gold, and the nose is almost belligerently forthright and has a blunt, gun-metal quality, the fruit being restrained almost to stuffiness. The taste is similarly sober and austere, with a life-is-real-life-is-earnest quality. So how did it get a three-glass rating? Well, some people really love severe, oaky wines, and for those people, this is an excellent buy. Price range: 750 ml, $2.25–6.49.

ŸŸŸŸ LOUIS M. MARTINI CALIFORNIA CHABLIS   Prepared & bottled by Louis M. Martini, St. Helena, California. Rating: 11+. Distribution: A. Here's a real value! A sunny, golden wine with a charming nose full of ripe fruit and sunshine, and a rich, elegant, mouth-filling taste. It's a fairly dry wine with good acid, a well-bred wine of pleasing dimensions, and a great bargain to boot. Price range: 750 ml, $2.49–4.49.

Ÿ LOUIS M. MARTINI NORTH COAST DRY CHENIN BLANC   Produced & bottled by Louis M. Martini, St. Helena, California. Rating: 8+. Distribution: A. This parchment-pale wine has a shallow iced-tea aroma that is unimpressive but acceptable. Although it's a bit thin in the mouth, it's also dry, zesty, refreshing, and full of barely ripe fruit. Price range: 750 ml, $3.18–5.29.

ỸỸỸỸ LOUIS M. MARTINI CALIFORNIA GEWURZTRAMINER 1980 Produced & bottled by Louis M. Martini, St. Helena, California. Rating: 11+. Distribution: A. You're going to like this lovely, lemon-colored wine. On one hand, it has a voluptuous, nectarlike bouquet that is deep, rounded, floral, full of fruit and fruit sugars. On the other hand, the taste is surprisingly dry and crisp, with lots of delicious, spicy fruit and a carefree feeling of expansiveness. The acid is a touch light, but you won't mind—everything else is so opulent and controlled you'll only have sensations of pleasure. Price range: 750 ml, $3.59–6.00.

MARTINI & ROSSI BIANCO DI CUSTOZA 1980 Produced & bottled by LE.GI., Bardolino, Italy. Rating: 7+. Distribution: C. A beautiful wine to look at: rich, lemony, golden. Not such a beautiful wine to smell: slightly baked. So how about tasting? Well, it's dry, somewhat tart, with decent acid and simple fruit. A decent, unexceptional wine. Price range: 750 ml, $3.99–5.49.

ỸỸ MASI SOAVE CLASSICO SUPERIORE 1980 Bottled by Masi Agricola, S.P.A., S. Ambrogio di Valpolicella, Italy. Rating: 9. Distribution: C. As a category, Soave wines have been termed "inoffensive and good-natured," which to a large extent describes this one.

The color is a charming greenish gold, and the nose is small, decent, and won't keep you up nights savoring its memory. The taste is dry, full of pleasant if somewhat unspecified fruit, and the acid balance is quite good, making it a nice, refreshing, inoffensive, good-natured wine. Price range: 750 ml, $3.49–5.49.

♈♈ MASSON LIGHT PREMIUM CALIFORNIA LIGHT CHABLIS   Made & bottled by Paul Masson, Saratoga, California. Rating: 9. Distribution: A. Thinness statistics: 7.1 percent alcohol, 49 calories per 100 milliliters. Tasting statistics: sunny gold color. Obliging, fruity, somewhat grassy nose. Dry, slender, light-hearted flavor, a bit thin, but cheerful and accommodating nevertheless, due to its refreshing acid balance. Price range: 750 ml, $2.25–4.39.

♈ PAUL MASSON RARE PREMIUM CALIFORNIA CHABLIS Made & bottled by Paul Masson Vineyards, Saratoga, California. Rating: 8+. Distribution: A. This is an attractive, genial wine, pale amber in color, with a decent if unexceptional nose. The taste is pleasingly fruity and would be even more pleasing with a slightly higher acid level. Still, it's amiable enough, and it doesn't cost an arm and a leg, so why carp? Price range: 750 ml, $2.21–3.99.

♈♈ PAUL MASSON CALIFORNIA CHENIN BLANC 1980 Produced & bottled by Paul Masson Vineyards, Saratoga, California. Rating: 9+. Distribution: A. The nose of this clear, golden wine is brash and aggressive, with a kind of pushy, green-fruit aroma that appeals to the satyr in me. The taste is off-dry, with a boatload of fruit and a second boatload of acid, which makes the whole production very refreshing indeed. Price range: 750 ml, $2.28–4.49.

PAUL MASSON CALIFORNIA FRENCH COLOMBARD 1980 Produced & bottled by Paul Masson Vineyards, Saratoga, California. Rating: 7+. Distribution: A. The color is straw, with flashes of green. The nose is unexceptional, fruity, and has a slight bitter note. The taste is decent enough, lightly sweet with fair acid, but marred by the same bitter note found in the nose. Price range: 750 ml, $2.28–4.49.

PAUL MASSON RARE PREMIUM CALIFORNIA RHINE   Produced & bottled by Paul Masson Vineyards, Saratoga, California. Rating: 7+. Distribution: A. The color is pale gold, and the nose is decently fruity. There's something in the taste, however, that holds this wine back. It's not its lack of acid, because most California Rhines have the same shortcoming. Rather, it's a faint, but definite, bitter component, and I'm afraid that it will keep it from becoming anyone's great favorite. Price range: 1.5 l, $3.69–5.75.

♟♟♟♟ PAUL MASSON RHINE CASTLE 1981   Produced & bottled by Paul Masson Vineyards, Saratoga, California. Rating: 11+. Distribution: A. This is a fresh, charming, youthful wine—quite sweet, of course— but very fetching in the way it's put together. The lemony color has flashes of green, the honeyed nose is full of ripe grapes, flowers, orchards, you name it. The taste is equally honeyed, smooth, fruity, a mouth-filling nectar. If Paul M. could just coax a tiny bit of acidity into it, it would score a full five glasses. Price range: 750 ml, $2.37–4.49.

ΨΨ MASSON LIGHT RHINE   Made & bottled by Paul Masson, Saratoga, California. Rating: 9+. Distribution: A. Many "light" wines seem like imitations of "real" wine, but this wheat-colored Rhine is not one of them. It has an innocent nose full of uncomplicated fruit, and the taste has a moderate sweetness, relatively low acid, and the same simple fruit found in the nose. It has more body than most "lights," and this, as much as anything, is what makes it seem more like its higher-alcohol brethren. Oh yes, I almost forgot: 7 percent alcohol, 50 calories per 100 milliliters. Price range: 750 ml, $2.25–4.19.

ΨΨΨ PAUL MASSON CALIFORNIA RIESLING 1980   Produced & bottled by Paul Masson Vineyards, Saratoga, California. Rating: 11. Distribution: A. This lemon-gold Riesling has a fresh, piquant nose, with an attractive grassiness and a generous quantity of assorted fruit. The taste fills the mouth with a moderately dry, full-bodied, fully-ripe flavor, and there are pleasing echoes of its fruit bouquet. Despite a slight lack of acid, it's a supple, drinkable, handsomely mature wine. Price range: 750 ml, $2.28–4.49.

ΨΨΨ PAUL MASSON CALIFORNIA DRY SAUTERNE   Produced & bottled by Paul Masson Vineyards, Saratoga, California. Rating: 10+. Distribution: A. There's a racy, outdoorsy quality to the nose of this lemon-gold Sauterne. It's assertive, rather grassy, and has spice and brambles in the background, along with lots of verve and sophistication. The taste is dry, crisp, lively, refreshing, and full of the same qualities as the nose. The fruit is mixed up with burrs and brambles and lots of other outdoor elements. It's a very nice wine, I think you'll enjoy it. Price range: 750 ml, $2.25–4.19.

♉♉♉ MATEUS WHITE Produced & bottled by Sogrape, Pôrto, Portugal. Rating: 10+. Distribution: A. I've always liked the funny, squat bottle Mateus comes in, and in the case of the white, I also like the contents. The color is light buff, and the nose is dry, decent, and dignified, with the fruitiness held somewhat in the background. The taste is moderately dry, has the same dignity as the nose, and offers a rather attractive hedgerow flavor of brambles and briers along with the fruit. The fact I like it doesn't mean you will, so since it's almost universally available, maybe you'd better try a bottle. Price range: 750 ml, $3.22–5.49.

♉ MAUI BLANC LIGHT DRY PINEAPPLE WINE Produced & bottled by Tedeschi Vineyard and Winery, Ulupalakua, Maui, Hawaii. Rating: 8+. Distribution: C. A surprisingly light and fruity little wine considering its origins in sticky-sweet, overripe, pineapple juice. Its pale color is reminiscent of the sun-drenched yet foggy slopes of Haleakala whence it comes. Unassuming, shy rather than nosy, it's the perfect accompaniment to a light Hawaiian meal of raw fish, opihi, salt pork, and poi. Price range: 750 ml, $4.32–6.49.

🍷 MIRASSOU 1981 MONTEREY COUNTY DRY CHABLIS
Produced & bottled by Mirassou Vineyards, San Jose,
California. Rating: 8. Distribution: B. This tawny
Chablis has a matronly nose and flavor that give it a
somewhat austere character. It's not a defect, it's just
that kind of Chablis, made more or less in the French
manner. It's dry, it has adequate fruit, and it probably goes best with a fish dish. Price range: 750 ml,
$2.73–4.99.

🍷🍷🍷 MOMMESSIN CUVEE SAINT PIERRE Shipped by
Mommessin, La Grange Saint Pierre, France. Rating:
10. Distribution: B. Mommessin has given us a
honey-colored wine with a dry, lightly fruity bouquet and a sprightly yet dignified taste. In the mouth
it's nicely dry and has good acid, along with a crisp,
slightly unripe flavor. It's one of those wines that will
let the flavor of a delicate fish dish shine through.
Price range: 750 ml, $2.99–4.99.

CK MONDAVI CALIFORNIA CHABLIS Made & bottled
by C. Mondavi & Sons, St. Helena, California. Rating: 7+. Distribution: A. The lovely greenish gold
color of this wine promises more than the wine delivers. Still, it's very drinkable, so don't go away. The
nose tries for the gravity of a French Chablis, but
misses by being a bit strident. The taste is moderately
dry, with a pleasant sweet-and-sour tartness, but on
the whole the wine seems a trifle oldish. Price range:
1.5 l, $2.97–4.49.

🍷🍷🍷🍷 ROBERT MONDAVI WHITE 1981 Produced & bottled by Robert Mondavi Winery, Oakville, California.

Rating: 12. Distribution: A. In this wine Robert Mondavi offers us a crisp, dry white with substantial oak aging. It's a nice wine with a sunny blond color, a well-bred, oaky nose, and a structured austerity in its taste. Don't expect flowers or a cornucopia of fruit—it's not that kind of wine. Look instead for a wine that's lean, aristocratic, and a darned good value! Price range: 1.5 l, $2.97–6.99.

ȲȲȲȲȲ MONTEREY VINEYARD MONTEREY COUNTY CHENIN BLANC 1981 Produced & bottled by The Monterey Vineyard, Gonzales, California. Rating: 13. Distribution: B. This is a lovely wine. Its straw color is brilliant. The nose is instantly accessible, generous, full of assorted fruits and flowers. It's a nice experience just to sit there and sniff it. But when you do get around to drinking, you'll find it a wine that's sprightly, supple, light on the tongue, and has a honeyed finish that will make you think you've been drinking diluted nectar. Maybe you have! Price range: 750 ml, $3.40–5.99.

ȲȲȲȲȲ MONTEREY VINEYARD SAN LUIS OBISPO COUNTY FUME BLANC 1980 Produced & bottled by The Monterey Vineyard, Gonzales, California. Rating: 13. Distribution: B. Another winner, friends! Color: barley, with flashes of green. Nose: lovely, ripe, round, outdoorsy, with a complex, oak-fruit bouquet and lots of wholesome energy and elegance. Taste: dry, vigorous, a broad range of flavors, the fruit and oak working nicely together. Good acid, lots of zip, lots of sunshiny flavor. One of the best, so by all means, give it a try! Price range: 750 ml, $3.98–6.49.

ȲȲȲȲ MONTEREY VINEYARD MONTEREY COUNTY
GEWURZTRAMINER 1981 Produced & bottled by The
Monterey Vineyard, Gonzales, California. Rating:
11+. Distribution: B. If you like wines with any kind
of sweetness, you will most certainly like this light,
sunny number! The nose is round and rich, and has
the delicacy of the bloom on a plum. The taste is
seductively sweet, with a charming nectar quality,
and light but decent acid. The whole thing is a lovely
union of ripe fruits, well proportioned, a handsome
wine indeed. Price range: 750 ml, $3.98–6.49.

ȲȲȲȲ MONTEREY VINEYARD MONTEREY COUNTY PINOT
BLANC 1979 Produced & bottled by The Monterey
Vineyard, Gonzales, California. Rating: 12. Distribution: B. The color is a sunshiny lemon. The nose is full
of ripe fruit, spice, and vigor, dignified but not
stuffy. The taste is dry, crisp, nervy. There's lots of
lovely fruit, zesty and tart, and enough spice and acid
to make drinking this wine a very exhilarating experience. Price range: 750 ml, $3.40–5.99.

ȲȲ MONTEREY VINEYARD MONTEREY COUNTY JOHAN-
NISBERG RIESLING 1981 Produced & bottled by The
Monterey Vineyard, Gonzales, California. Rating:
9+. Distribution: B. This sunny, golden wine has an
engaging fruit-sugar bouquet that is clean and fresh,
and a fruity, off-dry taste I think you will enjoy. It's a
moderately serious wine, not all hearts and flowers,
with a nice feeling of structure. Price range: 750 ml,
$4.45–6.99.

ᵀᵀᵀᵀ MONTEREY VINEYARD CLASSIC CALIFORNIA DRY WHITE 1981 Produced & bottled by The Monterey Vineyard, Gonzales, California. Rating: 11+. Distribution: A. This wine, the color of chaff, has a serious, upright, attractive nose that presents a bouquet of mature fruit with floral overtones. The taste is moderately dry, medium-bodied, with good acid and some lovely mature-fruit flavors. It's a graceful, quietly handsome, meditative wine, well proportioned, full of flavor, and with an excellent finish. Price range: 750 ml, $2.98–4.49.

ᵀᵀᵀ MOREAU BLANC VIN DE TABLE Bottled by J. Moreau & Fils, France. Rating: 11. Distribution: C. This is a rather formal wine, perilously close to being stuffy, but on the whole dry, pleasing, oaky, and dignified. The color is pale greenish gold, and the nose is clean and rounded, its fruit restrained by the oak. The taste mirrors the nose in its dignity and reserve, with the fruit similarly held back and transmuted into slightly more complex flavors. Altogether, it's a rather aristocratic, very refreshing white wine. Well worth a try. Price range: 750 ml, $2.99–4.99.

ᵀᵀᵀᵀ NORTH COAST CELLARS APPELLATION NORTH COAST CHARDONNAY Produced & bottled by North Coast Cellars, Geyserville, California. Rating: 12. Distribution: C. This is a dignified yet amiable wine that I think you'll like a lot. Its golden color has attractive greenish flashes, and its nose is ripe and full, with a deep summer richness. In the mouth it's a complex, sunlit compound of fruit and oak aging—you'll pick up the oak in the nose, too—and all of this, together with a good acid balance, makes it very charming indeed. Price range: 750 ml, $3.97–5.99.

☘ NORTH COAST CELLARS APPELLATION NORTH COAST CHENIN BLANC Produced & bottled by North Coast Cellars, Geyserville, California. Rating: 8. Distribution: C. This is a slightly somber, dryish wine with some light sweetness, plus a nice acid balance that helps it to score. The color is gold with olive tones, and the nose has a mild grassiness along with the fruit. All in all, it's slightly better than middle of the road. Price range: 750 ml, $2.59–4.49.

☘ NORTH COAST CELLARS APPELLATION NORTH COAST FRENCH COLOMBARD Produced & bottled by North Coast Cellars, Geyserville, California. Rating: 8+. Distribution: C. An ingenuous, lightly sweet wine, light gold in color, with a very decent, clean, if somewhat commonplace nose. There's lots of simple fruitiness in the mouth, along with relatively low acid. Bottom line: a pleasant, workaday wine with no great pretentions. Price range: 750 ml, $2.59–4.49.

☘☘☘ NORTH COAST CELLARS APPELLATION NORTH COAST WHITE RIESLING Produced & bottled by North Coast Cellars, Geyserville, California. Rating: 10. Distribution: C. This is a very respectable White Riesling, gilded lemon in color, with a clean, accessible, fruity nose. The taste is moderately dry, with good body, good acid, and a pleasant assortment of fruit flavors. There's no individual characteristic of this wine that will set you on fire, but you'll find that its

various components are all sound, and brought together with some skill and care. Price range: 750 ml,
$2.59–4.49.

♉♉♉ OLARRA BLANCO SECO RIOJA 1978 Produced &
bottled by Bodegas Olarra, Logroño, Spain. Rating:
10+. Distribution: C. It looks like pale honey in a
glass with just a flash of green. The nose is clean,
fresh, and fruity, with subtle, woody overtones. The
taste is dry, crisp, racy, and somewhat exotic. The
fruit is just ripe, and there's a good acid balance. On
the whole, it's a very pleasing, refreshing drink. Price
range: 750 ml, $3.00–4.99.

♉♉♉ ANGELO PAPAGNI BIANCA DI MADERA Cellared &
bottled by Papagni Vineyards, Madera, California.
Rating: 10. Distribution: B. This handsome, lemony
gold wine has a very accessible nose that's full of
fresh, ripe fruit. In the mouth it has a pleasantly viscous, nectarlike quality. It's not overpoweringly
sweet, but gently reminds you that the whole wine
process starts out with fruit and fruit sugars. I think
you'll like it. Price range: 750 ml, $3.99–5.99.

♉♉♉ ANGELO PAPAGNI CHENIN BLANC 1980 Grown,
produced, & bottled by Papagni Vineyards, Madera,
California. Rating: 10+. Distribution: B. You'll find
this deep, lemony-gold Chenin Blanc quite different
from the usual. Instead of having a simple, fruity
nose, this nose is full, serious, powerful, well-
rounded, mature. In the mouth you'll find it robust,
full, generous, and unexpectedly complex for a
Chenin Blanc. In spite of all this seriousness, the wine

is still zesty and fresh, because there's a nice acid balance. Price range: 750 ml, $4.65–5.99.

ỶỶỶỶ ANGELO PAPAGNI MUSCAT ALEXANDRIA 1979 Grown, produced & bottled by Papagni Vineyards, Madera, California. Rating: 11. Distribution: B. This wine, the color of ripe lemons, has a floral, round, handsomely mature nose that displays a pleasing variety of fruit aromas. In the mouth it's big (13.3 percent), semisweet, floral, full-bodied, expansive. There's a rich, voluptuous, nectar quality to the fruit, and in my book it would make a terrific dessert wine. Come to think of it, this *is* my book! Price range: 750 ml, $4.10–5.99.

ỶỶ PAPAGNI VINEYARDS CALIFORNIA WHITE WINE Produced & bottled by Papagni Vineyards, Madera, California. Rating: 9+. Distribution: B. Hold this lemony wine up to the light and you'll see hints of green. Swirl it and smell, and you'll find a slightly austere nose. Take it in your mouth, and you'll find it full and fresh, a harmonious blending of fruit flavors. It's not a remarkable wine, but it's a very pleasant one nevertheless. Price range: 750 ml, $2.49–4.59.

ỶỶỶ PARDUCCI MENDOCINO COUNTY CHABLIS 1981 Produced & bottled by Parducci Wine Cellars, Ukiah, California. Rating: 10. Distribution: B. Most French Chablis are unable to recognize their California cousins, especially if they're like this light-hearted, feminine wine. From its honey color to its ingenuous floral nose, this wine is all charm and affability, fruit and flowers, iced tea and girls in backless summer dresses. The taste is on the edge of dryness, yet it still has an aura of nectar and honey. I wish it had a bit more acid, but I still think you'll enjoy its buoyant simplicity. Price range: 750 ml, $2.98–4.49.

ŸŸŸŸ PARDUCCI MENDOCINO COUNTY FRENCH COL-OMBARD 1981 Produced & bottled by Parducci Wine Cellars, Ukiah, California. Rating: 11+. Distribution: B. Here is a parchment-colored wine that's clean and ingenuous, full of simple charm, well-made and enjoyable. The nose shows a mixture of fruit and iced-tea flavors, and the taste, which is just off dry, has attractive nectar qualities, touches of honey, good body, and a good finish. Overall, this is a supple, sunshiny wine of pleasing simplicity, a sort of all-purpose wine, and I hope you'll give it a try. Price range: 750 ml, $3.44–5.49.

ŸŸŸ PARDUCCI MENDOCINO COUNTY GREEN HUNGAR-IAN 1980 Produced & bottled by Parducci Wine Cellars, Ukiah, California. Rating: 11. Distribution: B. This pale, straw-colored Green Hungarian has a diffident, delicate, ripe-fruit aroma that's clean and full of life. The taste is dry and full of energy, light-hearted and zesty, bursting with healthy, fresh fruit. It has good body, good acid, and a good finish. I think you'll find it a very refreshing accompaniment to many dishes that call for a wine that won't overpower the food, yet still has its own pleasant statement to make. Price range: 750 ml, $3.88–5.39.

ŸŸŸ PARDUCCI VINTAGE WHITE 1981 1980 Produced & bottled by Parducci Wine Cellars, Ukiah, California.

Rating: 11. Distribution: B. The color is parchment yellow. The nose is clean, fresh, and ripe, with delicate, round fruit and a nice feeling of quality. The taste is medium dry, comely, and well proportioned, with tons of wholesome, ripe fruit. It's a wine with charm and suppleness, a sort of light fruit nectar with good body and decent acid, and well worth your trying. Price range: 1.5 l, $4.38–6.19.

�� PARTAGER VIN BLANC   Bottled by Barton & Guestier, Blanquefort, France. Rating: 9+. Distribution: C. This flaxen-colored wine has an austere nose that is dry and dignified. The taste is semidry, fruity, with decent acid, and some more of the somber restraint we associate with austere wines. Some people will say it's not just dignified, it's just stuffy, but I think it's a very decent wine for mealtime occasions when you want to make sure the wine doesn't overpower the food. Price range: 750 ml, $2.03–4.59.

♛♛♛ J. PEDRONCELLI SONOMA COUNTY CHENIN BLANC 1981   Produced & bottled by J. Pedroncelli Winery, Geyserville, California. Rating: 10. Distribution: B. "Wholesome" is the word for this wine. It has a wholesome pale honey color, and the nose, too, although rather shy, is healthy and clean. The taste is semidry, buxom, bursting with round, ripe fruit, and there's even enough acid to give it a modest, pleasing zestiness. Price range: 750 ml, $3.44–5.49.

♛ J. PEDRONCELLI SONOMA COUNTY FRENCH COLOMBARD 1981   Produced & bottled by J. Pedroncelli Winery, Geyserville, California. Rating: 8+. Distribution: B. This is a wine the color of light honey, with an accommodating, nicely fruity nose, and a semi-sweet, mature-fruit taste. You get a pleasant nectarlike sensation in the mouth, with minimum acid, and it's all very simple, unassuming, and rather pleasant. Price range: 750 ml, $2.99–5.29.

ŸŸŸŸ J. PEDRONCELLI SONOMA COUNTY GEWURZ-TRAMINER 1981 Produced & bottled by J. Pedroncelli Winery, Geyserville, California. Rating: 11+. Distribution: B. This fruity, floral wine is the color of ripe wheat. The nose is ripe and accommodating, a rich autumn harvest of fruit aromas. Taste it, and you'll encounter that same aromatic harvest—apricots, peaches, nectarines, everything full and round, ripe and feminine. The acid is modest but adequate. It's a great wine to serve with dessert. Price range: 750 ml, $3.99–5.99.

ŸŸŸ J. PEDRONCELLI SONOMA COUNTY JOHANNISBERG RIESLING 1981 Produced & bottled by J. Pedroncelli Winery, Geyserville, California. Rating: 10. Distribution: B. This pale, tawny wine has a charming, summery, fruit-bloom nose. In the mouth you'll find it lightly sweet, with decent acid. Over all, it has a luscious, midsummer freshness that I like very much. I think you will, too. Price range: 750 ml, $3.99–5.99.

ŸŸŸŸ J. PEDRONCELLI SONOMA COUNTY SONOMA WHITE WINE Produced & bottled by J. Pedroncelli Winery, Geyserville, California. Rating: 12. Distribution: B. Here's a nice, fresh, lively white wine that won't break the bank. It's straw-colored and has a spirited, grassy, puckish nose with lots of lovely fresh fruit. The taste is dry, almost tart, nicely textured, with the same fruity-grassy sensations you'll encounter in the nose. There's a nice feeling of breadth to this wine. It has decent acid, good body, and a good finish. I think you'll find it extremely pleasant. Price range: 750 ml, $1.99–3.49.

♟♟♟ PÈRE PATRIARCHE BLANC DE BLANCS   Bottled by Patriarche Père & Fils, Meursanges, France. Rating: 10+. Distribution: C. This is a pleasant, conservative, self-assured import that can match any number of delicately flavored dishes. The color is a rich gold, with flashes of olive. The nose is sober and dignified, with its somewhat reserved fruit, and the aroma is a bit closed in and tamed. The taste is similarly conservative, dry, full-bodied, a pillar of the community. It's a quality wine with no surprises, a well-made, well-balanced wine that you should pick up next time you happen across a bottle. Price range: 750 ml, $2.66–5.49.

♟♟♟ PINOT BIANCO DEL VENETO 1981   Produced & bottled by Cantina Viticoltori, Ponte di Piave, Italy. Rating: 10. Distribution: C. The color is pale gold. The nose is readily approachable, pleasant and uncomplicated, full of ripe fruit and a summery sweetness. The taste is semidry, crisp, fresh, full of barely ripe fruit. It's not a big wine, but it's a jovial one, full of youthful energy, a good wine to serve with those dishes that need the accompaniment of something refreshing yet delicate. Price range: 750 ml, $3.39–5.25.

♟♟ PINOT GRIGIO 1980   Produced & bottled by Cantina Viticoltori, Ponte di Piave, Italy. Rating: 9. Distribution: C. This lemon-gold wine has a clean, fruity, straightforward nose, and a dry, tart, energetic taste. It's a wine of no particular complexity, but its freshness and its crisp, generous helping of barely ripe fruit give it a vigor and attractiveness I like. Price range: 750 ml, $3.99–5.79.

♟♟♟♟ PORTO PALO VINO DA TAVOLA BIANCO   Produced & bottled by Cantina Settesoli, Menfi, Italy. Rating: 11+. Distribution: C. This Sicilian wine has a silvery, straw color, and a somewhat oaky nose that is clear and clean, and has an earthy wholesomeness. The taste is much the same—dry, crisp, oaky, with lots of fruit and lots of quiet vigor. It's a solid, well-made wine, handsome but not showy, the kind of wine you can drink over a long period without growing tired of it. Of course, if you want jolly fruits and flowers, you'll have to look elsewhere. This wine is serious, direct, and incidentally, quite a value. Price range: 1.5 l, $2.89–4.99.

♟♟ PREMIAT TARNAVE CASTLE RIESLING 1979   Produced & bottled in Romania. Imported by Monsieur Henri, New York, New York. Rating: 9. Distribution: B. Every now and then you want to drink a wine that's a bit different from your everyday fare. Well, this handsome lemon-colored wine from Romania is a candidate. The nose is racy, aromatic, tinged with a not unpleasant grassy-reedy quality. The taste is generously fruity, somewhat sweet, mouth-filling, a bit short on acid, and has the same grassy notes you detected in the nose. It's not for every night, but it would be nice now and then. Price range; 750 ml, $1.88–4.99.

♈♈♈ PREMIAT VALEA DRY RIESLING 1979   Bottled in Romania. Imported by Monsieur Henri, New York, New York. Rating: 10+. Distribution: B. Premiat's Valea is dry, spare, crisp, fresh, well balanced, and definitely a foreign experience. The nose is serious, spare, austere, and shows more bark and herbs than grapes. It's an interesting wine, a refreshing wine, a wine of quality. It's also one of your few chances to look behind the Iron Curtain. At least they have some good wine there! Price range: 750 ml, $1.88–4.99.

♈♈♈ PRINCIPATO CHARDONNAY DI TRENTO 1981   Produced & bottled by Nuova Organizzazione Enologica Soc. Coop., Ravina, Italy. Rating: 10+. Distribution: C. This is a sunshiny, expansive wine with a lot to offer for the money. The color is a pale, greenish gold. The nose is simple and clean, nothing to go into ecstasies about, but very decent and companionable. The taste is dry, clean, straightforward, with a slight, pleasant grassiness and a lot of attractive country vigor. It's full of lovely fruit, it has good acid, it's refreshing, what more do you want? Price range: 1.5 l, $4.00–7.99.

♈ PRIVILEGIO DEL REY SANCHO RIOJA 1980   Produced & bottled by Sogeviñas Elciego, Alava, Spain. Rating: 8+. Distribution: C. Here's the old question: Is it dignified or is it stuffy? The nose is so reserved and oldish you may vote with the stuffy contingent. On the other hand, the taste is so dry, tart, and uncomplicated you may decide, along with me, that the reserve and restrained fruit are indications of modest dignity. Price range: 750 ml, $3.79–6.25.

RIUNITE BIANCO Produced & bottled by Cantine Coop. Riunite, Reggio Emilia, Italy. Rating: 6. Distribution: A. Who am I to put down the largest selling import in America? I know that Riunite's effervescent sweetness has captured the hearts, minds, and livers of countless Americans, yet I have to say that this white version of the basic red Lambrusco has a nose that is rank and a taste that is banal. Too bad. Price range: 750 ml, $2.34–3.99.

RIVERSIDE FARMS CHENIN BLANC NORTHERN CALIFORNIA 1981 Made & bottled by L. Foppiano Wine Company, Healdsburg, California. Rating: 8. Distribution: B. This straw-colored wine has an attractive, small nose, clean and demure, with delicate floral accents. The taste is fairly dry, with lots of plain, healthy fruit, and a slight, but not uncommon, acid deficiency. Price range: 750 ml, $2.77–4.29.

RIVERSIDE FARMS FRENCH COLOMBARD 1981 Made & bottled by Foppiano Wine Company, Healdsburg, California. Rating: 7+. Distribution: B. This light, barley-colored wine has a mild, decent, unpretentious nose, and an equally mild, decent, unpretentious taste. It's simple, fruity, semisweet, low in acid, and sits squarely in the middle of the road. Price range: 750 ml, $2.77–4.29.

ŸŸŸŸ RIVERSIDE FARMS PREMIUM DRY WHITE Made & bottled by L. Foppiano Wine Company, Healdsburg, California. Rating: 11+. Distribution: B. Here's a sleeper, a lot of value for a very reasonable sum of money. Foppiano has given us a straw-colored wine with a lovely, fruit-bloom bouquet that is rich and refined, delicate and charming. It's as though clusters of clean, ripe grapes had been plucked from a flower garden. In the mouth you'll find it medium dry with hints of sweetness, medium-bodied, smooth, buttery, and full of round, comfortable, fruit flavors. It's a bit light on acid, but I think you'll agree this is a very modest flaw, given all the other goodies. Price range: 750 ml, $2.19–3.99.

SAINT-CROIX-DU-MONT 1980 Bottled & shipped by Dourthe & Cie, Gironde, France. Rating: 5. Distribution: C. A stuffy, strident, closed-in nose sets the tone for this gilded, honey-colored wine, and the taste is no better—sweetish, flat, and baked. Stay away. Price range: 750 ml, $3.99–5.49.

ŸŸ SAN MARTIN CALIFORNIA CHABLIS 1980 Produced & bottled by San Martin Winery, San Martin, California. Rating: 9. Distribution: B. This dry, parchment-yellow wine has an austere dignified nose with fruit present but held in restraint. In the mouth it gives a pleasing performance, and the total impression is one of dignity and reserve, a nicely balanced wine made from slightly underripe fruit, overall very crisp and refreshing. Price range: 750 ml, $2.78–3.99.

ŸŸŸ SAN MARTIN SAN LUIS OBISPO COUNTY CHENIN BLANC 1980 Produced & bottled by San Martin Winery, San Martin, California. Rating: 10+. Distribution: B. This lovely, pale, straw-colored wine displays an attractive collection of fruit and flowers in its nose. The taste is a pleasing blend of fruit and honey, full and round. It could use a touch more acid, but since it tastes so good, why quibble? Price range: 750 ml, $2.99–5.49.

ΨΨΨΨ SAN MARTIN SAN LUIS OBISPO COUNTY SOFT CHENIN BLANC 1980   Produced & bottled by San Martin Winery, San Martin, California. Rating: 11+. Distribution: B. The light honey color of this wine is the first sign of the wonders within. The aromatic nose has unusual spicy, musky overtones that may surprise you, but I think you'll find them quite appealing. The taste is also a pleasant surprise, a generous, honeyed basket of sweet, ripe grapes with hints of exotic spice. The other thing you should know about it is that, although it's not billed as a "light" wine, its alcohol content is only 8.2 percent! Give it a try. Price range: 750 ml, $3.89–5.49.

ΨΨΨ SAN MARTIN RHINE 1981   Produced & bottled by San Martin Winery, San Martin, California. Rating: 11. Distribution: B. This straw-colored wine has a mannerly, fruity, summery nose that is very attractive, and displays the honeyed flavors of peaches and blackberries in its taste. The acid is low, but on the whole I don't think that will bother you if you're looking for a well-structured, somewhat sweet white wine. Price range: 750 ml, $2.79–4.29.

ΨΨΨΨ SAN MARTIN RIVERSIDE COUNTY EMERALD RIESLING 1980   Produced & bottled by San Martin Winery, San Martin, California. Rating: 11+. Distribution: B. The color: light barley shot with green. The nose: fresh, sunny, crisp, harmonious, inviting. It has depth, roundness, touches of real class. The taste: medium dry, fully ripe fruit, mature and elegant, a wine with a formal structure and a good acid balance. It's a charming wine, a wine for adult tastes. And you are an adult, aren't you? Price range: 750 ml, $3.98–5.79.

♆ SAN MARTIN CALIFORNIA WHITE TABLE WINE   Produced & bottled by San Martin Winery, San Martin, California. Rating: 8. Distribution: B. This is a simple, well-made wine that will never set anyone on fire, but still has a quality that makes it better than middle-of-the-road. There's pleasant fruit in both the nose and the mouth, some moderate sweetness, a decent balance, and you can afford it. Price range: 1.5 l, $3.39–5.49.

♆♆♆ STA. HELENA 1979 Produced & bottled by Achaia-Clauss Wine Company, Patras, Greece. Rating: 10+. Distribution: B. Many people fear Greek wines because they think they're going to encounter retsina, that sometimes bitter pine resin that goes into many Greek wines. The Greeks, however, also make many wines that contain no retsina whatever, and taste very good to finicky American palates. Take this handsome golden wine. It has a serious, mature bouquet that is deep and mellow, and a dry, dignified, serious taste. The fruit sugars and acid are well balanced, and I think you'll find it has a surprising richness, maybe even a touch of elegance. Price range: 750 ml, $3.19–4.99.

AUGUST SEBASTIANI CALIFORNIA MOUNTAIN CHABLIS
Vinted & bottled by Sebastiani Vineyards, Sonoma,
California. Rating: 7. Distribution: A. The dank,
heavy nose belies the attractive light barley color. The
taste is oldish, flat, and rather ordinary. Price range:
750 ml, $1.98–3.49.

ŸŸŸ SEBASTIANI NORTH COAST CHABLIS 1981 Produced & bottled by Sebastiani Vineyards, Sonoma,
California. Rating: 10. Distribution: A. You'll like this
handsome, straw-colored wine. Its lively, aggressive
nose has some attractive citrus notes in among the
fruit, and it has a moderately dry, dappled-sunshine
taste that will make you think of birds singing in a
summer vineyard. If you don't hear birds, don't
blame me! Price range: 750 ml, $2.35–4.29.

Ÿ AUGUST SEBASTIANI COUNTRY CHARDONNAY 1980
Produced & bottled by Sebastiani Vineyards,
Sonoma, California. Rating: 8+. Distribution: A.
This Chardonnay has a light sunshiny color and a
somewhat bashful but nevertheless ripe, rounded
nose. In the mouth it's a bit on the light, thin side,
with the fruit somewhat held back. Altogether, it's a
decent though unremarkable wine with no particular
defect. Price range: 1.5 l, $4.69–6.59.

ŸŸ AUGUST SEBASTIANI COUNTRY CHENIN BLANC
1981 Vinted & bottled by Sebastiani Vineyards,
Sonoma, California. Rating: 9. Distribution: A. The
color is ripe wheat; the nose is simple, clean, uncomplicated, moderately fruity. In the mouth you will
find a mannerly mingling of attractive fruit, with a

faint note of brier. It's a modest wine that offers quite a bit. Price range: 1.5 l, $3.74–5.49.

ŤŤŤŤ SEBASTIANI NORTH COAST COUNTIES CHENIN BLANC 1981   Produced & bottled by Sebastiani Vineyards, Sonoma, California. Rating: 11+. Distribution: A. There is an artful blending of mature fruit flavors in both the bouquet and the taste of this wine. The color is deep and lemony, the nose is a fusion of ripe grapes, honey, and sunshine. Like many California Chenin Blancs it could use a touch more acid, but forget it—just enjoy its rounded, captivating flavor! Price range: 750 ml, $3.29–5.49.

Ť AUGUST SEBASTIANI COUNTRY FRENCH COLOMBARD 1980   Vinted & bottled by Sebastiani Vineyards, Sonoma, California. Rating: 8+. Distribution: A. Some wines are one-dimensional, some are three-dimensional. This one is two-dimensional. The color is a lovely gold, with green flashes. The nose is narrow and unamazing. The taste is semidry, fruity, and pleasantly unexceptional. Two-D, but what's wrong with that? Price range: 750 ml, $3.74–5.49.

ŤŤŤ SEBASTIANI NORTH COAST COUNTIES GREEN HUNGARIAN 1980   Produced & bottled by Sebastiani Vineyards, Sonoma, California. Rating: 10. Distribution: A. This pale, olive-gold wine has a slender nose with a surprising, fleeting note of anise in it. I get a licorice hint in the taste, too, which otherwise is fairly dry, full of fresh, ripe fruit, and balanced with just the right amount of acid. An interesting wine. Price range: 750 ml, $3.29–4.99.

�♰ SEBASTIANI NORTH COAST COUNTIES PINOT NOIR BLANC 1981   Produced & bottled by Sebastiani Vineyards, Sonoma, California. Rating: 11. Distribution: A. Sebastiani calls this wine "Eye of the Swan," and it's one of those tranvestite wines—red wine grapes walking around in white wine clothes. The trick is to separate the juice from the skins immediately on pressing, and the result, in this case, is a pale, attractive, peach-colored wine. The bouquet is modest, pleasing, a bit restrained, and the taste is moderately dry with a nice sweet-and-sour effect, a tart edge combined with a smooth, honeyed quality. Overall, it's a supple, generous wine with lots of fully ripe fruit, and it's certainly worth a try. Price range: 750 ml. $3.46–5.49.

AUGUST SEBASTIANI LIGHT COUNTRY WHITE   Produced & bottled by Sebastiani Vineyards, Sonoma, California. Rating: 6+. Distribution: A. You get 9.3 percent alcohol and 57 calories per 100 milliliters in this butter-yellow wine. You also get an aggressive, penetrating, rather coarse nose. The taste imitates the nose, unfortunately, and although the wine has more of the feel of a "real" wine than many of the lights—probably because of its alcohol content—it's not really much of a treat. Price range: 1.5 l, $3.89–5.49.

♰♰♰♰ SIMPATICO EUROPEAN WHITE WINE   Blended & bottled by Alfred Franzen, Alf/Mosel, Germany. Rating: 11+. Distribution: C. Imagine a wine with 86 percent Italian grapes and 14 percent French grapes that is blended and bottled in Germany. That's Simpatico. So what's Simpatico like? It's lemon-gold in color, and its nose is pleasing, clean, and crisp, with the raciness of just-ripe fruit. The taste is off-dry, with a kind of honeyed fruit flavor, light acid, and a very pleasing finish. It's a smooth, cheerful wine with a lot of innocent charm, and it's not hard for me to believe the claim that it's the largest-selling white wine in Germany. Price range: 750 ml, $2.99–4.49.

♟♟♟♟ SONOMA VINEYARDS WHITE TABLE WINE Produced & bottled by Sonoma Vineyards, Windsor, California. Rating: 11+. Distribution: B. This sunny, golden wine has a lovely, soft, flowery nose that is clean and rounded and full of life. The taste is medium dry, a captivating mixture of fruit and honey, wholesome, outdoorsy, generous, light-hearted. If you want to know precisely what you're drinking, the label tells you—36 percent French Colombard, 31 percent Johannisberg Riesling, 27 percent Chardonnay, 6 percent Thompson Seedless. These have all been assembled very nicely, and I think you'll like the result. Price range: 1.5 l, $3.99–5.99.

♟♟ SOUVERAIN APPELLATION NORTH COAST CHABLIS 1981 Produced & bottled by Souverain, Geyserville, California. Rating: 9. Distribution: B. A nice, straw-colored wine with a mannerly, rounded, moderately fruity nose, and an affable, light, uncomplicated taste. It's just off-dry, with good fruit and decent acid, and you should probably give it a try. Price range: 750 ml, $3.29–4.59.

♟♟♟ SOUVERAIN APPELLATION NORTH COAST CHENIN BLANC 1981 Produced & bottled by Souverain, Geyserville, California. Rating: 10. Distribution: B. This clear, straw-colored Chenin Blanc has a fruity, clean, forthright nose. There's a light, pleasant sweetness to the taste, rather nectarlike, and I start thinking not only about grapes, but peaches, nectarines, and God knows what else. In any event, it's a nice wine, and I think you'll like it. Price range: 750 ml, $4.15–5.99.

ȚȚȚȚ SOUVERAIN APPELLATION NORTH COAST COLOM-BARD BLANC 1981   Produced & bottled by Souverain, Geyserville, California. Rating: 11+. Distribution: B. It's my pleasure to tell you you will enjoy the sunny simplicity of this charming wine, from its clean, parchment color and the simple, comely fruit of its luscious nose, to its affable, semisweet taste. Take a sip, and you'll find clean, ripe fruit and honey fused into a sprightly, light-hearted, refreshing wine. Try it! Price range: 750 ml, $3.39–5.49.

ȚȚȚȚ SOUVERAIN APPELLATION NORTH COAST GREY RIESLING 1981   Produced & bottled by Souverain, Geyserville, California. Rating: 11+. Distribution: B. Some wine drinkers insist white wines be dry enough to shrivel their tonsils, and those people miss the joys of drinking a lightly sweet, fruity, honeyed wine like this straw-colored Grey Riesling. It has a lovely, harmonious, deep-summer nose that is simple, clean, and full of ripe fruit, iced tea, and sunshine. This stylish nose leads you carelessly to its alter ego, the flavor, which is round, seductive, and succulent, an experience sweet and lazy as an August afternoon. Do I embroider? I think not, but why not see for yourself? Price range: 750 ml, $3.39–4.99.

ϿϿϿ SOUVERAIN CALIFORNIA WHITE TABLE WINE   Produced & bottled by Souverain, Geyserville, California. Rating: 11. Distribution: B. This pale, clear wine has a slight tawny cast. The nose is clean, a soft fragrance with some mild floral notes, and the taste is relatively dry, with good body and lots of charming ripe fruit. It's round, clean, refreshing, shows some refinement, and has a good finish. Like several other wines that come only in the 1.5-liter size, it would make a good "house wine." Price range: 1.5 l, $4.19–5.99.

SUMMIT PREMIUM CALIFORNIA CHABLIS   Prepared & bottled by Geyser Peak Winery, Geyserville, California. Rating: 7. Distribution: B. The color is pale honey. As for the nose and taste, my notes read: "unimpressive, acceptable, middle-of-the-road, adequate, a bit too sedate." Quite drinkable, therefore, but nothing to race home for. Price range: 4 l, $4.69–5.99.

Ͽ SUMMIT PREMIUM CALIFORNIA RHINE   Prepared & bottled by Geyser Peak Winery, Geyserville, California. Rating: 8+. Distribution: B. The ripe-wheat color of this wine will lead you on to sniff its easily accessible and altogether satisfactory aroma of fruit. The taste is conventional—sweet, fruity, and lacking in acid, of course—but it's one level better than some of the other chill 'n' gulpers. The price is right, too! Price range: 4 l, $4.69–5.99.

ϿϿϿϿϿ SUTTER HOME MUSCAT AMABILE 1981   Produced & bottled by Sutter Home Winery, St. Helena, California. Rating: 14. Distribution: B. Here's a dessert wine that's a dessert all by itself! This straw-colored Muscat offers your nose a lavish bouquet of flowers, a basket of apricots, nectarines, and papayas in a rich, voluptuous setting. The taste is ambrosial, sweet but not cloying. It has heaps of fruit, and tastes as though someone made a raid on the jam and jelly pantry. It's smooth, supple, elegant, nectarlike, and it should go on your shopping list. Price range: 750 ml, $3.48–5.49.

ΨΨ SUTTER HOME WHITE ZINFANDEL 1981 Produced & bottled by Sutter Home Winery, St. Helena, California. Rating: 9+. Distribution: B. Here's another cross-dressing wine, a white wine made from what are traditionally red-wine grapes. It's tawny-peach in color and has a decent, fresh, unassuming nose whose fruit aromas are pleasant but diffident. The taste is off-dry, mild, clean, refreshing. It's well made, and there's lots of expansive fruit. It's probably just the ticket for serving after your summer-afternoon tennis match. Price range: 750 ml, $3.77–5.49.

Ψ TAYLOR CALIFORNIA CELLARS CHABLIS Cellared & bottled by Taylor California Cellars, Gonzales, California. Rating: 8+. Distribution: A. This wine has the color of pale clover honey, and a gentle, floral nose. The taste is unremarkable but pleasing, a bit flat, but with enough genial fruit to make drinking it a nice experience. Price range: 1.5 l, $3.59–4.99.

Ψ TAYLOR CALIFORNIA CELLARS LIGHT CHABLIS OF CALIFORNIA Cellared & bottled by Taylor California Cellars, Gonzales, California. Rating: 8+. Distribution: A. First, you get 8.2 percent alcohol and only 53 calories per 100 milliliters. Then you get a nose that is small, somewhat serious, and has an attractive, fruit-bloom, flower-garden fragrance. And there's more: you also get a dry, rather fruity taste that is decent but thin; in fact, it feels as though something essential has been removed. What's been removed, of course, is alcohol and calories, but light-wine drinkers have already agreed to accept this trade-off. Price range: 1.5 l, $3.78–5.39.

ȲȲȲȲ TAYLOR CALIFORNIA CELLARS CHARDONNAY OF CALIFORNIA   Cellared & bottled by Taylor California Cellars, Gonzales, California. Rating: 12. Distribution: A. The color is light gold, the nose is an opulent mosaic of fruit aromas, clean, rich, and joyful. In the mouth the wine is relatively dry, full of youthful energy and elegant fruit. It's a Chardonnay in the fruity style, outdoorsy, with no imprint of oak aging. The acid balance is good, and I think you'll find the whole thing delightful! Price range: 1.5 l, $4.79–6.49.

ȲȲ TAYLOR CALIFORNIA CELLARS CHENIN BLANC OF CALIFORNIA   Cellared & bottled by Taylor California Cellars, Gonzales, California. Rating: 9+. Distribution: A. The color will make you think of very dry sherry. The nose is modest, fruity, and pleasant, and I get a hint of lemon in it. The taste is smooth and honeyed, a trace lacking in acid, but it's still a nice wine, and after you've chilled it properly, it will be just the thing for a picnic in the sunny uplands. Price range: 1.5 l, $3.99–5.79.

♈♈ TAYLOR CALIFORNIA CELLARS FRENCH COLOMBARD
OF CALIFORNIA   Cellared & bottled by Taylor California Cellars, Gonzales, California. Rating: 9. Distribution: A. This sunlit golden wine has a ripe, amiable,
simple nose. The taste is sprightly and semidry, with
pleasing fruit flavors, decent acid, and a sunshiny
simplicity throughout. Price range: 1.5 l, $3.99–5.79.

♈♈♈♈ TAYLOR CALIFORNIA CELLARS RHINE WINE OF
CALIFORNIA   Cellared & bottled by Taylor California
Cellars, San Francisco, California. Rating: 11+. Distribution: A. A real winner! Color: pale straw with
greenish glints. Nose: honeyed, rich, floral, summery. Taste: lovely ripe apricots, peaches, iced tea,
somewhat sweet but balanced with more acid than
most California Rhines. All in all, a very pleasant
sensory experience if you're not looking for something dry and crackling. Price range: 1.5 l, $3.59–4.99.

♈ TAYLOR CALIFORNIA CELLARS LIGHT RHINE WINE OF
CALIFORNIA   Cellared & bottled by Taylor California
Cellars, Gonzales, California. Rating: 8+. Distribution: A. In the "light" tradition, this wine has 7.5
percent alcohol and only 57 calories per 100 milliliters.
The nose is presentable, although it doesn't have a lot
to say, and the taste has a moderate sweetness, good
body for a "light," good acid, and decent but ordinary fruit flavors. Price range: 1.5 l, $3.78–5.49.

♈♈ TAYLOR CALIFORNIA CELLARS JOHANNISBERG RIES-
LING OF CALIFORNIA   Cellared & bottled by Taylor
California Cellars, Gonzales, California. Rating: 9.
Distribution: A..This straw-colored Riesling comes

with a modest, but easily accessible bouquet of comely and delicate fruit. There's fruit in abundance in the taste as well, all very round and ripe and ready to enjoy. The acid's a little short, but so what? If we threw out all the California whites that were short on acid, there wouldn't be much left to drink! Price range: 750 ml, $4.79–5.99.

ŶŶŶ TAYLOR CALIFORNIA CELLARS SAUVIGNON BLANC OF CALIFORNIA   Cellared & bottled by Taylor California Cellars, Gonzales, California. Rating: 10. Distribution: A. This barley-colored wine is dry and light-hearted, lithe and personable, and has clean, racy fruit and decent acid. The nose is similarly clean, fresh, and zesty, and the whole performance is very enjoyable. Price range: 1.5 l, $4.79–6.49.

ŶŶ TAYLOR CALIFORNIA CELLARS PREMIUM CALIFORNIA DRY WHITE WINE   Cellared & bottled by Taylor California Cellars, Gonzales, California. Rating: 9+. Distribution: A. Ripe wheat color. Fruity, lemony nose. Sprightly, expansive taste, full of fruit just reaching the edge of ripeness. A trace thin perhaps, a trace short on acid, but still a very nicely put together wine. Enjoy! Price range: 1.5 l, $3.59–4.99.

ŶŶŶ TORRES VINA ESMERALDA 1981   Produced & bottled by Miguel Torres, Vilafranca del Penedēs, Spain. Rating: 11. Distribution: B. This wine displays a lovely, clean, unsophisticated quality in both bouquet and taste. It's a pale parchment color, and the nose is clean, upbeat, fruity, and eager to please. The taste is moderately dry with touches of sweetness. It's lovely and feminine, a lacy, light-hearted, floral nectar that offers a variety of exotic fruit flavors. It's a bit light on acid, but I don't think that will bother you. It's a charming wine with an air of refinement throughout, and a nice finish. Price range: 750 ml, $3.83–5.25.

ŦŦŦ TORRES VINA SOL 1981 Produced & bottled by Miguel Torres, Vilafranca del Penedēs, Spain. Rating: 10+. Distribution: B. This is a very pale wine with an attractive and quietly fruity nose. In the mouth you'll find it dry, crisp, and zesty, with an abundance of just-ripe fruit and a pleasing acid balance. It's a nice all-purpose, day-to-day wine, fresh and wholesome, and it helps to have it available in a 1.5–liter bottle as well as the 750 ml. Price range: 750 ml, $2.99–4.39.

ŦŦŦŦŦ TORRES GRAN VINA SOL RESERVA 1981 Produced & bottled by Miguel Torres, Vilafranca del Penedēs, Spain. Rating: 13+. Distribution: B. The pale lemon-gold color of this lovely wine is matched with a fresh, lively, floral nose that somehow manages to fuse energy with charm and elegance. The taste is moderately dry with a pleasant tart edge, supple, well proportioned, and bursting with sunshiny fruit. It's a handsome wine with a graceful finish, youthful yet complex, and I think you'll enjoy having a bottle on your table. Price range: 750 ml, $4.18–6.49.

ŦŦŦŦ TRAKIA BLANC DE BLANCS 1980 Produced & bottled by Vinimpex, Sofia, Bulgaria. Rating: 11+. Distribution: C. In color, this Bulgarian wine is a light greenish gold. The nose is clean, fresh, sunshiny, full of healthy fruit. The taste is semidry, with lots of ripe, round, honeyed fruit. It's a refreshing wine with a good balance, and with lots of demure charm and refinement. Don't miss it! Price range: 750 ml, $2.79–4.79.

ΥΥΥ TRAKIA PINOT CHARDONNAY 1979 Produced & bottled by Vinimpex, Sofia, Bulgaria. Rating: 11. Distribution: B. The Bulgars have made themselves a very nice white wine, and now you can enjoy it, too. It's a ripe barley color, with a direct, fresh, not terribly complicated nose that has a generous helping of fruit in it. The taste is dry, clean, fresh, and well rounded. The wine has a lot of life and some complexity. It's well made, and you definitely won't find another Chardonnay like it at the price. Price range: 750 ml, $2.79–4.79.

ΥΥΥΥΥ TRAPICHE CHARDONNAY 1980 Produced & bottled by Establecimiento a Exp. 01019, Mendoza, Argentina. Rating: 13. Distribution: C. Argentina makes a lot of good wines, and this is a terrific example. The color is pale with olive tones, the nose is racy and athletic—rounded, structured, with some complexity, and showing lots of energy, clean fresh fruit, and Argentinean sunshine. The taste is moderately dry, delicate, fresh, a beguiling collection of fruit flavors. It has good body, good acid, a good finish, and I think you'll agree it's a wine of very high quality. Price range: 750 ml, $4.26–6.29.

ΥΥΥΥ VALBON WHITE TABLE WINE Produced & bottled by Bouchard Père & Fils, France. Rating: 11+.

Distribution: C. This is one of the serious wines—pleasantly serious, I'm happy to say, but serious all the same. It's lemon-gold in color, and the nose, although amiable, is not what you'd call light-hearted. Although it's clean and decorous, it's also quite oaky and conservative. The taste is solid, husky, masculine. The fruit is there, but on a speak-when-spoken-to basis, everything perfectly under control, and no fooling around. It's a good wine for the long haul, the kind of wine you don't tire of. Try some. Price range: 1.5 l, $4.49–6.50.

🍷🍷🍷 VERDILLAC BORDEAUX SUPERIEUR 1981 Produced & bottled by Bouchard Père & Fils, France. Rating: 11. Distribution: C. This parchment-pale import takes itself seriously, but in quite a different way from the Valbon just above. For one thing, it has a much more cheerful nose, soft and rounded, with a charming floral touch here and there, and the taste, while dry and conservative, offers more fruit and less oak. Like the Valbon, it's the kind of wine that wears well, and the difference between the two is principally in point of view. They're both serious, but this one enjoys a little off-color joke now and then. Price range: 750 ml, $3.99–6.00.

🍷🍷🍷🍷 VILLA ANTINORI BIANCO 1977 Produced & bottled by Marchesi L.e.P. Antinori S. Casciano V.P., Firenze, Italy. Rating: 11+. Distribution: C. The color is a deep, rich, molten gold. The nose is aromatic, full, mature, dignified, a congenial matron, extremely handsome and respectable if not actually exciting. The taste is similarly mature and sedate, and it's a wine of ample proportions and good breeding, dry, with an attractive, oaky quality. It has a "hand-rubbed" quality, quiet, well made, and full of things to think about. Start thinking. Price range: 750 ml, $4.19–5.59.

🍷 VILLA BANFI SOAVE CLASSICO SUPERIORE 1979   Bottled by P. Sartori, Negrar, Italy. Rating: 8. Distribution: B. A nice, unpretentious wine. Sunny, light gold in color. Uncomplicated nose, with fruit, a trifle closed-in. A decent, workaday taste, dry and tart, with fair acid. You could do a lot worse. Price range: 750 ml, $2.99–4.49.

WAN FU VIN DE TABLE BLANC   Bottled by Michel Montadour, France. Rating: 7. Distribution: C. Here's a wine nobody needed, a wine specifically designed to answer that burning question, "What shall we drink with Chinese food?" Well, the color's nice—buttercup yellow—but the nose and taste are stodgy and ponderous, and both have a slightly baked character. The label says it's "enchantingly dry," but I find it somewhat sweet. I guess the burning question is still unanswered. Price range: 750 ml, $3.40–5.49.

🍷🍷🍷🍷🍷 WEIBEL MENDOCINO COUNTY WHITE CABERNET SAUVIGNON 1981   Produced & bottled by Weibel Vineyards, Mission San Jose, California. Rating: 14. Distribution: B. Now and then someone makes a white wine out of red-wine grapes, and it really works! Such is the case with this white Cabernet from Weibel. It's the color of a ripe peach, and it has a nose that any wine, white or red, could be proud of—

lovely and sensuous, full of life and sophistication, with a variety of complex fruit scents. The taste is rich, smooth, and silky, just off-dry, with good body and good acid. It has elegance, power, harmony, and gorgeous fruit. Don't miss it. Price range: 750 ml, $3.49–6.39.

WEIBEL NORTH COAST MENDOCINO CHENIN BLANC 1980 Produced & bottled by Weibel Vineyards, Mission San Jose, California. Rating: 7. Distribution: B. This is a-middle-of-the-road Chenin Blanc, a lovely wine to look at, gold with greenish glints. The nose is rather formal and a tiny bit dank, and the taste is fruity, slightly sweet, certainly not unpleasant, but still a bit closed-in and stuffy. Price range: 750 ml, $2.29–4.99.

♆♆ WEIBEL CALIFORNIA GREEN HUNGARIAN Produced & bottled by Weibel Vineyards, Mission San Jose, California. Rating: 9. Distribution: B. This medium-gold wine has a clean, ingenuous, vibrant nose that calls up ripe fruit and clover. It's not a big nose, just a nice one. The taste is semisweet, a sunshiny, ripe-fruit nectar, simple and honeyed, with low acid. Price range: 750 ml, $3.68–4.99.

♆♆♆ WEIBEL MENDOCINO COUNTY PINOT NOIR–BLANC 1980 Produced & bottled by Weibel Vineyards, Mission San Jose, California. Rating: 11. Distribution: B. Weibel calls the white wine it makes from red Pinot Noir grapes "Eye of the Partridge." It has a pale, tea-rose color and a rather reticent nose, decent but small and restrained. The taste is moderately dry, with good body and good acid, and with a kind of elegance that derives from the style and authority of its fruit. Personally, I'd rather have a red wine made from Pinot Noir grapes than a white one, but if you're set on having a white, this is a nice one. Price range: 750 ml, $3.19–5.49.

❦❦❦❦ WEIBEL NORTH COAST MENDOCINO GREY RIESLING 1980 Produced & bottled by Weibel Vineyards, Mission San Jose, California. Rating: 11+. Distribution: B. This is a dry, crisp, stylish wine: lean, clean, and athletic. The color is pale straw, with glances of green. The nose is small and classy, and has a nice bouquet development and a feeling that someone started with good ingredients and proceeded carefully. It's the kind of dry white wine that goes well with delicate dishes. It won't overpower them, but it still has enough character to stand up and make its own harmonious contribution. Price range: 750 ml, $2.80–4.79.

❦ WEIBEL MONTEREY JOHANNISBERG RIESLING 1980 Produced & bottled by Weibel Vineyards, Mission San Jose, California. Rating: 8+. Distribution: B. The color is a lively greenish gold. The nose is unpretentious but pleasing, with a better-than-average fruit aroma, and the taste, while somewhat predictable in its low acid, has plenty of fruit and simple summer charm. Price range: 750 ml, $2.49–5.29.

❦❦ WEIBEL NORTH COAST MENDOCINO JOHANNISBERG RIESLING 1980 Produced & bottled by Weibel Vineyards, Mission San Jose, California. Rating: 9+. Distribution: B. This lemony-green Riesling has a presentable nose that is ripe and fruity, and a charming, light sweetness in the mouth. It has a touch more dignity than its brother from Monterey, mentioned above, and has fair acid and an attractive fusion of fruit flavors that goes well beyond hearts-and-flowers. Price range: 750 ml, $3.59–5.49.

TTT WEIBEL MENDOCINO COUNTY WHITE ZINFANDEL 1981   Produced & bottled by Weibel Vineyards, Mission San Jose, California. Rating: 10+. Distribution: B. Here's another go at making a white wine from red-wine grapes, and it turned out just fine. It's pale salmon in color, and has a clean, modest, unassuming nose. The taste hovers near the dry/sweet boundary, tilting slightly toward sweet, and it delivers a truckload of fruit. It's a nice, easygoing, sunshiny wine, too sweet to serve with fish, but just right to accompany a dessert or be served as an apéritif. Price range: 750 ml, $3.68–5.49.

TTTT WENTE BROTHERS LE BLANC DE BLANCS   Produced & bottled by Wente Brothers, Livermore, California. Rating: 11+. Distribution: A. The color is a sunny gold, the nose is lively and racy, very approachable, with a pleasant, new-mown grassiness. The taste is moderately dry, again lively and grassy and fresh, with lots of ripe fruit and energy. It's a clean, well-made wine with a good finish, and I earnestly commend it to your attention. Price range: 750 ml, $2.50–4.99.

♟♟ WENTE BROTHERS BLANC DE NOIR   Produced & bottled by Wente Brothers, Livermore, California. Rating: 9+. Distribution: A. Wente's white-wine-from-red-wine-grapes is a pale salmon color, and has a somewhat closed-in nose—nothing terrible, understand, just a little hard to find the fruit. The moderately dry taste has a rather pleasant sensation of sweetness, a lot of clean, ripe fruit, and good acid. A bit of the slightly stuffy nose carries over into the taste, but it's still a very pleasant wine, with an air of quality about it. Price range: 750 ml, $3.49–4.99.

♟♟ WENTE BROTHERS CALIFORNIA CHABLIS   Produced & bottled by Wente Brothers, Livermore, California. Rating: 9+. Distribution: A. This is a moderately dry wine, pale greenish gold in color, with a very accessible nose that is penetrating, outdoorsy, and grassy. The taste is moderately dry and dignified, with lots of ripe fruit. It's a simple, pleasant wine for lots of simple, pleasant purposes. Price range: 750 ml, $2.53–4.29.

♟♟♟♟ WENTE BROTHERS CALIFORNIA GREY RIESLING 1981   Produced & bottled by Wente Brothers, Livermore, California. Rating: 12. Distribution: A. Color: pale gold with amber tones. Nose: quiet, mature, rounded, velvety. Clean and fresh. Easily accessible. Taste: dry, supple, round, generous, full of juicy ripe fruit, healthy, outdoorsy, wholesome. You'll like the way it fills your mouth, you'll like the acid balance, you'll like the finish. Need I go on? Price range: 750 ml, $2.50–4.99.

ΨΨΨ WENTE BROTHERS LIVERMORE VALLEY DRY SEMIL-
LON   Produced & bottled by Wente Brothers, Livermore, California. Rating: 10. Distribution: A. The
wine is the color of pale lemon juice. The nose? It
combines the aromas of grapes and wet grass—nice,
clean, wet grass beside a clear stream. The grassy
character carries over into the taste, which is dry,
crisp, sturdy, and has lots of zip. It seems to me the
kind of wine that would appeal to satyrs, goats,
rakes, and roués. After that, I'm almost afraid to say it
appeals to me, but it does. Price range: 750 ml, $3.67–
5.29.

9

Pink Wines

▼▼▼▼ ALMADÉN CALIFORNIA GAMAY ROSÉ 1981 Produced & bottled by Almadén Vineyards, San Jose, California. Rating: 11+. Distribution: A. This pink Gamay has a clear, clean, red-orange color. The nose is straightforward, fruity yet slightly serious, and the taste is semidry with a slight tart edge, with plenty of ripe fruit and good acid. It's a rosé with structure and character, even a certain amount of complexity. If you like pink wines at all, you'll like this one. Price range: 750 ml, $2.69–3.99.

▼ ALMADÉN CALIFORNIA GRENACHE ROSÉ Vinted & bottled by Almadén Vineyards, San Jose. Rating: 8. Distribution: A. The color is tawny pink. The fruity nose is nicely accessible and shows a modest hint of breeding. The taste is semidry, somewhat reserved, the fruit held back, and the acid rather low. A pleasant enough wine, but nothing special. Price range: 750 ml, $2.25–3.79.

ALMADÉN CALIFORNIA MOUNTAIN NECTAR VIN ROSÉ
Vinted & bottled by Almadén Vineyards, San José,
California. Rating: 7+. Distribution: A. This medium-red rosé has an approachable but unimpressive nose—the fruit's there, but so what? To go with
the nose it has an acceptable but fairly uninspiring
taste. Chill 'n' gulp. Price range: 750 ml, $2.25–3.59.

ᵀᵀ ALMADÉN LIGHT ROSÉ Vinted & bottled by Almadén Vineyards, San José, California. Rating: 9+.
Distribution: A. Here's the box score on this "light":
7 percent alcohol, 53 calories per 100 milliliters. The
other vital statistics are as follows. Color: darkish
rosé. Nose: pleasant and clean, lots of mature fruit,
respectable if not overwhelming. Taste: modestly
sweet, soft, fruity, light acid, everything simple, a
wine without pretense but still capable of giving enjoyment. So, cool it down on a hot afternoon and who
knows? Price range: 1.5 l, $3.57–4.99.

ᵀ BEAULIEU VINEYARD BEAUROSÉ 1980 Produced &
bottled by Beaulieu Vineyard, Rutherford, California.
Rating: 8+. Distribution: A. The color is a clean, light
cardinal. The nose is shy, conventional, fruity, adequate. It's a simple, sweet wine with a pleasant fusion of fruit flavors, and my advice to you is: Drink it,
enjoy it, and don't spend too much time thinking
about it. Price range: 750 ml, $3.65–5.25.

ᵀᵀ BULLY HILL VINEYARDS SPACE SHUTTLE ROSÉ WINE
1981 Produced & bottled by Bully Hill Vineyards,
Hammondsport, New York. Rating: 9+. Distribution: X. This handsome, orangey-red wine has a shy,

subtle aroma that is charming, upbeat, and youthful. Although the label calls it semidry, I call it semisweet. Whichever it is, it's a pleasing combination of sunshiny fruit flavors and moderately low acid. Price range: 750 ml, $3.49–5.25.

ϓϓϓ CHRISTIAN BROTHERS LASALLE ROSÉ   Produced & bottled by The Christian Brothers, Napa, California. Rating: 10. Distribution: A. If you don't like sweet wines, you can tune out right here, because this one is very sweet. You also may or may not like the fact it's quite effervescent and makes a lot of bubbles in your mouth. On the other hand, it's a wine with a definite personality. It has a deep, sonorous nose, reserved and rather masculine, plus a taste that displays a touch of breeding. There's also lots of sweet, ripe fruit. Price range: 750 ml, $2.99–4.49.

ϓϓϓ CHRISTIAN BROTHERS CALIFORNIA NAPA ROSÉ BRAND   Produced & bottled by The Christian Brothers, Napa, California. Rating: 10. Distribution: A. This wine is rather dark for a rosé, a deep reddish pink with orange overtones. The nose is captivating, rounded, full of mixed fruits and a kind of buxom maturity. There's moderate sweetness in the taste, and it has more body than many rosés. Along with some developed fruit sugars, it also shows indications of having come from a good family. Price range: 750 ml, $1.99–3.99.

COLONY CALIFORNIA CLASSIC ROSÉ   Vinted & bottled by Colony Wines, San Francisco, California. Rating: 7+. Distribution: A. The color is a light scarlet, and the nose is diffident and conventionally fruity. The taste is sweet as Grandma's grape jelly, and it's an acceptable, if predictable, wine. Price range: 1.5 l, $2.99–4.29.

♉ CONCANNON CALIFORNIA VIN ROSÉ 1981 Produced & bottled by Concannon Vineyards, Livermore, California. Rating: 8+. Distribution: B. The nose of this crimson-pink wine is fresh, clean, simple, and upbeat. The taste is fairly dry for a rosé, which means that it's only moderately sweet, and it has lots of ripe, simple fruit, and a certain amount of zest derived from its modest acid. Price range: 750 ml, $2.49–4.29.

♉♉♉ CONCANNON ZINFANDEL ROSÉ 1981 Produced & bottled by Concannon Vineyard, Livermore, California. Rating: 10. Distribution: B. The light, clear, cherry color of this wine is the first of its plusses. The second is its modest, clean, ripe-fruit nose. The third, of course, is its taste, which is sprightly, dry, pleasantly tart, with a good acid balance and a lot of fruit. It even has *character*, which isn't an easy accomplishment for a pink wine! Price range: 750 ml, $2.77–4.99.

♉♉ CRESTA BLANCA MENDOCINO GAMAY ROSÉ 1981 Produced & bottled by Cresta Blanca Vineyards, Ukiah, California. Rating: 9. Distribution: B. This is a genial, accommodating wine with a light, clear, raspberry color and a decent if unspectacular nose. The taste is slightly sweet, just on the edge of dry, with an adequate acid balance. The overall picture is of a fruity pink wine that's not remarkable but stands well ahead of many others. Price range: 750 ml, $2.79–4.69.

🍷🍷🍷 CRIBARI CALIFORNIA NAPA GAMAY ROSÉ 1981 Made & bottled by Cribari & Sons, Lodi, California. Rating; 10+. Distribution: B. Cribari comes through very nicely with this handsome, light scarlet wine. The nose is clean, unassuming, full of ripe fruit, and the taste has a modest sweetness not really far from being dry. The acid balance is good, the wine is well made, and the price is right! Better get a bottle right away! Price range: 750 ml, $1.99–3.49.

CRIBARI CALIFORNIA PINK CHABLIS Made & bottled by Cribari & Sons, Lodi, California. Rating: 5. Distribution: B. This light scarlet wine has a stale, sweat-sock nose that won't entice you, and a somber, though fruity, taste, with a bitter note. Sorry. Price range: 750 ml, $1.79–3.29.

CRIBARI CALIFORNIA MOUNTAIN VIN ROSÉ Made & bottled by Cribari & Sons, Lodi, California. Rating: 6. Distribution: B. The color is a clear, baby-shower pink, and the nose is commonplace, with a faint bitter note. There's fruit in the taste, and some acid, but that bitterness still comes through to keep the score low. Price range: 4 l, $5.19–6.49.

🍷🍷 FETZER PREMIUM ROSÉ MENDOCINO TABLE WINE Produced & bottled by Fetzer Vineyards, Redwood Valley, California. Rating: 9+. Distribution: B. The color is lovely, a kind of peachy pink. The nose is

delicate, ingenuous, and softly fruit
gently sweet, charming, light-hearted
with a very modest amount of acid
sweetness. Price range: 750 ml, $2.69–

🍷🍷 FRANZIA CALIFORNIA LIGHT ROSÉ M~~ade & bottled~~
by Franzia Brothers Winemakers, San Francisco, California. Rating: 9+. Distribution: A. Another "light"
wine. Alcohol, 7.5 percent, 57 calories per 100 milliliters. Color orange-pink, nose commonplace. The
taste is a surprise—medium dry, light, crisp, lively,
full of sunny, ripe fruit. There's not a lot of complexity, but there seldom is in a rosé, so let this wine
refresh you, and figure it's done its job. Price range:
1.5 l, $1.79–$3.19.

GALLO PINK CHABLIS OF CALIFORNIA Made & bottled
by Gallo Vineyards, Modesto, California. Rating: 7+.
Distribution: A. This is a sweet, flat, predictable
wine, but decent and acceptable if pink wines are
your thing. The color is a lovely peach. The nose is
sweetish and prosaic. The taste has fruit and sweetness, and that's about all the conversation you can
have about this wine. Price range: 1.5 l, $2.99–3.99.

🍷 ERNEST & JULIO GALLO ROSÉ OF CALIFORNIA Vinted
& cellared & bottled by Ernest & Julio Gallo, Modesto, California. Rating: 8. Distribution: A. This
light scarlet wine has a simple, forthright nose, and a
light, fruity taste. It's semidry, or should I say it's
semisweet? Anyhow, it's a decent rosé, a bit lacking
in acid, but that's life. Price range: 1.5 l, $2.99–3.99.

ALLO RED ROSÉ Made & bottled by Gallo Vineyards, Modesto, California. Rating: 7. Distribution: A. There's something of a stuffy cellar quality in the nose of this crimson wine, not terrible but not wonderful either. The taste is respectable, fruity, syrupy. Try pouring it on waffles. Price range: 1.5 l, $2.99–3.99.

🍷 GALLO VIN ROSÉ OF CALIFORNIA Made & bottled by Gallo Vineyards, Modesto, California. Rating: 8. Distribution: A. The color is a rosy amber. The nose is of the garden variety, civil and conventional. The taste is similar, fruity, pleasant, prosaic, with moderate sweetness and moderate acid. Okay, but no big deal. Price range: 750 ml, $2.48–3.99.

🍷🍷🍷🍷 GEYSER PEAK SONOMA COUNTY ROSÉ OF CABERNET SAUVIGNON 1981 Produced & bottled by Geyser Peak Winery, Geyserville, California. Rating: 11+. Distribution: B. This rosy, clear wine has a light, charming nose, full of fruit sugars. In the mouth it's semidry, with pleasing flavors of fruits, berries, and fresh tea. It's a carefully assembled wine, and it has a good balance. If you like pink wines, don't miss this one. Price range: 750 ml, $3.59–5.49.

GIACOBAZZI ROSATO Produced & bottled by Grandi Vini Giacobazzi, Nonantola, Italy. Rating: 5. Distribution: A. This wine looks lovely, a dark garnet color, but the nose has an unpleasant, decaying vegetable aroma. The taste is not as bad as you might expect from the nose, but it's still too mawkish and bitter for any real enjoyment. Price range: 750 ml, $2.69–3.99.

GIUMARRA VINEYARDS VIN ROSÉ OF CALIFORNIA 1980 Produced & bottled by Giumarra Vineyards, Edison, California. Rating: 7+. Distribution: C. This pale, orange-red wine has a satisfactory nose, clean and properly fruity, and a sweetish, low-acid taste. There's nothing particularly wrong with it. It's just predictable and rather ordinary. Price range: 750 ml, $2.19–3.49.

♥♥♥♥ INGLENOOK NORTH COAST COUNTIES VINTAGE CABERNET ROSÉ 1981 Produced & bottled by Inglenook Vineyards, Rutherford, California. Rating: 12. Distribution: A. The color of this wine is somewhat dark for a rosé, but not quite dark enough to be classified as a red. The nose is assertive, rounded, and thanks to the Cabernet grapes from which it is made, more complex than most pinks. The taste is fruity and semidry, fresh and honest with an obliging sweet-and-sour effect. I think it's an outstanding pink wine. What do you think? Price range: 750 ml, $3.29–5.25.

JACARÉ CLASSIQUE ROSÉ Vinted & bottled by Jacaré Wine Merchants, San Francisco, California. Rating: 7+. Distribution: A. The color is red-orange, the nose has an aggressive, sharp edge, with passable fruit. The taste is sweet, decent, and uninspired. The way to drink it is to chill it to about 33 degrees and gulp it. Price range: 750 ml, $2.27–3.99.

♆ JACARÉ WHITE ROSÉ Vinted & bottled by Jacaré Wine Merchants, San Francisco, California. Rating: 8+. Distribution: A. I love this wine's brilliant peach color. The nose is not spectacular, but it's very presentable nevertheless, and has lots of clean, ripe grapes for you to sniff at. The taste is sweet, clean, full of sunny fruit, unremarkable, but quite enjoyable all the same. Price range: 750 ml, $2.27–3.99.

CHARLES KRUG CALIFORNIA VIN ROSÉ Produced & bottled by Charles Krug Winery, St. Helena, California. Rating: 6+. Distribution: A. Color: light, clear crimson. Nose: routine, with a faint stuffy cellar component—not awful, just not for sustained sniffing. Taste: sweet and fruity, with a slight bitterness. Price range: 750 ml, $2.33–3.99.

♆♆ LANCERS VIN ROSÉ Bottled by J. M. da Fonseca, Lisbon, Portugal. Rating: 9+. Distribution: A. The dusky vermilion color of this wine is dark for a rosé. The nose is decent, unspectacular, serious, the fruit muted, with a slight whiff of the cellar. The taste is medium dry, slightly effervescent, with lots of serious fruit—somber, tamed, held back. There's a touch of austerity and a feeling of quality, but it's not enough to carry it to a higher rating. Price range: 750 ml, $2.99–4.49.

LOS REYES VINO ROSADO Produced & bottled by Pedro Domecq, Los Reyes, Mexico. Rating: 4. Distribution: C. This pink is a very dark pink, almost a sweet Sherry color. The aroma seems to come not from Mexico, but from Akron, Ohio; it smells like an old tire. The taste is no better. Price range: 750 ml, $2.99–4.69.

♟♟♟ PAUL MASSON CALIFORNIA GAMAY ROSÉ 1981 Produced & bottled by Paul Masson, Saratoga, California. Rating: 10. Distribution: A. This orange-pink Gamay has an unusual nose and taste you may or may not like. I happen to like it, not for every night, but as a pleasant and interesting change from more conventional wines. The nose is very civil, with an unusual grassy note and—you're not going to think this is very nice, but it is—a delicate sort of cigar-box aroma. These attributes also appear in the taste of the wine, which is dry and has plenty of fruit. Price range: 1.5 l, $5.49–7.29.

♟♟ PAUL MASSON RARE PREMIUM CALIFORNIA ROSÉ Made & bottled by Paul Masson Vineyards, Saratoga, California. Rating: 9+. Distribution: A. This tawny peach-colored wine has a pleasing, ripe-fruit-and-tea aroma, and a sweet, summery, honey-and-nectar taste. It's the kind of wine that summons up visions of dancing maidens in diaphanous gowns, and if they could only figure out how to pump some acid into it, it would score a lot higher. Price range: 1.5 l, $3.99–5.99.

PAUL MASSON CALIFORNIA VIN ROSÉ SEC   Made & bottled by Paul Masson Vineyards, Saratoga, California. Rating: 7+. Distribution: A. This is another peach-colored rosé wine. It has a decent, garden variety nose without any major defects, and the taste is almost dry enough to be called semidry. Its fruit is modestly restrained, it has low acid, and it's one of those wines that's acceptable but not terribly exciting. Price range: 1.5 l, $3.99–5.99.

ŶŶŶ MASSON LIGHT ROSÉ   Made & bottled by Paul Masson, Saratoga, California. Rating: 10. Distribution: A. This pale, orange-pink wine has 7.1 percent alcohol and 54 calories per 100 milliliters. More important, it has a pleasant, upbeat nose that offers a cheerful fruit-nectar aroma, and a taste that is rather sweet, but at the same time clean and ingenuous. It's a wine with a summery charm that goes with bare shoulders and dappled sunlight. Sweet-wine lovers should give it a try. Price range: 1.5 l, $3.99–5.99.

Ŷ MATEUS ROSÉ   Produced & bottled by Sogrape, Pôrto, Portugal. Rating: 8+. Distribution: A. The color is a clear pink, and the nose is rather nondescript. There's some fruit in it, but nothing very fetching, and it has a faint chemical note. The taste is medium dry. Despite the dryness, the wine has a pleasing sensation of fruit sweetness, and it's fairly refreshing, although the finish has a tinge of bitterness. This is a terribly popular wine in the United States, so you have to wonder how come? Could it be those beautiful television commercials? Price range: 750 ml, $3.22–4.99.

MIRASSOU SANTA CLARA COUNTY PETITE ROSÉ 1981 Produced & bottled by Mirassou Vineyards, San Jose, California. Rating: 7+. Distribution: B. The color is a light, lipstick red. There's not a lot to the nose, and what there is is rather commonplace. The taste is semisweet, acceptable, unimaginative. Not a terrible wine by any means, but it won't keep you up nights thinking about it. Price range: 750 ml, $2.73–4.49.

CK MONDAVI CALIFORNIA VIN ROSÉ Made & bottled by C. Mondavi & Sons, St. Helena, California. Rating: 7+. Distribution: A. A pale ruby wine with a reluctant, but otherwise acceptable, nose. It's not as sweet as most rosés, but plenty sweet nevertheless. Like many another wine, it has minimum acid and plenty of fruit. Right down the middle of the road. Price range, 1.5 l, $2.97–5.25.

ΥΥ ROBERT MONDAVI ROSÉ 1981 Produced & bottled by Robert Mondavi Winery, Oakville, California. Rating: 9. Distribution: A. This vermilion wine has a dry, fruity, zesty nose with a slight, pleasant grassiness. In the mouth the taste is semidry, with lots of ripe fruit, and the grassy note adds interest and character. It's not a blockbuster wine by any means, but at least it's not flat and boring like 80 percent of the other rosés on the market. Price range: 1.5 l, $2.97–6.49.

ΥΥ MONTEREY VINEYARD CLASSIC CALIFORNIA ROSÉ 1979 Produced & bottled by The Monterey Vineyard, Gonzales, California. Rating: 9. Distribution: A. The color is a tawny, dark rosé. It has an engaging yet dignified nose, modestly sophisticated, with restrained fruit. The taste is slightly sweet, with attractive ripe fruit, and it's jaunty and refreshing in spite of its light acid. Price range: 750 ml, $2.98–4.49.

ΥΥ MONTEREY VINEYARDS MONTEREY COUNTY ROSÉ OF CABERNET SAUVIGNON 1981 Produced & bottled by The Monterey Vineyards, Gonzales, California. Rating: 9. Distribution: A. This lovely clean pink wine has a slight reedy quality in the nose and mouth. In the mouth the Cabernet lineage gives this wine a feeling of structure and backbone that many pink wines lack. The taste has dignity and restraint, lots of just-ripe fruit, and a good acid balance. Price range: 750 ml, $3.40–5.49.

ΥΥ NECTAROSÉ VIN ROSÉ DE FRANCE Produced & bottled by Maison J. H. Secrestat Aine, St. Hilaire–St. Florent, France. Rating: 9+. Distribution: A. This flame-orange import has a somewhat stern nose with a slight mustiness that nearly covers the fruit. There's lots of lively, sunshiny fruit in the taste, however, which is moderately dry and enjoyable. It has life, vigor, refreshing acid, and a display of character, and it's only the mustiness of the nose that keeps it from scoring higher. Price range: 750 ml, $2.59–5.79.

ΥΥΥΥ PAPAGNI VINEYARDS CALIFORNIA ROSÉ WINE Produced & bottled by Papagni Vineyards, Madera, California. Rating: 12. Distribution: B. Few rosés are as dark as this one, which is a lovely, churchy red. The nose is delicate and congenial, nicely rounded, with some spiciness and a fruit-bloom bouquet. The taste is moderately dry. It's a wine with character and subtlety, with spice and supple elegance, with sophisticated, developed flavors and zesty acid. So why are you sitting there? Get thee to a wine shop! Price range: 750 ml, $3.39–4.99.

ΨΨ ANGELO PAPAGNI MADERA ROSÉ 1980   Grown, produced, & bottled by Papagni Vineyards, Madera, California. Rating: 9. Distribution: B. This blood-red
wine has an obliging, modestly refined nose that is
both subtle and fruity. The taste is sunshiny, mouth-
filling, lightly sweet, and, in spite of low acid, quite
ingratiating. You could enjoy this wine a lot on a hot
day! Price range, 750 ml, $3.79–5.29.

Ψ J. PEDRONCELLI SONOMA COUNTY SONOMA ROSÉ
WINE   Produced & bottled by J. Pedroncelli Winery,
Geyserville, California. Rating: 8. Distribution: B.
This is a good, workaday rosé wine, pale ruby in
color, with a simple, fruity, and relatively conven-
tional nose. The taste is cheerful, fruity, and simple.
It's moderately sweet, and a bit short on acid. Worka-
day is the key word. Price range: 750 ml, $1.99–3.49.

ΨΨΨΨ J. PEDRONCELLI SONOMA COUNTY ZINFANDEL
ROSÉ 1981   Produced & bottled by J. Pedroncelli Winery, Geyserville, California. Rating: 11+. Distribution: B. The color is a bit dark for a rosé, but very
handsome nevertheless. The nose is easily accessible,
with a pleasant bouquet of ripe fruit. The taste is the
real payoff, however. It's joyful, supple, generous,
full of ripe, sweet apples and pomegranates, mildly
sweet, and has a moderate acid balance. I like it a lot,
and think you will, too. Price range: 750 ml, $2.99–
5.25.

RIUNITE ROSATO   Produced & bottled by Cantine
Coop. Riunite, Reggio Emilia, Italy. Rating: 4. Distribution: A. Color: amber-peach. Nose: awkward, bit-

ter, cooked. Taste: awkward, bitter, cooked. How come it sells like hot cakes? Price range: 750 ml, $2.10–3.99.

℞ RIVERSIDE FARMS PREMIUM DRY ROSÉ   Made & bottled by L. Foppiano Wine Company, Healdsburg, California. Rating: 8+. Distribution: B. This vermilion wine has a very presentable, fruity, uncomplicated nose, and a semidry, refreshing flavor. Its fruit spectrum is narrow, but the acid balance is quite decent. The bottom line is that it's a pleasant, rather crisp rosé wine of some modest charm. Price range: 750 ml, $2.19–3.99.

℞℞ SAN MARTIN CALIFORNIA ROSÉ TABLE WINE   Produced & bottled by San Martin Winery, San Martin, California. Rating: 9+. Distribution: B. This scarlet rosé is almost dark enough to be called a red. The nose, too, is deep and serious for a rosé, with a slight reedy-grassy quality. The taste is near the edge of dryness, but still has to be classified as semisweet. It's full of mouth-filling, ripe, round fruit, and has fairly decent acid. At the price, it's quite a good pink‥wine value. Price range: 1.5 l, $3.33–4.99.

℞℞℞ SAN MARTIN ROSÉ 1981   Produced & bottled by San Martin Vineyards, San Martin, California. Rating: 11. Distribution: B. The color is a tawny rosé. The nose is congenial, fetching, full of simple summer fruit. The taste is moderately sweet, rounded, sunshiny, a bit lacking in acid, but still a graceful fusion of ripe fruit flavors. Quite nice. Price range: 750 ml, $2.78–4.29.

⏺ AUGUST SEBASTIANI COUNTRY GAMAY ROSÉ 1981
Produced & bottled by Sebastiani Vineyards,
Sonoma, California. Rating: 8+. Distribution: A. The
nose of this light strawberry-colored wine doesn't
give you much to love, but not much to hate, either.
The taste is semidry with a slight tart edge, lots of
fruit, and a good balance. Not a spectacular wine, but
a decent one. Price range: 1.5 l, $3.74–5.25.

⏺⏺⏺⏺⏺ SEBASTIANI SONOMA VALLEY
GEWURZTRAMINER ROSA 1981 Produced & bottled by
Sebastiani Vineyards, Sonoma, California. Rating:
13. Distribution: A. What an unusually lovely wine!
The color is pale peach, with a golden rim. The nose is
all charm and style, fruit and flowers, demurely complex. The taste is modestly sweet, with enough acid
to give it an attractive zestiness, fruity, floral, feminine, youthful. I see young girls in flowing tunics
foot-racing through leafy bowers. What do you see?
Price range: 750 ml, $3.46–5.59.

⏺ AUGUST SEBASTIANI CALIFORNIA MOUNTAIN VIN
ROSÉ Vinted & bottled by Sebastiani Vineyards,
Sonoma, California. Rating: 8+. Distribution: A. The
color is vermilion. The nose is satisfactory, without
being surprising or exciting. The taste is semisweet,
pleasantly round and juicy, with fair acid. Unpretentious, but pleasant. Price range: 750 ml, $1.98–3.49.

SEBASTIANI NORTHERN CALIFORNIA VIN ROSÉ 1981
Produced & bottled by Sebastiani Vineyards,
Sonoma, California. Rating: 7+. Distribution: A.
This scarlet wine has an undistinguished nose and a

sweet, predictable taste—fruity, with low acid. It's just another rose on life's highway. Price range: 750 ml, $2.35–3.99.

ΨΨΨ SOUVERAIN APPELLATION NORTH COAST PINOT NOIR ROSÉ 1981   Produced & bottled by Souverain, Geyserville, California. Rating: 10. Distribution: A. Color: light, clear vermilion. Nose: decent and respectable, an unassuming blend of fruit and fruit sugars. Taste: charm without sophistication, a lovely ripe-fruit sweetness balanced by adequate acid. Put it all together and what do you have? A pleasing, ingenuous wine. Price range: 750 ml, $2.68–4.49.

Ψ SUMMIT PREMIUM CALIFORNIA VIN ROSÉ   Prepared & bottled by Geyser Peak Winery, Geyserville, California. Rating: 8. Distribution: A. This clear, light pink wine has an ingenuous, upbeat nose, simple and sunny, not at all complex. The taste is decent and clean, and it's an acceptable, garden-variety sweet wine without any particular defects other than a shortage of acid. Price range: 4 l, $4.69–5.99.

TAYLOR CALIFORNIA CELLARS ROSÉ WINE OF CALIFORNIA   Cellared & bottled by Taylor California Cellars, Gonzales, California. Rating: 7+. Distribution: A. The color is pale cherry, the nose is obliging enough, and has a reasonable fruitiness. In the mouth there's a rather pop-wine sweetness, and I guess you'd say it's decent, but commonplace. Price range: 1.5 l, $3.59–4.99.

ŸŸ TAYLOR CALIFORNIA CELLARS LIGHT ROSÉ WINE OF CALIFORNIA   Cellared & bottled by Taylor California Cellars, Gonzales, California. Rating: 9. Distribution: A. The alcohol is 8.6 percent and there are 58 calories per 100 milliliters. The color is light crimson, and the nose is simple, a bit candied, but still decently in the middle of the road. The taste is better than the nose, with some dryness and lots of simple fruit. It all adds up to a decent, plain, rosé wine, well made but nothing to shout about. Price range: 1.5 l, $3.78–4.99.

ŸŸŸŸ TORRES DE CASTA 1981   Produced & bottled by Miguel Torres, Vilafranca del Penedẽs, Spain. Rating: 12. Distribution: B. This import has a deep, rich, pink color and a subtle, delicate nose, a bit reticent but clean and attractive. The taste is silky and elegant, moderately dry, with charming fruit flavors and a feeling of refinement and sophistication. It's a light-hearted wine, perfect for drinking in deck chairs or hammocks on a summer afternoon. Price range: 750 ml, $2.99–5.25.

WEIBEL MONTEREY CABERNET SAUVIGNON ROSÉ 1979 Produced & bottled by Weibel Vineyards, Mission San Jose, California. Rating: 7+. Distribution: B. Here's another dark rosé, reddish with just a touch of orange. The nose is aggressive and rather ordinary, and the taste is sweet and decently fruity. It's not at all the kind of thing you'd expect from a wine with Cabernet Sauvignon in its title. Don't get me wrong, it's not a bad wine, it's just an underachiever. Price range: 750 ml, $3.59–5.49.

♟♟♟♟ WEIBEL CALIFORNIA VIN ROSÉ Produced & bottled by Weibel Vineyards, Mission San Jose, California. Rating: 11+. Distribution: B. Let's split a bottle of this russet-colored *vin rosé* right away! Then we can both enjoy its stylish nose, its pleasing initial rush of aromas, and its zesty complexity of spice and berries. We can also chat about its flavor, its moderate sweetness and spiciness, its structure and breeding, its acid, its good finish. What do you say? Price range: 750 ml, $2.79–4.49.

Appendices

Sources of Supplies

A few places you can get corks, bottles, and all kinds of wine-making extracts and equipment, in person or by mail order:

Oak Barrel Winecraft
1201 University Avenue
Berkeley, CA 94710
(415) 849-0400

Wine and the People
907 University Avenue
Berkeley, CA 94710
(415) 549-1266

Great Fermentations
87 Larkspur
San Rafael, CA 94901
(415) 459-2520

Milan Laboratory
57 Spring Street
New York, NY 10012
(212) 226-4780

Books on Making
Your Own Wine

Some books to investigate in case you decide to make your own wine. Successful amateur winemakers of my acquaintance particularly recommend the first five.

Grapes into Wine, by Philip M. Wagner. Knopf, New York, 1974. Paperback.

Guidelines to Practical Winemaking, by Julius H. Fessler. Julius H. Fessler, 1965, P.O. Box 2842, Rockridge Station, Oakland, CA 94618. Paperback.

Progressive Winemaking, by Peter Duncan and Bryan Acton. Amateur Winemaker Publications, Andover, Hants., England, 1967. Paperback.

Technology of Winemaking, by Maynard Amerine. AVI Publishing Co., Westbury, Conn., 1971 (3rd edition). Hardcover.

Commercial Winemaking, by Richard Vine. AVI Publishing Co., Westbury, Conn., 1982. Hardcover.

Easy Guide to Home-made Wine, by B. C. A. Turner. Mills & Boon, Toronto, 1968. Paperback.

First Steps in Winemaking, by C. J. J. Berry. Amateur Winemaker Publications, Andover, Hants., England, 1973. Paperback.

Making Wines like Those You Buy, by Bryan Acton and Peter Duncan. Standard Press, Andover, Hants., England, 1973. Paperback.

Successful Winemaking at Home, by H. E. Bravery. ARC Books, New York, 1961. Paperback.

Winemaking with Concentrates, by Peter Duncan. Amateur Winemaker Publications, Andover, Hants., England, 1974. Paperback.

Grapegrowing and Winemaking, by David Jackson and Danny Schuster. Altarinda Press, Orinda, California, 1981. Hardcover.

Catalog

If you are interested in a list of fine Paperback
books, covering a wide range of subjects
and interests, send your name and address,
requesting your free catalog, to:

McGraw-Hill Paperbacks
1221 Avenue of Americas
New York, N.Y. 10020